New Land, New Lives

Scandinavian Immigrants to the Pacific Northwest

NEW LAND
NEW LIVES

Scandinavian Immigrants to the Pacific Northwest

Janet E. Rasmussen

Foreword by Odd S. Lovoll

Norwegian-American Historical Association Northfield, Minnesota

University of Washington Press Seattle & London

Printed in the United States of America
Typesetting by Charles Ellertson,
Paste-up by Steve Frame,
Tseng Information Systems, Inc.
Design by Audrey Johansen Meyer

Library of Congress Cataloging-in-Publication Data

Rasmussen, Janet Elaine.
New land, new lives : Scandinavian immigrants to the Pacific Northwest /
Janet E. Rasmussen ; foreword by Odd S. Lovoll. p.   cm.
Includes bibliographical references.
ISBN 0-295-97288-2 (alk. paper)
1. Scandinavian Americans—Northwest, Pacific—Social life and customs.
2. Scandinavian Americans—Alaska—Social life and customs.
3. Scandinavian Americans—Northwest, Pacific—Interviews.
4. Scandinavian Americans—Alaska—Interviews.   5. Immigrants—
Northwest, Pacific—Interviews.   6. Immigrants—Alaska—Interviews.
7. Northwest, Pacific—Social life and customs.   8. Alaska—Social life
and customs.   I. Title.   F855.2.S18R37   1993
979.5′004395—dc20   93-22999   CIP

The paper used in this publication meets the minimum requirements
of American National Standard for Information Sciences—
Permanence of Paper for Printed Library Materials, ANSI Z39.48-1984.

Contents

v

Part Three / **New Lives: Work** 169

Foreword

In *New Land, New Lives*, Janet E. Rasmussen tells us what she, as a thoughtful and compassionate listener, found to be instructive and emblematic in the personal accounts of ordinary people whom she and her assistants interviewed orally over a period of several years. The narrators all shared a common experience of emigration from one of the Nordic countries—Norway, Sweden, Finland, Denmark, or Iceland—and they all found a home in the Pacific Northwest.

Their evocative recollections cover a broad array of human experiences, ranging from the festive to the mundane tasks of everyday living, and give precious insights into their time and place in history. They all emigrated as children or young adults during the early decades of this century. Distant memories and emotions are recaptured as retrospective accounts of their childhood surroundings in the old country, the meaning of their arrival in America, and their lives as strangers in a new land. Here they for the most part entered the culture of the working class in occupational pursuits common to the earlier Nordic immigrants settling on the west coast of the United States. It is the voices of unknown everyday people, the participants in history who rarely speak directly to us, that we hear in these life histories.

Janet Rasmussen demonstrates her mastery of oral history in these interviews. She uses them with great care, with sensitivity, and with knowledge of the literature on the investigative techniques. She thereby avoids the pitfalls associated with this kind of documentation. The recorded narratives ring true to the historical situation and provide vivid impressions only possible in oral history of individual attitudes and values. She is currently Vice President for Academic Affairs and Professor of Modern Languages at Nebraska Wesleyan University. Rasmussen's major scholarly focus, as evidenced in publications of high merit, has been on women and their life choices. In addition to a series of in-depth studies of Norwegian female literary figures, she has investigated and published articles on domestic service, marriage patterns, familial values, and feminist ideologies among Scandinavian immigrant women. Some of the latter pieces grew out of the same project as the present oral history anthology.

Finally, I wish to thank the University of Washington Press, and most especially its managing editor Julidta Tarver, for enjoyable and efficient collaboration on this important project. And, again, it is my pleasure to acknowledge with much gratitude the contributions of Mary R. Hove, my editorial assistant, in preparing the manuscript for publication.

Odd S. Lovoll, Editor
The Norwegian-American Historical Association
St. Olaf College

Preface

An experimental course on Scandinavian women in the Pacific Northwest that I taught during the spring of 1979 provided the initial impetus for documenting the life experiences of Scandinavian immigrants. My students eagerly sought out local female informants in order to learn about such things as food traditions, home remedies, and ethnic organizations. At the same time, they learned the value of first-person testimony.

In the months that followed, two of the students and I launched, with support from the President's Office at Pacific Lutheran University (PLU), the recording of oral history interviews with persons of Scandinavian heritage. For this pilot project, we focused on individuals who had played important roles in the history of the university.

Expansion of the collecting effort was made possible by a two-year grant from the L. J. Skaggs and Mary C. Skaggs Foundation of Oakland, California. The grant allowed us to define a broader target population—first-generation Scandinavians who had settled in the Pacific Northwest during the early decades of the twentieth century. The grant-sponsored interviewing and tape processing began in 1981, with dedicated involvement by several PLU students, former students, and staff members. Additional funding for the development of an oral history archive came from the Joel E. Ferris Foundation of Spokane, Washington, and the Norwegian Emigration Fund of the Royal Norwegian Ministry of Foreign Affairs in Oslo.

The resulting oral history archive is housed in the Scandinavian Immigrant Experience Collection in the Robert A. L. Mortvedt Library at Pacific Lutheran University. The interview material presented here has been drawn exclusively from that archive. As such, it represents a new source of information about the Scandinavian presence in North America.

I am very grateful for the capable assistance rendered by fellow interviewers Inger Nygaard Carr, Cynthia S. Klein, Donna Mallonee, and Morrene Head Nesvig. Serving as student assistants for the project were Linda Carlson, Carol Skog Fox, Becky Husby, Kimberly Labes, Andrea Leuenberger, Phillip Nelson, Karen Olson, Julie Peterson, Patricia Sargent, Laura Schubert, and Laurie Stumme. Media services supervisor Layne Nordgren and his student assistant Damon Kirk helped with specific tasks, as did community volunteer Patricia Nelson. As Director of Corporate and Foundation Relations, Molly Edman facilitated the requisite outside funding. Isabel Watness and other members of the PLU Humanities staff provided essential office support.

Mary Sue Gee supplied valuable research assistance during the final stage of project activity and helped me select the interviews for this book. PLU archivist Kerstin Ringdahl shared her expertise and enthusiasm throughout. Both Kerstin and Mary Sue have my deep thanks. I also gratefully acknowledge the indispensable advice and encouragement of Norwegian-American Historical Association editor Odd Lovoll. Other friends and colleagues who smoothed the way for this publication include Sue Davidson, Bjørn Jensen, Pat Kelley, Joanne Klein, Steve Murray, Harald Naess, Tiina Nunnally, Audun Toven, and Solveig Zempel. My work also benefited greatly from a sabbatical leave and a Regency Advancement Award from Pacific Lutheran University, a grant-in-aid from the American Association for State and Local History, and a Faculty Growth Award from the American Lutheran Church.

Of course, none of this activity could have gone forward without the cooperation and generosity of the people we interviewed. Their stories enriched and inspired me, both personally and professionally. To them and their families I owe a profound debt of gratitude.

This book is dedicated to my husband Ulf Rasmussen, whose path to the United States from Norway wove the saga of the immigrant experience into the fabric of my day-to-day existence. His unflagging support, including the sacrifice of countless weekends and evenings of companionship, made it possible for me to complete the necessary research, transcribing, editing, and writing. For his patience, good humor, and constant encouragement, he deserves, as the Scandinavians say, a thousand thanks!

Janet E. Rasmussen
Lincoln, Nebraska

New Land, New Lives

Scandinavian Immigrants to the Pacific Northwest

Introduction

There's a lot of history in your life, isn't there?" With a note of surprise, Magnhild Johnsen offered this observation while responding to an interviewer's questions about when and why she had left the country of her birth. Like most others with whom we spoke, Magnhild did not readily view her personal experiences as historically significant. Yet the events she recounted were both dramatic and revealing.

Born in Kristiansand, Norway, in 1909, Magnhild arrived in the United States at the age of twenty, a single woman planning to do housework for a year and then return home for further education. When she did finally return, she brought a husband and two young children and the year was 1939. Caught in Norway by World War II, the Johnsens aided the resistance movement through the trying years of German occupation. After the war, the family crossed the Atlantic again, eager to renew their American identities.[1]

A life like Magnhild Johnsen's does indeed contain "a lot of history." So, too, do the lives of the more than two hundred other immigrants whose oral history interviews have been deposited in the Scandinavian archives at Pacific Lutheran University in Tacoma, Washington. The present work draws upon a selection of their stories to portray the dynamics of Scandinavian immigration to the Pacific Northwest during the early decades of the twentieth century.

These personal accounts sketch the intricate patterns of family life in turn-of-the-century Scandinavia. They communicate the emotions that attended the leave-taking and convey striking details of the journey to a new home across the ocean. In lively and sometimes poignant fashion, the reminiscences illuminate the process of adapting to American society and the avenues for perpetuating the cultural heritage. Everyday life and associations, not politics or theological controversies, are the subject of the first-person narratives. The words come from "ordinary" persons, as opposed to persons with established public reputations.

In two respects this approach constitutes a unique contribution. First, no previous book on the Scandinavians in North America has been based on oral testimony. Several collections of immigrant letters are available, the most recent being Solveig Zempel's *In Their Own Words: Letters from Norwegian Immigrants* (1991). Letters offer a contemporaneous and often intimate record from which a concrete image of the immigrant experience can emerge; oral history relies on memory and the direct solicitation of information to reveal how individuals value and interpret various aspects of the past. The two types of first-person source material thus not only supplement in important ways the official historical record, but also complement each other. Second, much inquiry and analysis in regard to the Scandinavian presence in the Pacific Northwest after 1910 await the attention of researchers. This presentation suggests relevant parameters and themes and thus aims to stimulate systematic investigations of the period and the region.[2]

The Legacy of the Homeland

The immigrants carried the imprint of their native cultures and values into, and through, the new lives they established in the United States. Recent studies of settlements in the Upper Middle West document in detail how communities could be "transplanted" from Scandinavia, so that kinship and other interpersonal ties remained intact and key institutions like the church were replicated.[3] Broadly speaking, both chain migration—members of a family or neighbors following after one another—and the maintenance of regional homeland loyalties were important features of Scandinavian immigration to the Pacific Northwest as well.[4] Still, it might reasonably be argued that the links were less compelling and less fundamental to the shape of the immigrant experience in the Pacific Northwest than was true in the Midwest, given that the major influx of Scandinavians into the Pacific Northwest occurred during a later phase of the mass migration and that urban environments received a good share of the twentieth-century new-comers.[5]

The interview excerpts that follow provide a way to examine the fabric of Scandinavian culture within the Pacific Northwest immigrant experience. With oral history, the focus shifts from "hard" indicators like census, tax, and church records into the "soft" realm of personal experience and expression. Out of the personal particulars, general patterns of behavior and sentiment emerge and invite interpretation. In the case of these immigrants to the Pacific Northwest, the patterns suggest an intricate and sturdy web of homeland influences. Familial ties and connections can be discerned across geographical space. Child-hood values and childhood habits resonate in the vocabulary used to describe occupational choices. The choice of a mate, the response to American lifestyles, the articulation of ethnic identity—in these and other aspects of immigrant life the informants reveal the dynamics that marry cultural continuity to cultural transformation.

The five parts of the anthology are designed to illustrate this process. The homeland is explored through memories of family and child-hood and then viewed in the context of the decision to emigrate. The new land is encountered and analyzed, both physically and psycho-logically, on the immigrant journey and during the early years of ad-justment. New lives are forged around work and family, but remain informed by tradition.

In the early decades of the twentieth century, the typical Scandina-vian emigrants were young, unmarried adults, motivated by economic pressures to seek employment overseas. Among them were a large number of women; by 1905, between thirty-five and fifty percent of the emigrants from the individual Nordic countries were female. In recog-nition of this fact, and to counter the male bias of earlier research in the field, the documentation of women's experiences served as a priority for the oral history project. The shape of this book has also been in-fluenced by a strong commitment to inclusiveness. Because immigrant women typically filled the role of tradition bearers, their insights and actions are critical to an understanding of the legacy of the European homeland.

To set the context for the individual immigrant voices, I offer an overview of the emigration from Scandinavia followed by a discussion of the oral source material and the editorial principles that have guided me in presenting the material in written form.

The Emigration from Scandinavia

During the late nineteenth and early twentieth centuries, the Scandinavian countries sent a high percentage of their populations to North America. Altogether, some two and a half million residents of Denmark, Finland, Iceland, Norway, and Sweden traversed the Atlantic during the period of mass emigration. The magnitude of the population movements is illustrated by the fact that Norway lost as many citizens as had comprised her total population in 1800.

The rate of emigration fluctuated in response to economic and social conditions in both Scandinavia and the United States. But overall, there was a mushrooming effect—the greater the number of emigrants, the greater the returning stream of America letters and the greater the number of both published and informal accounts of American life available to the populace in Scandinavia. Such firsthand information instilled confidence in those who remained behind. Prepaid tickets sent by relatives in the new land and energetic promotion efforts by steamship and railroad agents added to the enticement. For those infected with "America fever," the only cure was to venture across the ocean.

Groups of Scandinavians arrived in North America during the first half of the nineteenth century, and by the 1850s the movement was clearly established.[6] The peak of emigration was reached during the 1880s. The flow tapered off during the 1890s, when the United States suffered an economic downturn, then picked up again after the turn of the century. The First World War reduced out-migration to a trickle; and soon after the war, the United States government enacted restrictions on the number of immigrants permitted annually from any one

INTRODUCTION

country. This quota system took effect in 1921; a stricter quota introduced in 1924 took final form in 1929. The allotted quota spaces were used almost to capacity throughout the 1920s, but the Great Depression finally halted the tide of mass emigration. In fact, taking Sweden as an example, more persons returned to the homeland than emigrated to the United States between 1930 and 1934.[7]

Areas of Scandinavian settlement developed in the Upper Midwest, particularly in Illinois, Wisconsin, Iowa, Minnesota, and North Dakota. Then, after the settling of the middle western territories, the immigrants began turning their faces farther westward and a favored destination became the Pacific Northwest, the Puget Sound region in particular.

Prior to the 1870s, only a few Scandinavians found their way to the west coast. One source reports sixty-five Norwegians in Washington and forty-seven in Oregon Territory in 1870.[8] But by the 1880s, when the railroads reached the Pacific Northwest, a sufficient influx of immigrants caused Scandinavian churches and organizations to be established in the urban centers. Tacoma, Washington, provides a good example. A Swedish Lutheran congregation began in Tacoma in 1882 and a Norwegian Lutheran congregation in 1887. The Swedish Valhalla Lodge was founded in 1884, the Normanna Chorus in 1888, and the Danish Brotherhood in 1889. Both the Swedish-language newspaper *Tacoma Tribunen* and the Norwegian-language *Tacoma Tidende* began publication in 1890. All this activity suggests the emergence of a vibrant Scandinavian presence.

Between 1890 and 1910, more than 150,000 Scandinavians settled in the Pacific Northwest, an average annual influx of about 7,500. Washington received the bulk of these persons. By 1910, Scandinavians comprised the largest ethnic group in the state, constituting over twenty percent of the foreign-born population. It was not uncommon for immigrants to move west in stages, finding their way to the coast after two or more years of work in the Midwest. The evidence suggests that persons from the Nordic region felt a kinship with the natural surroundings and economic base of the Pacific Northwest. Fishing, lumbering, and farming were leading industries in the Northwest, just as they were in Scandinavia, and the mountains, lush forests, and protected waters resembled those of the homeland.[9]

Cities like Seattle, Spokane, and Tacoma welcomed a great many of these immigrants. By 1940, almost 20,000 first-generation Scandinavians were living in Seattle, a number equal to thirty percent of the city's foreign-born population.[10] Some smaller communities also developed obvious ethnic profiles. Selah in central Washington became home to Swedish farmers and members of the Mission Covenant Church. Poulsbo in western Washington attracted Norwegian settlers. Astoria, at the northern border of Oregon's coast, offered Finnish immigrants jobs in the fishing and wood-products industries. Danish farmers found their way to Enumclaw, Washington, and Icelanders to Blaine. To these examples could be added other towns like Silverton and Junction City, Oregon, and Stanwood, Washington.

The imprint of the Scandinavians remains strong in the Pacific Northwest, as evidenced by a rich array of ethnic festivals and organizations.[11] But, by and large, the present-day participants are members of the second and third generations. Nationwide, the number of first-generation Scandinavians shrank from around one million in 1940 to around three hundred thousand in 1975. Since the majority of those who emigrated prior to the Depression were born before 1910, their ranks have thinned considerably during the past fifteen years. With a few exceptions, the resource represented by the actual immigrants from early in the century is now gone. That demographic reality heightens the value of the oral history material on which this book draws.

The Oral History Project

The general significance of preservation activity—saving historically important buildings, artifacts, and texts—is rather well understood in today's society. The whys and hows of oral history research are less familiar. Louis M. Starr of Columbia University has provided this now standard definition of oral history: "Oral history is primary source material obtained by recording the spoken words—generally by means of planned, tape-recorded interviews—of persons deemed to harbor hitherto unavailable information worth preserving."[12] Interviewing itself is a time-honored tool of journalists and folklorists, but tape recording has given new dimensions to the scholarly use and interpretation of interviews.

As indicated above, New Land, New Lives draws on recorded life histories to depict the personal experiences of those who participated in the last waves of mass emigration from Scandinavia. In deciding to seek grant funding for, and to engage my students in, the interviewing of first-generation Scandinavians, I was motivated by three specific advantages of the oral history method. First, as Louis Starr stresses in his definition, oral history makes it possible to retrieve specific, otherwise unavailable information. Second, oral history enables us to broaden the historical record. Women, ethnic minorities, workers, and others whose experiences and perspectives are seldom rendered in official documents or written autobiographical form may be heard and recognized. Third, oral history affirms human experience as the stuff out of which the fabric of history and culture is woven. Thus, it compels us to pay tribute to the roles of individual human beings. Oral historian James Bennett points out that affirmation of the importance of individuals is especially critical in an era when we otherwise confront "massive forces that grind up and spit out our humanity." Bennett continues, "By preserving the experiences we deem important by whatever particular criterion, we symbolize and show respect for human beings in general, as ends in themselves rather than always as means to reach other things, in endless processes of consumption and repetition."[13] Humanistic oral history suggests an affinity between personal narrative and literary narrative. When we listen to people's stories in their own words, we reconstruct the texture of life as it is lived.

The goal of the interview project was the establishment of a tape archive for Pacific Lutheran University. Those interviewed emigrated between 1900 and 1930 from Denmark, Finland, Iceland, Norway, or Sweden and settled, either immediately or eventually, in the Pacific Northwest. The interviews were all conducted as mini-life histories. Deriving from a single encounter with an elderly immigrant, the recording session covered a wide range of topics. Project interviewers were equipped with a standard questionnaire (see Appendix) but were instructed to follow the contours of the individual's own special circumstances rather than to move mechanically through the prepared questions. As a result, each conversation produced an oral record with slightly different characteristics and emphases.

Fewer than a fifth of all the interviews, forty-five out of 240, are presented here. The choice of whom to include was dictated by the desire to offer a balanced selection, as well as by the desire to highlight lively and engaging storytellers. Needless to say, these two factors sometimes tugged against one another and necessitated compromises. In addition, there was the practical need to create a manageable and welcoming selection. Suffice it to say that the first draft incorporated twice as many immigrant voices as found in the present volume. As noted above, a conscious decision was made to include a generous representation of women's stories.

The tapes were transcribed—a painstaking and never-perfect task—followed by an equally painstaking and imperfect task, namely the editing of the transcriptions. An oral history interview is a conversation, steered by the interviewer; as such, multiple interpersonal dynamics affect narrator response. The most faithful record of the conversation would include all the interviewer's questions and comments along with the responses. To highlight the first-person narrative, as I wished to do, required radical editing. All questions have been eliminated. Material has been freely moved and combined, and much has been omitted. But, with the exception of an occasional translation, factual correction, or pronoun reference, nothing has been added. The words on the page are the words of the narrator. Necessary notations and explanations have been placed in brackets or notes.

Because these selections reflect oral speech, aspects of the text require the reader's indulgence. Interference from the native language is stronger in some cases than in others; but throughout, there are ample instances of imperfect grammar and inconsistent verb tenses. I trust that the attempt to retain the flavor of immigrant speech does not impede the reader's understanding or convey an unintended lack of respect for the individuals who generously shared their impressions and experiences.

The interviews were conducted in a spirit of trust—trust that the narrator would respond openly and honestly. Yet one must constantly keep in mind that the narrators were asked to review events from many decades past. Some accomplished this with more agility than others, though in all cases the process of reflection tints the story being told. It is a bit disconcerting to review interviews with three siblings and to discover that each presents different information about the parents; in some respects the stories complement each other, but they also contradict each other with regard to certain dates and events. Folklore enters some of the reminiscences, too; an uncanny number of the immigrants, or their friends and relatives, just missed the fateful voyage of the *Titanic*.

As part of the editing process, many details have been checked and questionable items eliminated. Still, the reader is cautioned that "true" history as remembered by one witness may not be factually or representatively "true" and also that certain aspects of the situation may have been omitted or repressed. Further, it is worth stressing that one cannot claim statistical validity for the demographic patterns and the circumstances revealed on the tapes. In fact, the perspectives presented here may be skewed, in that referrals to interviewees derived, in large part, from a network of church and ethnic organizations. "Unaffiliated" Scandinavians were not so easily identified, nor were the "nonsurvivors" available to offer their side of the story. It should also be pointed out that the information supplied is not always as complete as one might wish; the identification of family photographs, for example, is sketchy.

Such interpretive and presentational difficulties do not diminish the general significance of the memories captured on tape and now on the printed page. They are a unique source of sociocultural and historical information. In particular, they highlight the human experiences and values that make up the immigrant legacy from the "top of Europe."

NOTES

1. Magnhild Johnsen's story will be found in Part One below.

2. See the Bibliography for additional publications of immigrant letters and diaries and for the major studies of early Scandinavian settlement in the Pacific Northwest.

3. See the essay by Ann Marie Legreid, "Kinship and Crossing: The Role of Family and Community in the Migrations from Inner Hardanger, 1836–1900," in Øyvind T. Gulliksen, Ingeborg R. Kongslien, and Dina Tolfsby, eds., *Essays on Norwegian-American Literature and History Volume II* (Oslo, 1990), 57–72. A major study of the phenomenon is Robert C. Ostergren, *A Community Transplanted: The Trans-Atlantic Experience of a Swedish Immigrant Settlement in the Upper Middle West* (Madison, Wisconsin, 1988).

4. One striking example is provided by the Selbu community in eastern Washington; see Marvin G. Slind, "Norse to the Palouse: The Selbu Community," in *Bunchgrass Historian*, 10:4 (1982), 10–19. See also Slind and Fred C. Bohm, *Norse to the Palouse: Sagas of the Selbu Norwegians* (Pullman, Washington, 1990).

5. Scandinavian emigration during the nineteenth century is generally seen as dominated by families and that of the twentieth century by young adults. See, for example, the chapter "Change and Unrest, 1865–1915" in Ingrid Semmingsen, *Norway to America: A History of the Migration*, trans. by Einar Haugen (Minneapolis, 1978), 106–120.

6. Scandinavians had, of course, a presence in North America well before this. A Swedish colony was established in Delaware already in 1638. And Viking expeditions had reached the shores of eastern Canada by the year 1000.

7. See Hans Norman and Harald Runblom, *Transatlantic Connections* (Oslo, 1988) and Sture Lindmark, "End of the Great Migration," *Swedish Pioneer Historical Quarterly*, 20:1 (1969), 25–41.

8. Carlton C. Qualey, *Norwegian Settlement in the United States* (Northfield, Minnesota, 1938), 188.

9. See chapter II, "Settlement Patterns and Occupations," in Jorgen Dahlie, *A Social History of Scandinavian Immigration, Washington State, 1895–1910* (New York, 1980).

10. Calvin F. Schmid, *Social Trends in Seattle* (Seattle, 1944), 99. Foreign-born Scandinavians made up five percent of Seattle's total population in 1940, with the heaviest concentration of Norwegians and Swedes living in the area of the city known as Ballard.

11. For striking photographic documentation of this ethnic presence, see Kristina Veirs, ed., *Nordic Heritage Northwest* (Seattle, 1982).

12. Louis M. Starr, "Oral History," in *Encyclopedia of Library and Information Science*, 20 (New York, 1977), 440.

13. James Bennett, "Human Values in Oral History," in *Oral History Review*, 11 (1983), 5.

Part One / **Homeland**

Spread across the northern roof of Europe, the Scandinavian countries have been marked physically, economically, and culturally by their position on the periphery. The climatic conditions and challenging landscapes of the Far North influenced settlement patterns and circumscribed resource-based occupations like farming and fishing. Compared with other parts of western Europe, industrialization arrived late, and traditional lifestyles persisted to some extent into the early decades of the twentieth century. Precious literary and folk treasures like the sagas, ballads, and folktales were preserved in unique quantities, while modern artistic giants like Henrik Ibsen fled Scandinavian cultural provincialism to nurture their creative talents on the Continent.

Counterbalancing this image of life at the margins is the historical record of vigorous Scandinavian interactions with other cultures, most dramatically represented by the Viking expeditions, which reached both across the North Atlantic and deep into Russia. By the nineteenth century, the seafaring industries—shipping and whaling—and the steady emigration of Scandinavians to North America—and to a lesser extent other parts of the world—confirmed that Scandinavian isolation, never total, was crumbling rapidly in an era of improved transportation and communication.

Climatic conditions vary from the marine-influenced regions of Denmark and coastal Norway to the sub-polar continental zones of Finland and northern Sweden. The heavy forests of Sweden and Finland give way in the west to the mountains and fjords of Norway and in the southwest to the wind-blown heaths of Denmark. Out in the mid-Atlantic, Iceland's hot springs and lava fields present a stark and arresting landscape. In much of the region, farmers struggle with rugged terrain and marginal natural vegetation. The spectacular light summer nights contrast with a winter palette of eery blues and blacks.

The ties among the five countries are long-standing and too complex to enumerate fully here. The historian Franklin Scott writes that the Scandinavians "have a common cultural tradition, have been in and out of various political combinations with one another, and think of themselves as a group. They have their differences, each of the five nations is an entity, yet each is far more different from other nations outside the group than it is from any of the brother nations within the group."[1] Of primary importance to this family relationship are the linguistic ties that make it possible for the majority of Scandinavians to communicate with each other without formal translation.

In 1900, when the immigrants featured here were being born, the five countries boasted a combined population of 12,500,000. Denmark, Finland, and Norway were roughly equal in size, with 2.5, 2.7, and 2.2 million inhabitants respectively. Sweden's population numbered 5.1 million. Iceland was still part of the Danish kingdom.[2]

Industrialization came to the Nordic region during the latter half of the nineteenth century. Whereas agriculture still dominated the economic landscape in 1870, a fundamental shift had occurred by the turn of the century, and the manufacturing and service industries had begun to assume a leading role. Finland retained its rural profile longer than did Denmark, Norway, and Sweden; sixty-six percent of the Finnish population was still employed in agriculture and related fields in 1910. The four decades immediately prior to the First World War were a time of high economic growth, as exports increased, industry expanded, and emigration absorbed much of the natural population growth. People moved into the urban centers to take service and factory jobs and gradually the conveniences of modern life entered their homes.[3]

The oral history narratives document the continuation of subsistence farming alongside the development of an urban, money-based economy. Torvald Opsal notes, "You had plenty to eat, but there was no cash." In order to pay for Torvald's trip to Bergen to be cleared for emigration, the Opsal family sold one of their cows. Food and clothing

Andrew Johnson and family at his mother's home in Sweden (see p. 47)

production required steady and energetic workers. Ester Sundvik says of her mother, "She was never idle. When she sat down, she knitted stockings and spun wool and linen and all kinds of things that she was busy with." Moreover, Ester's mother ran the farm single-handed, raised three daughters, preserved and stored foods in the era before refrigeration, and served as the local midwife. Remarkably, this demanding lifestyle produced few complaints, perhaps in part because "we didn't know anything else." Torvald Opsal's maternal grandmother was likewise a model of endurance—"just a quiet, hardworking woman, light, small, could outrun any sheep until the day she died."

Torvald Opsal emphasizes the unrelenting physical labor of rural life: "Working, that was something we had to do when we started to walk. There was no playing; even going to school we never had any time to play." According to Martin Rasmussen, the schoolteacher knew "how to use the rod" and his mother how "to keep us in line." Likewise, when Martin left the farm to become a machine-shop apprentice, a strict disciplinary system applied—"the boss, he would hit you."

On the whole, life in the country was quiet and peaceful. The daily routine revolved around survival tasks. Pleasure came principally from good hearty food. Christmas served as a cherished respite from routine fare and labor. The pastor and the schoolteacher functioned as the principal authority figures. People relied on each other for assistance. Ina Silverberg's family had more resources than most, so her father distributed seed to the neighbors in the spring; in return, the neighbors helped him at harvest time.

At the same time, much was changing. Martin Rasmussen chronicles some of the innovations on their rather large farm in southern Denmark, including the transition from manual labor to farm machinery and the introduction of fertilizer. There was also substantial migration from the country into the cities. Else Goodwin tells of her father and his eleven siblings, "They were raised out in the country, but most of them drifted into Copenhagen." Farm laborers became streetcar operators, prison guards, and small business owners.

The city dwellers recognized the importance of maintaining contact with the land. Gretchen Yost describes how the government would send children to stay with families in the country and how her mother always kept flowers in the kitchen window—a bright contrast to the dreary tenement apartment. Else Goodwin also received a school vacation in the country; what is more, her family leased a colony garden— "all these plots of land where you put up a little summer house and have your garden." For Bergljot DeRosa, outdoor recreation as a skier and hiker provided the vital link with the natural world—"I could walk alone and just look around and be perfectly at ease and peace."

Just as women filled a central role in the farm economy, so women often bore major responsibility within the urban setting. Gretchen Yost's mother was a widow who relied upon her own manual labor and the odd jobs undertaken by the children in order to make ends meet. Else Goodwin's mother helped run the family's mangle shop. With Bergljot DeRosa's father often at sea, her mother raised six children and managed the household; like her grandmother, she was "really, really strong."

The traditional household units were not as static as one might imagine. One reason households fluctuated was the early departure of children to live and work outside the home. Large families and limited resources made it practical, even mandatory, for children to leave home. A young person might be attached to another household to receive training and provide labor; often the employers were relatives or neighbors. A second major reason for the volatile household composition was parental absence, caused by work, emigration, or death. Seamen and fishermen were absent for long periods of time; and their occupations, like many others, carried physical risks. The death of a parent was a childhood experience faced by a remarkably high number of the interviewees.

The Scandinavians had a high rate of literacy. Public education was nurtured from early in the nineteenth century. A public school law was introduced in Denmark as early as 1814, in Norway in 1837, in Sweden in 1842, and in Finland in 1866. As the school systems evolved, attendance was expected from the age of seven to the time of confirmation, although the school term in rural districts lasted at most twelve weeks a year.[4] Upon confirmation, usually at age fourteen, a young person was considered an adult, responsible for his or her own welfare.

The school curriculum included a solid introduction to the Bible and to Lutheran doctrine. The Lutheran Church has been the state church of the Scandinavian countries since the Reformation. Persons are born into the Lutheran church and well over ninety percent of Scandinavians remain members throughout their lifetimes; but the church has not escaped criticism or the development of rival religious bodies. Where the state church failed to satisfy the spiritual needs of the population, parallel lay organizations sprang up, typically centered in a prayer house or mission house. Andrew Johnson offers an interesting account of his family's involvement with the Swedish Mission Covenant.

Political events of the early twentieth century color some of the individual stories. Finland experienced great turmoil when the Russian tsar extended his domination of this neighbor to the west. Many Finns fled the country in 1901–1902, in response to a new conscription law that demanded that Finnish males fight, as necessary, in and for Russia.[5] The Danes of North Slesvig, including Martin Rasmussen, found themselves drawn into World War I on the German side, in spite of their fervent anti-German sentiments.

In examining the reasons why these immigrants left the land of their birth, the gender stereotyping familiar from novels of the emigration—man as bold adventurer and woman as reluctant companion—fails to apply. For just like their male contemporaries, Scandinavian women actively sought new opportunities and new horizons. In a nuanced presentation of life in northern Norway, Henny Hale gives powerful expression to the forces that restricted her at home and those that beckoned to her from across the sea. She recalls the heavy burden of physical labor, the constant specter of death at sea, and the confining physical landscape—symbolic of her limited options. As she emphatically states, "I felt like I was choking, 'cause I couldn't see over the mountains."

Thus driven, or pushed, by negative features of her Norwegian environment, Henny Hale simultaneously experienced the allure of America. She heard fantastic stories, especially from her father, whose own desire to go to America remained unfulfilled. "We thought America was lined with gold all over the place," she says. Many of her relatives had already emigrated and they sent back beautiful presents. The fancy clothes in particular impressed the young country girl. With America, Henny associates luxury, sophistication, and relatives. With Norway, in spite of the memories of loving parents and lovely summer nights, she associates drudgery, death, and despair. At the age of twenty, she found herself obsessed with the idea of emigration—"I wanted to go to America, *period.*"

Magnhild Johnsen journeyed across the Atlantic just in time to be caught in the grip of war. But her 1938 journey was from west to east. As a remigrant to Norway, she lived through the German Occupation, a participant in the resistance movement and a witness to much suffering. The family decided to return to the United States in 1948, because of "too many sad memories from the war." The Johnsen family represents an important segment of the twentieth-century immigrant population, namely those who remigrate. As many as one in five returned to live, for a time at least, in the Scandinavian homeland. Frequent trips back and forth were also not uncommon. In some cases, the "emigrants" never actually settled down on this side of the Atlantic, but rather "commuted" for a number of years in response to seasonal work patterns.

Overseas migration was one of several unstable elements in the lives of Scandinavian families during the early part of the century. Still, the geographical and cultural space that came to separate family members as a result of emigration distinguished the transatlantic move from the partings otherwise woven into the rhythm of family life. Not surprisingly, then, the leave-taking sparked emotions that were otherwise kept in check. Sometimes the parents refused a formal good-by, fearing an unseemly flood of tears. Sometimes the kiss or tear or solemn word of love did find expression, as when Ina Silverberg's father placed his hands on her head and offered his blessing. These unusual circumstances made a lasting impression upon the departing offspring, although to judge by their testimony, the emigrants themselves found that excitement and anticipation overshadowed much of the pain and guilt of departure.

Then, too, the emigrants could look ahead to an established network of relationships in the distant western United States, where relatives and neighbors had already established homes. A study of Swedish-American Line passengers between 1922 and 1930 showed that two-thirds of them were joining relatives in America, one-fifth of them traveling on prepaid tickets.[6] Seen in this light, emigration was not abandonment of the family; by and large, it was an extension of well-established social patterns and priorities.

The interviews in this section are arranged to give first a picture of rural life and then an impression of urban childhoods.

NOTES

1. Franklin D. Scott, *Scandinavia* (Cambridge, Massachusetts, 1975), 1.

2. B. R. Mitchell, "Statistical Appendix 1700–1914," in Carl M. Cipolla, ed., *The Fontana Economic History of Europe*, 4 (London, 1973), 747–749. Iceland was granted status as a separate kingdom under the Danish crown in 1918; in 1944, it became an independent republic.

3. Lennart Jörberg, "The Industrial Revolution in the Nordic Countries," in *The Fontana Economic History of Europe*, 399, 377–378.

4. B. J. Hovde, *The Scandinavian Countries, 1720–1865*, 2 (Boston, 1943), 606.

5. Reino Kero, "The Background of Finnish Emigration," in Ralph J. Jalkanen, ed., *The Finns in North America: A Social Symposium* (Hancock, Michigan, 1969), 58.

6. Florence Edith Janson, *The Background of Swedish Immigration 1840–1930* (1931; reprinted New York, 1970), 484.

Henny Hale

"I couldn't see over the mountains."

*Born in Eidet, Vesterålen, Norway, in 1903, Henny Hale
emigrated in 1923 on a ticket supplied by an uncle in
Tacoma. She did domestic work and became involved
in activities at Tacoma's Normanna Hall, where she
met her husband. Upon marrying, she quit work.
The Hales had two daughters.*

My family was a good family. They were well thought of and they were hardworking. I guess we were very poor. We didn't know we were poor, because we had a happy home life. And we had God-fearing parents; I think that made a lot of difference.

My father was a fisherman and a farmer. Father would go to Finnmarken in the late spring to fish, until he had to come back to work on his farm; and in the winter he went to the Lofoten Islands for cod.* My mother died when she was thirty-six, leaving six children. She was a slender, pretty little thing, and she shouldn't have had to die so young. I remember her going down to the sea to get the heads of the fish and go home and boil them up and bring them to the barn for the cows. Mother used to crochet curtains and she had a loom and wove all the rugs for our floors. She was very handy. How she found the time I don't know. Besides that, she was a seamstress and sewed for other people.

We used peat for heat; we had peat bogs all over the place. My dad

---

*Finnmarken refers to the northernmost district in Norway; the Lofoten Islands are a prime fishing ground just off the coast of northern Norway, close to the island group where Henny grew up.

Henny and Louis Hale, Tacoma

would cut off about six thousand peat squares every spring; and we children had to slice these squares in six little slices with a spade. That was heavy work. We with our little legs would stand there and slice up all these and then set them to dry. It was marvelous fuel. We had a *kamin* [stove] in the front room; it was very beautiful, with several tiers of iron where we could set coffee pots to warm.

After mother died, it was just me and my older sister that had to take over. I was twelve; my sister Mary was fourteen. We had to do the milking and the baking. Maybe I sound like we worked ourselves to death, well, we did. But that's how we lived up in the north; it was hard going.

In the winter, now here was I, twelve years old, had to hack a road through the snow, hack holes in the river in the ice, carry about fourteen buckets every other day to the barn for the cows and the sheep. We had it to do and so we did it.

We took the sheep in from the barn and I clipped them in the kitchen. I was so short, I sat on the sheep's back and clipped the wool off of it. There was a lady that used to come to the house all the time and I didn't like her. She was running after my dad when he was a widower. One time, I was clipping the wool of this sheep and she was sitting at the kitchen table having a cup of coffee. And I happened to clip the skin of the sheep and he didn't like it one bit, so the sheep leaped into that lady's lap and spilled her coffee and I was so glad. Isn't that terrible?

I was the tomboy. Mary was the lady. I ran out and played ball with the boys and went swimming in the river and I'd go fishing with my dad. Summer nights when he was home and the midnight sun was shining, we'd take the little boat and go way out and fill the bucket with little *gjedde* [pike]. We'd sit out on the water till the sun came to the sea and went up again.* And then we'd go home and cook up a pot of that fish. We worked hard, but there were times when we enjoyed our life, too.

I was confirmed at fifteen and then I quit school. I stayed home for a couple of years just to help. I left home when I was seventeen, though. I went to a neighboring farm where I stayed for about two years and then I came back to work for my schoolteacher. I liked her very, very much and then I decided to go to America and she said, "If you stay another year, I'll give you a silver spoon for Christmas." Well, I didn't want to stay.

Why I wanted to go to America? Maybe it was born in me. Because my dad wanted to go to America when he was a young man. But one after another his brothers and sisters left and came to America, and he didn't want to leave grandfather alone with the farm so he and

---

*She is describing the summer midnight sun, when the sun touches the horizon but never sinks beneath it.

his brother Martin stayed home. Of course, we thought America was lined with gold all over the place. My father and everybody else told stories about this. My Uncle George was over here, and Aunt Minnie, and Uncle Ed and Arnt, and Nick and Albert, and Aunt Ellen was here. They were all over here and they wrote home and they'd send packages. Blouses with beautiful lace on—oh it was so beautiful, all of it. High-button shoes.

But I think more than anything was that I couldn't *see*. I wanted to see more of the world. There was a hill up above our house and where I really decided to go to America was on that hill. I had a Sunday off from this place where I was working and I came home and I walked up on that hill and I stood on tiptoe. I actually stood on tiptoe. I felt like I was choking, because I couldn't see over the mountains. And I decided, I'm just not going to live like this. And I went home and I sat down that Sunday afternoon and I wrote to my uncle George Johnson in Tacoma if he would send me a ticket, please, so I could come to America. In short order, I had a ticket.

I was twenty. I left October 10, I think it was, 1923. I got the ticket, and like I say, I had hardly been off of the farm. I didn't know what the world was all about. But I had to take the boat and go into the nearest city, I think it was Svolvær, to get my papers in order. That's the first time I saw an electric light. No kidding. I didn't know what I let myself in for, but I wanted to go to America, *period*; so I went to get these papers in order and I made it. I was here about three weeks before Christmas. I don't know what drove me. I was possessed; I just wanted *out*.

What I remember more than anything was my little brother going with me down to where we took the boat to row across; and he stood there with his fists like this and he stuck them in his pocket and he wasn't going to cry. My dad went with me; he rowed me across that sea there. Then there was a small place, maybe four or five blocks long, to walk from the boat and over to the ship that I was going on. My dad helped me with my suitcase and he walked half of the way with me. And I turned around and I kissed him before I left—the only time in my life I kissed my father. I never did kiss my mother. Because you didn't have emotions; you weren't supposed to. He turned around and walked home again. He was really glad that I could get out of there.

We lived out by the North Sea, right on the sea. The North Sea would come over the rocks and I'd stand there petrified looking at it. It was really fantastic. Our young friends, as well as families, died one after another out on the sea. I remember one Sunday afternoon, a bunch of us friends had been to what they called the *ungdomsmøte* [youth fellowship] and one of the boys said, on the way home, "In the morning I'm going to take the boat and I will not come back until after *potetopptakinga* [the potato harvest]." You know, he went out in the morning and we never saw him again. We don't know what happened to him. He could have gone away some place, or he could have drowned. This sort of thing made an impression on me. I don't think there was any thought of getting out of it and go to America and marry, because I was going back home again in five years. But you never do, you never do.

We sailed from Eidet down the coast and we stopped in Bodø where my sister worked at that time, so she came to the boat and gave me a blanket. In Bergen, we took the train to Oslo. I was alone till I came on the train; then we met people that was going to America and we got to talking. In Oslo, we had to stay overnight and we went out for a tour of Karl Johan [the main street] and it was fun. I thought I had an awful lot of money, so I went into a *butikk* [store] and I bought myself a green hat and I paid thirty crowns for it. Oh, gee, I paid thirty crowns for a green hat, a green silk hat. I remember that green silk hat all my life. And I came to Tacoma with, I think, forty-two cents.

I have been back to Norway twice. In 1977 I went for the first time and in 1979 I took my two daughters with me for the family reunion; that was a joyous trip. They say when you have been away from home, anything looks different and smaller. Well, that is not just imagination. I am so sure that all the hills were smaller, absolutely. The hills where I used to run chasing the cows and the sheep, they were smaller and they were much rockier and the river where I used to go swimming was a trickle. But I took my girls up to that place where I stood on tiptoe and that was quite a moment.

Ester Sundvik

"We never knew what real medicine was."

Born in the Åland Islands, Finland, around 1903, Ester
Sundvik emigrated in 1922 and spent several years doing
domestic work for families in New York, Connecticut,
and Massachusetts. Following marriage and the birth of
a daughter, Ester continued to work. The family moved
to Vancouver, Washington, in 1943. There Ester became
the head cook at a shipyard and was chosen to christen a
Navy aircraft carrier.

I come from the Åland Islands, just between Finland and Sweden.
From our town it took seven hours to get to Turku with a boat, and
it took about the same length of time to get to Stockholm. Finnish people are living there, but they speak Swedish. Schools, churches,
everything is in Swedish.[*]

My father was a baker. Mother met him working in a bakery—she
sold bread and he baked—and then they got married. I don't know
anything about my father, that's the saddest thing, because we were
separated from him. I was three months old when he left for America.
There were just two older sisters, Wilhelmina and Ingrid. When my
aunt found out mother was deserted, she said we should go to the
family home and stay there, because it was empty.

We had the most beautiful relationship with our mother. She was a
remarkable person. She never complained. She was never idle. It was
marvelous, really; we had all the security from her.

Mother raised cows from calves and when they were ready to have

---

[*]Although the population of the Åland Islands identifies culturally and linguistically
with Sweden, the island group constitutes an official län or province within Finland.

their first calf, she sold them, and that was part of her living. She sold butter and milk, and she was the midwife in town. I don't think she was educated for it, but people thought she was like a doctor. Every child in our town, my mother delivered. And then, when they got older, she took them home and taught them kindergarten. When she sat down, she knitted stockings and spun wool and linen, and she kept the house so nice. She really did work hard and she was in good health. You don't die from overwork, that's for sure!

We had a little farm, maybe seven acres. This little place belonged to Saltvik, but it was called Ödkarby. It was a very beautiful place. The woods—fir and pine trees—was right back of the house, and we were close to the water. We walked to the water and swam. Sometimes we went in the morning to take the cows to the pasture, and mother made up a picnic lunch, and we stayed there all day to bring the cows home to be milked in the evening.

We had quite a big lawn and a woodshed and a barn, and we had a little house, not attached to the house but by itself, and there we kept all our food. We didn't have inside plumbing; we had that outside, too.

I can see it when my eyes are closed, and I dream about it so many times, that I am there, sleeping in the same bedroom where I slept. We had a little round fireplace made out of tiles in the corner of our bedroom. They call it *kakelugn*. When the tiles got warm, it kept the room warm all night. Every night in the wintertime, about six o'clock, mother made a fire. She said, "Now we're going to have a little rest and we're going to sit and enjoy the fire." We didn't put the lights on; we just sat there and looked at the fire in the dark. It was so beautiful. My girl friends used to come over and sometimes mother give us something to eat, which we enjoyed very much.

My mother was a beautiful cook and she was a little different than some women around our neighborhood because she had worked in the bakery and helped to make such lovely food there. We had carrot pudding and we had *leverlåda*, that was made out of ground liver and rice and raisins and then an egg custard on top of it and baked in the oven. It doesn't sound good, but to us it was very, very good. Then she made meatballs and pork roast and side pork. She always butchered a pig and a calf each fall and that had to be salted, because it wouldn't keep otherwise, and a brine put over it. And that we lived on the whole winter. She made sausage and head cheese and all kinds of things.

We had not every vegetable that they have nowadays. We had beets and cabbage and carrots and rutabagas and potatoes, and we kept that in the root cellar. It was dug pretty deep down in the dirt and lined with bricks. The walls didn't come up very far, because it was to keep cool in the summer and not freezing in the winter. There was a roof with shingles on it and you walked down about three or four steps to go down into it. And there we kept our milk and butter in the summer and it kept very nice and cold. It was not so convenient as to open up the refrigerator door, but it worked quite beautifully and we didn't know anything else, so it wasn't a hardship for us. Everybody had it that way.

Mother made us children plant the flowers and fix up the flower beds, so she could do the things we couldn't do. First of all, we had lilacs. And we had calendulas and many different kinds of those blue cornflowers. I can't think about the irises we had and many other flowers: forget-me-nots, they were so cute, and violets, and lily of the valley. There was flowers all over in the woods, wildflowers. I can't remember all their names, but they called them *vitsippa* [wood anemone].

There were very many wild berries—blueberries and lingonberries and a little bit of cranberries. And we had something they called *smultron*, like small wild strawberries, very, very nice. Mother made jam out of them and also out of the lingonberries.

Mother made a liniment out of turpentine. There were some other ingredients in it, ammonia and cream. We had to shake the bottle every time we used it, because the cream separated; but it didn't curdle or anything, it was very creamy and nice, and that we used whenever we got a pain. It was just marvelous. Then she also made black currant juice and kept that all winter. She heated it and give it to us and that was good for colds and croups. Then she used to make chamomile tea for us to drink when we had bad colds. We never knew what any real medicine was; we never had an aspirin in the house or anything like that. I never had been to a doctor all the time I was home. I was nineteen when I came over to America and I had to have an examination. The doctor said, "You are very healthy. Here, go. You can take off any day."

Christmas was so beautiful at home and we had Christmas for twenty days. Every neighbor had a party. And we had our Christmas tree that we cut down from the woods, snow up to the waistline. We shook the snow out. We had a veranda that went across the whole house and mother used to keep it there and put paper under it so it wouldn't ruin the floor. Then when it was dry enough, we took it in and the whole house smelled from the fir. We didn't have any bought decorations. We made stars out of paper and little baskets of paper that were woven— slips of different kinds of paper, blue and green and red and all kinds— with a handle on it. Then we put a little candy or raisins or prunes in it, so the day the tree was taken down we could eat all those goodies. There were strips of colored paper that we made a garland out of and put around the tree. It was very cute when we got done with it. We had candleholders on the branches and we stuck candles in there, and we never had an accident or anything with the candles burning.

The first of May we had really big, big fires. We used to go up on the mountain and build the fires and then we could see all over town and all the church steeples. The mountain was not far from our house. We used to climb up there and make the fires and we used to sing, "Idag det första maj, maj, maj; idag det första maj," today is the first of May.

Midsummer was also one of the highlights in our lives. They cut down birches and decorated the outside of the house with birch trees. Just at that time, the birch leaves were all out and they were so pretty. Some people even made a little house with just birches all around it and then the entrance to go in; and there was a little table and you could go in there and have your coffee.

They did have a lot of superstition there, and when I was a child I really was scared. We had a woodshed and they said some lady—I don't know if she lived in our house or what—was there chopping wood and she had been dead for years and years and years. It took me a long time before I could go out to the woodshed and get wood without being scared. And then we had some hills to go up on the road, and they always said that there was somebody on the hill. And that scared me, too, because I had to go up that hill when I walked from the minister. I hoped that, my goodness, nobody is coming that I would be scared of!

I went to school about six years. You went longer if you wanted to go to another school, but I didn't do it, because I was more for the domestic. I liked cooking, sewing, embroidery, weaving, and all those kind of things. So I quit at fourteen and went to confirmation class. I had to go away; it was too far to walk from our house to the parsonage where they had class. Another girl friend and I lived in a little house with a lady. We took food with us from home and the lady helped us cook it. We went a long time, too; it isn't like here. We started in the fall and went the whole school year to confirmation class. We had two pastors, one was for the catechism and the other was for the Bible history.

I stayed home for a while and then I had a very good friend that wanted me to come to Stockholm. So I was there a year. I worked for a captain's widow. She had fixed up her house for a guest house. She had seven or eight people living there at a time. They called it a private hotel, but we served just coffee and coffee bread and cakes for breakfast. I worked hard there and she didn't give me enough food either. I was very homesick, but I didn't want to let them know I was homesick at home, so I stuck it out a year.

Then I was home for a while and helped mother and then I started working for a minister. I did a lot of little things. I knitted stockings and took care of the plants and got the wood in from the woodshed. We had to have fires in all the fireplaces every morning and that was my job. I stayed there until I went to America [1922].

I didn't really decide; it just came on me all of a sudden. My friend Edith said she was going to America and I thought I would go, too. She said, "Come with me, because I would be so lonesome without you." My poor little mother didn't want me to go off, because she thought it was too much and too far away and I didn't speak English. The minister didn't want me to go. He said, "Other people live here, so you can also live here. That big place New York, you wouldn't like that." I didn't pay much attention, because I went.

I promised mother that I would come home as soon as I paid my fare coming over here and saved enough money. And that I did, because I made ninety dollars a month in Boston, which was very good at that time. I saved every penny I possibly could, and I went home to visit my mother and sisters and that was really a lovely, lovely time. I came home for Christmas. There was so much snow and we went to church at night with a horse and sleigh. I forgot how beautiful it was in the wintertime.

Ina Silverberg

"I get so lonesome for Finland."

*A 1907 emigrant from rural Finland, Ina Silverberg
planned only a brief visit with her brothers in southwestern
Washington. Instead, she married a logger of Scandinavian
descent and settled in Astoria, Oregon, where she held various
service jobs and raised a daughter. Her contacts with the homeland included three return trips and regular correspondence.*

I have been born in 1889 in farm country—Kaustinen, Finland. My
maiden name, Aino Elisabet Huntos.

Huntos, that's a Russian word. We used to be underneath the
Russia.* In my homeplace, where I was born, was a Russian military
hospital. An old man, nobody know what nationality he was, he stay
years and years as kind of caretaker that place. He used to have a dog,
Hunt, and if somebody come along, he say, "Ooshs, ooshs," that means,
get in. Then they started to tell [call] that place Huntos. My daddy, he
had been born "Pentala." When he buy this place, they start calling him
"Huntos."

At the farm Pentala, they got four boys and they make just living. My
daddy was the youngest boy. He used to do farmwork and blacksmith.
And he went to Russia. In Karelia there was good carpenters; they built
so many church I can't name it.† They went to Russia and they start

---

*Resistance to Russian domination has been a constant part of Finland's history;
especially significant in this context was the policy of Russification begun by the
tsar in the 1890s. Strident Finnish demands that their self-rule be respected had little
effect, until the Russian Revolution of 1917 provided the opportunity for Finland to
declare itself an independent republic.
†Karelia refers to the region along the Russo-Finnish border.

building the famous church in Petersburg, they call it Isaac's Church. My daddy work there.

I remember when we used to have farm. First thing, early the morning, my daddy built a fire; we had the open fireplace in the corner of the house. Then he went to take care the cows, give them something to eat, and take care the horses. Then he came in and then I used to be up. He cook coffee and calling to mommy to come have a coffee. They drink coffee and he take me in his lap. When he was through with the coffee, then he dress up me and fix my hair. We used to have always a working girl. [But] I have been so fussy; I didn't let anybody touch my hair. I always holler, running after daddy, "Daddy, don't go. You brush Aino's hair, Aino's hair." And daddy had to always fix my hair. I have been really my daddy's girl.

We make living. They talking about poor Finland, how poor. I used to say, "America is good country. I am citizen. I like. But I want to tell true, I never been hungry in Finland." I didn't know even others that be hungry. We have everything; we had plenty. We just had a good farm, growing always our grains, barley and rye and oats. Early in the spring, most everybody there, they start to make something from what they had, a little piece of land. They ask my daddy [for] rye. He just tell them, "How much do you need? Just help yourself." And they did that, the poor families. And they asked him to pay, he said, "No, just come help out when we start digging up the potatoes." He gave how much they need, if they just come help when we need the help. Same with barley and everything.

They was so glad to come help, especially young girls and boys. At my place they get really good eats; mother make good meat and many dish. My mother was really good cook. Then the evening, we was through with picking potato and cutting rye, then we have a big place, really smooth, let us play. So we play ring around the rosie sometimes, singing. Daddy just sitting in the porch, laughing. My daddy says, "You people have to have some fun. You let them to play home, then they don't run away, they stay home. You don't have to worry; you know where they are."

Ina Silverberg

I went to private schools. They don't have too many, what they call here grade schools. My neighbor boy and me, we was same age; we have a private teacher. We didn't know city life. I had been two times inside of city before I came this country.

We celebrate Christmas in Finland just almost like here, but little better. Here, people more careless, they don't care how they dress. But we Finnish, came Christmas, it was so big honor. We fix ourself, best clothes, and we try to act really nice way. We went to church.

My mommy and daddy, they was really religious persons. When I read the Bible stories, I get the craziest ideas; and then I went asking to mommy those crazy things. Then my mother have temper. She pulling my hair. Then I start asking daddy. My daddy said, "Mommy's not mean to you, what? She have only one girl, she try to teach you be just as good woman like she is." He put it such nice way. He was really active at church. Every Sunday, he used to sing in the church.

Just before I left [for] this country, my cousin's wedding and I was best girl. We used to have three days dancing and celebrating. We make outside, flowers and branches. When we have a wedding party, we have sixty-three couples. We walk hand in hand. Then they give a soda pop to us and others they was drinking wine and some mans they was drinking whiskey. Then we started dancing about two o'clock. We was through six o'clock; it last four hours before we was through. We have many violins and accordion.

I didn't come to work here. I just came see my brothers in Naselle, Washington, just across the [Columbia] river. I have been three months old when the oldest one left home and the second one I have been already a year old. I came here I was eighteen, 1907. They wanted me to come, see. My mother and daddy, they have let me to go, and give me money.

I had been born in the farm country and I hadn't learn to do anything but just sweep the floors and mop the floors and cook a little bit something. I used to say, like snails with horns, you have to have those horns a little bit ahead and listen and go slowly. That's what I try to do.

I have been here now seventy-two years and I get these kind of spells, just like sickness. I get so lonesome for Finland. I tell truth, I like here and everything good; but I don't stay here if I don't have my daughter here and if I don't have two grandson and four great grandchildren and I love children. I can't go. I love Finland and everything so good there. I have good friends I like to visit there. I have first cousins and lots of second cousins. I get once in a while letter from Finland. And I have tapes, they playing to me tapes and singing.

I can talk a whole week. I have in my mind, when my daddy say good-by to me, when I left Finland. He gave a prayer. We went to Kokkola, where the train left. The steps for the train, I stand there, and he stand one step lower. Then he put his hands over my head, and he say, "Now our little girl is going to the world. I can't give you riches or gold or silver, but take my blessing and keep it. Remember the old folks' prayers and this will always help you." No matter what happens, I have my father's blessing.

Martin Rasmussen

"When I was a child,
we ate out of a common big dish."

Martin Rasmussen was born in 1896 to Danish farmers
living in what was then German territory. He went through
a traditional apprenticeship and served in the German army
before his path led to Denmark and on to the United States
in 1923. After several years in the Midwest, Martin moved
to Tacoma, where he designed and made machinery for
a plywood plant.

It was Germany at that time. North Slesvig, the Germans called it. Now the name is Sønderjylland [southern Jutland]. It used to be a Danish province, before 1864, that's where they had the war between Germany and Denmark. It went back to Denmark in 1920; I saw the king driving over the border to take possession.

My father was born in Denmark and my mother in North Slesvig. I had four brothers and one sister. My oldest brother, Søren, inherited the farm. We brothers were all in German military service between 1914–1918, in World War I. One of my brothers fell in Poland—Peder Rasmussen; he was around twenty years old.*

My father had a nice farm. It was good-sized—a hundred and fifty acres or something like that, fourteen to eighteen cows, and six or seven horses. You had to work on the farm. You had to get the cows out in the field and everything in order before you went to school in the morning. Later on, you had to be out and pull up the rutabagas and turnips and so forth. We had some hired help, too.

*Some six thousand Danes from Slesvig died in German uniform during WWI; an additional seven thousand ended the war as invalids.

Martin Rasmussen's unit, German Army, World War I

Potatoes, we'd get a special vacation for potatoes, two weeks in September or August. Then the whole family was in the potato field; that was nasty and cold. Had a wonderful appetite when we got home at five or six o'clock. There was a couple of men digging; the rest of us were gathering the potatoes in sacks. In many cases, there was dug a big hole in the ground, the potatoes down there, and straw on the bottom, and straw on the top, and dirt on it, and they would last all winter. There would be quite a few rotten ones, though. That was the same way with rutabagas—hauled to a hole and then covered up, but you didn't dig down as deep.

In those days, we didn't have much machinery, so we cut the straw for the horses by hand, with a hand machine. Out in the fields, the rye was harvested first. There would be four or five manfolks with a scythe cutting down. The women, they would gather the grain; they had some kind of a fork, and then they didn't have any string, so they would use a handful of straw and bind it. I did that many times; it takes a certain amount of skill. Later on, we got a harvesting machine; we would have to go after and tie it up.

The womenfolks, they would be out helping in the field quite a bit. And they would do the milking of the cows. They had to be milked three times a day: in the morning, at noon, and around eight o'clock at night. A milkman came around in the morning and hauled all the milk from that village to the dairy to be processed. When the cream was taken out, the skim milk came back to feed the hogs and the calves. That was the ordinary procedure. The milk was the main income, and selling hogs.

In wintertime, snow would be plenteous; sometime the snow would go up to the roof. We would play in the snow. We did some skiing in the meadows. For entertainment, we kids did card playing, what was called *sort peder* [*sorteper* = Old Maid], blackjack, something like that. In summertime, the boys would all go bathing. We had a creek that went through there. And we played this here football, soccer. That was our entertainment. And then, of course, we all had a bicycle. But the cattle had to be taken care of on Sundays and every day. Work was the main thing. On Sundays, we would ride the horses sometimes. Sometimes my dad, he would buy a wild one that nobody could stay on.

My mother, and then there was usually one or two girls, they did the sewing. My mother did the weaving; she was a good weaver. The clothes, of course, was made by a tailor, usually very heavy clothing.

And then, of course, there was the fall butchering; that was another occupation for the womenfolks, they were helping. And then the baking. We had a big oven. My dad, he usually fired it up in the forenoon, made it real hot with wood. Then my mother would bake the white bread. The pumpernickel were put in the oven after the cake and cookies was baked. The pumpernickel would be about a foot-and-a-half long and there would be about thirty of those. They was put in and stayed in there for hours. After it was baked in the afternoon, these pumpernickel was taken out and laid upside down on the bed, I don't know why, but that was the rule.

When I was a child, we ate out of a common big dish. Everybody had a spoon and dipped. My mother had an old-fashioned stove with wood or coal, and then it had a big pan on there. What we mostly had for dinner was sidepork and potatoes. Beans was conserved in a big jar, salted. And then the beets was stored in big jars, pickled. They would hang the hams around the stove and then they would put them on the top floor, in big caskets with grain. Upstairs over the living quarters, that's where the grain would be stored. So it was a very warm building. The windows were single, not double like today. There would be flower pots in all the windows. The beds were enclosed, and then there was curtains in front.

Ghost stories, an awful lot of those. They had seen a woman without a head walking past the graveyard. Oh, that was very dangerous. They'd seen this and they'd seen that. The graveyard was something—you didn't pass by there at night. Sometimes with a wedding, the horses would stop, and that was a bad omen.

Going to church, manfolks sit on one side and womenfolks sit on the other side. No mixed affairs, no. There was, like usual, singing, but there was no dancing. That was the Lutheran church. The minister, he was speaking Danish, because the majority were of Danish descent. There was a few Germans in the neighborhood up there, too, but it was all Danish [in church]. The pastor has a farm, but, of course, the farm was rented out to some other farmer. But he lives in that farmhouse; he lives nice and well.

For confirmation preparation you had to go there once a week, one forenoon each week, for half a year. In the lectures for confirmation, we had to learn a lot of songs and to know about the Bible. Then for confirmation the boys had to stand on one side and the girls on the other side. They [congregation] was sitting in the pews and we were standing up there. He asked each one certain questions; I almost remember what he asked, it was something special from the New Testament. We had to answer and we'd better knew the answer, too.

The grownups went to church Christmas Day. That was very important. But Christmas Eve was the greatest affair for the children. You usually had a Christmas tree in the biggest room, the hall. There was no

electric lighting in those days, we had candlelight. We were all dancing around our Christmas tree. Before that we had our best and finest
dinner in the year. That usually consisted of pork and all the things that
goes with it, because that was extraordinary. After dancing around the
Christmas tree, we got the gifts. After that they had *pebernødder* [pepper-
nuts, small cakes]. They are prepared before Christmas. We helped cut
those in the evening and they had big bags of it, that was especially for
the kids. My dad put out the grain for the birds; everything had to be
taken care of right.

New Year's Eve, we boys went out in the afternoon to the relations,
far off, with these Chinese fireworks and then we usually got cookies.
That was us kids. Then in the evening the grown-ups would come
around in droves. You go from one farm to another and then they
would shoot fireworks and then they would be invited in for coffee,
cake, and cookies. And that was up to twelve or one o'clock. But then
after that, some of the neighbors would come and get into the cow barn
and steal the wheelbarrows and take the gates away from the fence and
things like that, be mischievous. They would haul things way up on the
hillside or put it on the roof or things like that. That was the grown-up
boys. My brothers had to be awake all evening so they didn't do too
much damage. That was New Year's Eve.

I went to a German school, quite strict, and finished my eighth grade.
German in school. Well, we had two hours of Danish Bible class. Our
schoolteacher, he could talk Danish, too. The pastor, he was the head
of the schools in that district; there were probably five or six schools.
The teachers didn't like to see him, because it meant criticism. Everything was very strict in those days. The teacher, he knew how to use
the rod. And at home it was the same thing. My mother, she had a nine
cat tail [cat-o'-nine-tails] that was used to keep us in line. But life was
still wonderful.

I went to be an apprentice in a machine shop in Vojens. I was apprenticed for four years; I started in 1910 and I get out in 1914. I lived among
the people down there. You had to pay a certain amount for room and
board. Father had to pay that because we didn't get hardly any wages
for an apprentice, started in with five cent an hour. Apprenticeship was

very strict. The boss, he would hit you. I stayed home one Christmas. It was that week between Christmas and New Year and I could help with the threshing. When I came back, he hit me right and left—I didn't have permission.

The journeymen, they were allowed to wear a hat, kind of round and old-fashioned; but the apprentice wasn't allowed to wear that. When someone tried, they'd just throw that hat off and down in the dirt. The journeyman, he told me one day to oil his shaft. I thought I didn't have to do that, but maybe I should have done it because he sure gave me a dandy licking. *Ja*, they were tough. I think we were about twelve apprentices to the place. And we became powerful after a while because there was almost more apprentices than journeymen. They changed a little bit.

After I was through apprenticeship four years, then I went down to Hamburg in 1914–15. The war had begun at that time. I went out on the *Flugplatz*, the flying field in Hamburg. There I was doing some machine job. These big balloons—zeppelins—would go from there up along the coastline and watch out for the fleet and they would go to England, too. One day, it was kind of blowing. They didn't have enough [men] to haul the zeppelin down, so we from the shop had to go over and help haul that thing down and get it into the big hall. We held on and then a storm, a kind of heavy wind, came and it went up. I let go, most of them just let go. But there was a couple that kept hanging on to that darn thing, and they went up with it! Of course, they came back down. Then I saw the bombs—the ones that they used against England. They were stacked outside; they were kind of pear-shaped.

Then I came home. My oldest brother, he was a strong Dane and my sister, too. They went across the border and had their meetings over there. The Germans were not always too sweet. You couldn't sing. The newspapers could be anti-German, but if you had festivities, certain hymns you couldn't sing. There was a wedding in town and there was some of those younger guys that want to sing these here songs that they were not supposed to sing. This Hans, he was from Jutland, but he was a strong German. So he mentioned about this here singing they did. The judge and some of those Germans found out and they went to court about that. And right close to the border, they had some rough guys that went into the school. There was usually three pictures on the back wall. That was the Kaiser, the former Kaiser, and Kaiser Wilhelm. And they had damaged the pictures. That was very serious. They had to skip the country; they got up to ten years in prison. That was terrible to damage the image of the Kaiser.

Then I was drafted into the service. When you're young like that, you hear them talk about all what went on, war and so forth—you hear it from school. It was worked on you constantly, this here propaganda about how wonderful war was. We had a teacher, he knew our Danish sentiment. He didn't like that. He was from further down in Germany. I didn't have any special interest in going off to a German war, because our sentiment was rather Danish. But still, I liked to see what went on, so I could tell when I came back what I'd seen. Boys, they have that kind of spirit.

There was two million students in Germany that volunteered. When they came to the front, they found out they didn't like it. And I had the same experience. The frontline, that's where reality shows up. There is nothing beautiful about a war. If there is a hell on earth, it is right there. I was down in France. Then I contacted typhus and came back to German hospitals and was taken well care of by the nuns. Especially one, she was the sweetest. I wasn't supposed to have any black bread or any pumpernickel, but she come after work and give me something. I don't want to go on about the war.

After the war, in 1918–19, we could come to Denmark; the border was open. I had my four years of apprenticeship that was necessary to enter the engineering institute in Copenhagen. We got a good education there, about three and a half, four years. After my schooling, I got a job in a dairy machinery outfit in Kolding, Denmark.

I went to the United States in 1923. I was getting to be up in years, twenty-seven. There was not enough work in Denmark. They couldn't use all the technical men they made. I had been 'round in the world, been working in Germany, in the war. To go to America, I didn't think there was much to that!

Sigfrid Ohrt

"He slipped out of the country."

*Sigfrid Ohrt left Norway with her mother in 1901, at the age
of ten. They settled in the Dakotas, and Sigfrid held many
different jobs while obtaining a business education. She and
her husband moved to the Pacific Northwest in 1919. They
raised four children.*

We lived in Eidsness, a rural community up on a fjord, and my father made his living by working in Bergen. He did various things. He worked for a newspaper, wrote articles and witty things, and was involved in a bank. My mother had a child every year. She came from a mountain family where they had been in dairying. She did the farmwork; it was a small, small acreage.

In those days, the families made their own clothes. They had sheep and used the wool. My mother had a spinning wheel and I can remember winding up yarn for her. She had a dressmaker come in to sew for us, a shoemaker come in to make shoes. She did a lot of things, but she couldn't do everything. So, that's the kind of a family we were on a small place. I was born September 26, 1891.

I remember being quite an active child. My brothers would make a big swing between two trees, one boy on each tree; they'd swing me almost around in a circle. We played with boats in the little inlet and we did fishing. In the winter, you could skate on the lake. I don't recall ever swimming there. Girls could wade, but boys could swim. One of my brothers snared birds. We frown on that today, but then it was sport. We played games with rocks. We'd pick up little rocks and throw them up in the air, and they'd land on the back of our hand, and we'd throw them up and catch them again. That was one of our favorite pastimes.

We started school at the age of seven and had school six days a week, Saturdays as well as other days. I was very excited the first day of school. My sister Inger and her friend, who were three years older than I, took me to school. They each held a hand and escorted me into the school-room. The schoolmaster was a young man who sat me in a seat and gave me some instructions. He asked me to write a "4." I wrote it up-side down. He said, "In our school, we do it this way." We used slates and slate pencils. I was given one and felt very important.

We had to memorize our lessons. I used to get up real early every morning to do my studying. We were very well disciplined; we did our work. I was not the best student, but I did try to memorize. Religious training was done in the school. We had catechism and Bible history.

On Sunday, the neighbors used to gather. They had a big boat, big enough for the neighbors who wanted to [go to] church. About four men would row across the fjord to the church. They were long ser-vices. My mother used to have us children on the floor in front of her. The seats were high-backed seats so we couldn't be seen. We'd be play-ing on the floor there while the service was going on. I don't know how she kept us quiet; she was a very good disciplinarian. After the services, we looked forward to getting out and looking at the graves [in the churchyard]. I can still remember admiring the beautiful roses.

My grandfather Eidsness was a very fine old man. When I was a little wee girl, grandfather used to hold me on his knee and sing to me, "*Ride, ride ranke, hesten heter Blanke.*"* He was living with his second wife in one part of the house. The house was built with two stories and we had half of it, the bigger half. Grandfather and grandmother had their room and a storeroom. We were never allowed to visit them without permission. But I used to follow grandfather around the grounds; and when he went fishing, he'd have me in the boat with him. Grandmother had a great big apron she wore and whenever she went out some place away from the house, she'd gather up sticks and things for her stove. They were very thrifty and she was especially so.

Our mother seldom left her home; she was so busy there. But she did

*Nursery rhyme similar to "Ride a cock-horse to Banbury Cross."

go to the Christmas program at the schoolhouse with us. We danced around the Christmas tree and sang Christmas carols. They had one ring of adults. And the next [ring] would be coming the opposite direction with teenage children and at the outside were the little ones. We'd go in different directions. That was the highlight of our celebration. It was a free and easy evening. That was where I drank my first cup of cocoa; we really thought that was something special.

And the community celebrated the Seventeenth of May.* They would get together and march two by two to the schoolhouse and back home. Somebody would be carrying a big flag at the head of it, and each one of the children would carry a small flag. We looked forward to that.

We left Norway when I was ten. I had been in school three years. My father was the kind of a man who was quite talented and he was very, very generous with his time and talents—to the extent that his family was neglected. In time, he got himself into trouble. He couldn't fulfill his financial obligations, so he slipped out of the country. That I understand was quite common in those days. His income wasn't sufficient to take care of his big family, so the house was about to be taken away.

So my mother's father, and also a brother, came to our home and helped her pack and dispose of things. She had to get out of there, and she was doing the best she could. She had three brothers in South Dakota who had farms. They were just young men who had recently come to America. They sent money for the tickets so she could pack her family to America. Also, they needed help in South Dakota, so my sister Inger who was then thirteen and John who was sixteen were sent tickets to come over by themselves, before we were ready to go.

I can remember my mother hiding things in the hayloft for her family. She hid a saddle in the hay and there must have been other things, too. She brought her hand sewing machine and her spinning wheel with her; she couldn't part with them.

The day that we left, I had a special friend that I wanted to say good-bye to. And when the rest of the family were carrying the stuff to the boat landing, I slipped around to this house to say good-bye to that

*Norwegian Constitution Day, the national holiday.

family. And my grandfather came down. He was very sad and he said, "I know I shall never see any of you again." He wandered back to the empty house with tears rolling down his cheeks.

We were loaded into that big community boat and the neighbors rowed us over to the little landing where the boat picked us up. We stayed overnight in Bergen and the following day we were taken by boat across the North Sea to England.

When we left Norway in 1901, we really never got together as a family anymore. We were scattered through no fault of our own, just circumstances. So that's it.

Andrew Johnson

"We were raised like regular puritans."

*Andrew Johnson and his family left Sweden for Tacoma in
1914. Andrew was fourteen years old and wanted to go to
school or learn a trade; instead, he took a series of factory and
caretaker jobs before becoming a machinist during the Second
World War. He married an American of Swedish descent and
had two daughters. As a young immigrant, Andrew endured
a rather hostile reception.*

My name, Anders Johansson, was changed in the immigration
papers. I was told to call myself Andrew and change Johansson to Johnson. I don't know why. I was born in Hallarum,
Jämjö parish, Blekinge province. That's in the southeast part of Sweden,
right on the coast of the Baltic. I was born March 4, 1900.

My mother was born out on an island. Her folks were small farmers
and fishermen. My father's folks were crofters. A crofter is a person that
gets a piece of land from a larger farm; he uses it as he wants to, only
he pays a rent. He has to pay either in money or in labor, so many days'
labor a year, to the big farm.

We were also in a way crofters. We first started in a small house that
was on this farm, with no land, and then we got some land. Later on,
we owned a building and put it on the land. But the land belonged to
this big farm and we paid fifteen crowns* a year, or fifteen days of labor

---

*The crown has been the monetary unit of Denmark, Norway, and Sweden since the
Scandinavian monetary union was formed in the 1870s. There are one hundred öre/
øre in each crown. The exact worth of the crown varies slightly among the countries;
the present exchange rate is approximately six crowns to one U.S. dollar.

in task tax, for that land. That's what we had when we sold the place and came to this country.

We lived close to a village that mainly existed on brick manufacturing. My father was a brickburner. To bake the bricks, you have to be skilled. You have to know exactly how hot it is. If you get it too hot, it will melt together. And if you don't get it hot enough, you get a brick that is not any good. I played there all the time. That's where I got my love for machinery, because I was always helping somebody doing something.

We're eight, four boys and four girls. I'm the oldest. Mother took care of us. She was the boss and she knew how to work both ends against the middle. She had to. Father was gone quite a bit. When the brick plant was down for improvements, he worked in the sugar-beet fields in Skåne.*

In Sweden, I finished what they call grade school. I was supposed to go to school for seven years; but I skipped a class, I only went for six. School started at nine o'clock and we started out walking about seven o'clock. We usually were three or four in company, so we were never lonesome. The first three years, I had a very, very, very strict teacher. I didn't get along too well with her. Then we had a young woman teacher and I fell in love! The last two years, we had a man teacher. He was understanding and had a way about him. I have to admit, I was more relaxed and learned more. He had care of the manual training. Manual training was very important for the boys; the girls, of course, had their classes of sewing and so on. I really enjoyed school. I loved to study.

I was confirmed in Sweden, too. We didn't break away from the state church, but our religious affiliation was missionshus, mission house. A lot of people were dissatisfied with the way the state church kept its services; they were much too formal. So, the laymen got together and held services in chapels all over. They were freer and you were allowed to express yourself; it was more of an awakening. That's how the Covenant Church started. In Swedish, it's called missionsförbundet, mission cove-

*Province at the southern tip of Sweden.

nant. Waldenström favored these mission houses and became a leader among them.[*]

There was a lot of trouble in Sweden. It was against the law to have a religious meeting in a home or in a chapel unless the parish minister was present. The statutes were finally taken out of the books about 1850.[†] The pressure got so hard on the state church that they had to change; it wasn't the religious freedom that people liked.

On my mother's side, people were very religious. Out the islands there, many of these old fishermans know the real thing. When my mother was small, sailors used to come out to her dad's house; they had private prayer meetings together. And she used to tell me, some of them, they had long whiskers and they used to pray and sing, and be real happy in the Lord together. My mother grew up under that influence and she made sure we got it, too.

Christmas Day, early in the morning, we always had a julotta [Christmas morning worship] in the Lutheran church. When I was small, the service started at four o'clock in the morning. On Christmas Eve, we give presents and had a tree. Sometimes we managed to get some lutfisk[‡] and we loved gröt [porridge] made out of milk and rice. And, of course, my mother was a good baker. She baked all kinds of coffeebread and cookies.

Then we had another thing we ate, and were famous for down there—kroppkaka. You take potatoes and you grate them, and you take all the starch out and you put flour in so it has a consistency. You make a ball and on the inside you put meat. Only we'd put onions and pepper inside with the meats. Then you boil them. Kind of a potato dumpling; we liked that.

Of course, we lived out close to the water and there was a lot of fish

---

[*]The Swedish Mission Covenant Church was founded in 1878. Paul Peter Waldenström (1838–1917) was an engaging preacher who played a major role in the establishment of the independent local congregations that comprised this free church.
[†]The penalties for holding private religious meetings were abolished in 1858, although some restrictions on free preaching remained in force until 1868.
[‡]Literally, lye fish; see also the interviews with Gretchen Yost and Torvald Opsal.

to eat, especially cod. Then around March we had a Baltic herring that was running. They would catch tons of it. It was bigger than smelts. You used to fillet and fry them and my memory is that it tasted just wonderful. [Also] they used to take this herring and salt it and use it anytime.

We had chickens and we had rabbits and then we always killed a pig in fall. And my mother knew how to make all kinds of sausage. It's too bad that we lost that; none of us took a hold to learn it. And we took the rye to the flourmill and had it ground and mother did the baking. We had a great big oven and we made a big, big fire in that. Then they raked all the coal and everything out of it. Mother had a wooden shovel; she put so many big round cakes in there and closed the door.

We made pie in Sweden, because so many Americans had come back and they taught people how. There was a tremendous influence by people that had come back for a visit. It was tremendous, really. They almost committed suicide, the Swedes. Everybody left.

About 1907, there was hard times in Sweden. The brick plant was shut down and my dad could not get anything to do. An aunt, my mother's sister, was over for a visit in Sweden from this country. She had a boarding house down on "I" Street in Tacoma. "Well," she said to my mother, "I can take Alfred"—that's my dad—"he can come over to Tacoma and stay with me for a while." It only cost thirty dollars for a ticket. So it was decided that 1908, he come to the United States. Dad was in the militia and they wouldn't let him go; he had to write to get a special permit from the high court in Stockholm. So he was delayed a couple months.

Dad was working here in Tacoma in one of these fuel yards selling wood and coal. He was a teamster, them days. Then 1912, my mother's brother Magnus and my sister's husband John came back from America and they were going to stay [in Sweden]. But John had been back two months and he says, "No, I'm not staying. I'm going back to United States." Then my mother wrote my dad, "I'm not going to stay all by myself."

In 1914, we all came over. My mother sold everything. You put an ad in the paper that you intend to sell your home and there would be an auction. You auction off all your chairs and furnitures and all your belongings at a certain date. Then we sold the house and the contract that we had with the farmer to somebody else. The money we used for a ticket. At that time there were a lot of competition between the different steamship companies, because they wanted the immigrant trade. We got leaflets from Scandinavian-American Line, from the Cunard Line, from the White Star Line, heaven knows what we didn't get from. And agents even come and visited us.

I had a good time in Sweden. When I was in my teens, I would have gone back any chance I had. At that time, there was an awful lot of jokes and fun made of the immigrants. I could never open my mouth and talk without somebody making fun of me. It happened fifteen, twenty times every day. "You goddamm Swede, go back where you come from." At work, you heard that all the time. "You dumb Swede," and so on. I come out with the rough and tough workers and all other nationalities and they just cussed you down something awful sometimes, they really bore down on you. I just hated it! I hated to go to work; I hated to be here; I hated everything here.

Even in our Swedish church I was very unhappy. Most of the young people that went there were born in this country and they kind of looked down on you, as what they call a greenhorn. I was surprised at the attitude they took, that you were very ignorant and didn't know nothing. Even in church.

The only thing I went to was the Scandinavian church, for the simple reason that we were raised like regular puritans. It was wrong for us to play cards, it was wrong for us to dance, and these lodges and so on were not where we belonged. I can remember they were dancing at home [in Sweden]. But the people that were dancing, they nearly always got drunk and there were fights, bloody fights. We were supposed to be separate; we were brought up this way. Now I realize that some of that was wrong, because you lived in a cage.

Torvald Opsal

"Home you had plenty to eat, but there was no cash."

After spending the summer of 1929 in the Midwest, Torvald Opsal came west to Washington. There the nineteen-year-old Norwegian began a long association with the fishing industry. Ten years later, he married. While Torvald fished seasonally in Alaska and California, his wife worked as a bookkeeper in Tacoma.

My mother's maiden name was Kjersti Fatland and my dad was Torkel Opsal. They were born and raised in Vikedal, Norway. Vikedal is just a hamlet. Stavanger is the main town; it's two hours by ferry. The Gulf Stream came by there, so it was mild. It would snow for a week and then it would rain for two weeks. Walking to school, you could feel the cold slush on the open heel of your wooden shoes. I feel it still!

My granddad on my dad's side and his two brothers had a shipyard. They built good-sized sailing ships for a living. When they sold the shipyard, they bought a farm apiece. His name was Amundson, but he bought the Opsal farm, and that's how the Opsal name came in. You see, my granddad became Ole Amundson Opsal after he bought that farm.*

I never knew my granddad on my mother's side, because he died early, but my grandmother, Ingeborg Fatland, got to be ninety-eight or ninety-nine. She lived on a farm halfway up in the valley, had nine kids. She was just a quiet, hard-working woman—light, small, active, could outrun any sheep until the day she died. Those old-timers made

---

*A person's last name typically derived from the name of the farm. Place names remained stable, whereas personal names might shift.

Torvald Opsal (left) and his brother Ole, ca. 1912

practically everything; did the spinning, all the weaving. It was a hard
life, but still she had all she needed.

My dad went over to Minnesota and North Dakota and stayed for six
years. He came back in 1906 and took over my granddad's place, started
raising a family. We were four kids, three boys and a girl. It was a small
farm, seven, eight cows and a horse. They had boats, did a little fishing on the side. And they had woods, cut timber and sell. They pretty
much lived the same way the whole area—a little farming, a little two-
bit logging, and some fishing. To meet the bills, they would sell things
on the farm, like pigs and sheep. We raised quite a few sheep.

They had good grade schools. Even as old as my grandmother was, she had gone to grade school like the rest of us. When I started school, I was six years old and I had the same teacher my dad had gone to. They were kind of foxy, those old teachers; they wouldn't do anything to embarrass somebody that was a little slower. We had so many classes in one room. That was good, because we could be two, three years behind and we could listen to what the teacher was teaching the higher-ups. We caught on to something before we got there ourselves.

Everybody had to go to church. The minister had three churches; he alternated, every third Sunday, but he lived in Vikedal. The church was state-owned; they were state-paid. We had Sunday School every Sunday, except that Sunday we had church, in what you called bedehuset [the meeting house]. That was community-owned and operated. There was three, four that would teach Sunday School. We all had to go.

Then you had religion half an hour a day in school, every day. Bible history was a book in itself and it was practically all dates. You had to learn it at home and tell the teacher the next day. You didn't know when you'd be called on, so you couldn't get away from it.

What we got out of Christmas wasn't presents like now; it was food, good food. That's what we looked forward to. I don't remember ever having a present or giving one until the last year or two before I left. Nobody did. Christmas Eve, the guy went up to church and started ringing the bell. Everybody had the holidays off. There was no police or anything like that, so there was nothing to have open. It was quiet, peaceful.

Christmas Eve at our place was mostly meat, a roast, and risengrøt [rice porridge]. That was a must. I remember when we were real young, we had a big bowl, a tureen, that sat on a stand. It was cooked so fine and so nice you wouldn't know it was rice. It was floating in butter and they had this red sauce on top. That was the best stuff. We all took a spoon and ate out of that bowl. That's the custom of that time. Later on, we had our own plates. We went to church, everybody, Christmas morning. Then mother would usually leave church a little early and go home and get the food ready for the rest of us. We had meat and potatoes. We lived good.

Sandbakkelse and *krumkake* and all that [typical cookies] was kept in a big tin can, so you had it for weeks after New Year's. Of course you didn't get all you wanted; that was more or less rationed. When people came to the house, they had to have coffee and goodies. We never went anyplace and nobody ever came to us from an invitation; it was always, if they stopped by. We didn't have much of anything except we had good food. At least it tasted good to us! I never tasted *lutefisk* * until I came here to Normanna Hall [Tacoma, Washington], and I didn't like it. Nobody had it where I came from.

Good heavens, for money I started to work when I was just a little tyke. Our neighbor was quite well-to-do, had a big, big farm, and did a lot of hiring, especially in the haying and cutting the grain. My brother and I were just small ones and we were cutting grain for money. It was raining. We had made kind of a headgear out of gunny sacks and that got soaked wet and you were wet. But you stayed all day long, day in and day out. Working, that was something we had to do when we started to walk. There was no playing; even going to school we never had any time for play.

While I was confirmed, I worked in a granite rock quarry. We hauled *gatestein*, cobblestones, down to the dock and the steamers came in and picked it up. There was no power equipment; your arms and hands did it all. Then I went on a road gang. We made a highway going up to the valley. You had a long plank and a wheelbarrow and a pick and shovel. It was all done by hand, every bit of it. You got into rocks, then you had the experts dynamiting it. That's all I did until the time I came here [to United States].

I grew up with people that had been in this country. I'd say just about half of the population home had been here. My gosh, you could go down to the stores and they would sit there and talk English, and even talk Norwegian, about the old logging days out here [in the Pacific Northwest] and fishing in Alaska and farming in the Midwest. They all liked it out here [Pacific Northwest], the climate and it was just like back

---

*Lutefisk, dried cod which is treated and soaked before cooking, is widely identified as an ethnic trademark among Norwegian Americans.

home—trees, water, boats, and what have you. As much like home as you can get, on a bigger scale.

Through the quota system, I signed up to go to a farm.* My dad's three brothers lived in North Dakota, so I sent some papers to them and one of them signed a guarantee. The next thing I knew, I got a notice that I was accepted and had to go to an American doctor in Bergen. It took money to go up to Bergen and I didn't have any money. Home you had plenty to eat, but there was no cash. So my dad had a cow he was going to sell, says to take it along to town. So I took the cow along to town, sold it in Stavanger, got the cash for it, and went to Bergen.

The doctor checked your teeth for cavities and checked you for hernia and then filled out some papers. That was about all. I was eighteen in May and went to the doctor in the fall the same year, 1928. I didn't go [emigrate] till March of 1929.

I made my own trunk, spent weeks on that thing and made it good. Mother was pretty good up until the last day. She made breakfast and I ate good. And then right after breakfast, she decided to go out and I could see that she just couldn't be there when I left the house. So she went out in the barn. As I walked out, why I glanced to the side and I could see her through the window in the barn.

My dad took me down to the dock. Of course, he had been here; it was nothing to him. He was glad that I could get out, because he knew very well that there was nothing to do at home. It's silly to keep the kids at home, if there's nothing for them.

*Through the quota laws of 1921 and 1924, the United States government began restricting immigration into the country.

Gretchen Yost

*"We had to find out ways for ourselves
how to make things go."*

Ten-year-old Greta, or Gretchen as she became known
in English, emigrated with her mother and brother
in 1919. From 1920 she lived in Tacoma. On her own
at the age of fourteen, Gretchen worked in a cafeteria
and later baked and sold pies. She shared favorite food
customs with her three children, but cultivated no
formal ties with her Swedish heritage.

My name was Greta Karlsson. I was born July 25, 1909, in Malmö, Sweden. Malmö was a very busy metropolis.[*] I remember its cleanliness and I remember the birch trees down the inner section of the roads. But no small homes; they were building apartment complexes. There would be a cement court in the middle and then all these apartments around. You went in through like a gate, actually not a gate but an opening. Inside, they would have a level up where all the little outhouses were, because there wasn't any indoor plumbing. The courtyard was a place for the children to play. It was a fabulous place, because [at Midsummer] the big maypole would be put up and the violins and the accordions would come and everyone would dance.

That was fish country. I remember the fishermen coming in this courtyard with a cart and calling out "Limhamnssill, Limhamnssill." Limhamn was a little fishing country [village, now suburb of Malmö] and sill of course meant fish [herring].

You came into a hallway. It was quite dark. Then it had a small kitchen where my mother always had flowers of some kind growing. I remem-

[*]Located at the southern tip of Sweden, Malmö had 83,000 inhabitants in 1910.

57

ber very vividly that she'd have nasturtiums and how bright they were in the window. Then there was one small bedroom and one a little bit larger. We ate in the kitchen. It was just very small. No indoor plumbing as far as the toilet facilities was concerned, but yet we had water. All these little outhouses were locked, so I had the key around my neck when we'd be out playing.

My mother was a widow. My father was drowned when I was six months old. He was a fireman on a ship. And so, from then on it was hard work. My mother couldn't make enough and us children had to help. She was cleaning office buildings or whatever menial labor she could get. My brother had a job working for a fruit company where he would haul the fruit in a wooden cart; and when the fruit got ripe we were very happy, because he could bring it home if it got too ripe.

In those days there wasn't the fear of children being on the street or in a crowd. My brother was a real promoter. He was old for his age. And he'd get this type of a job and that type of a job. He had this job selling newspapers and magazines and he involved me in it. I used to sell magazines and papers in the depot when I was five years old. My brother was five years older than myself; he'd hide behind the post to see that I didn't get away with anything and they bought a lot from me. Of course, I wasn't old enough to go to school and he was, so I had to stay at home in the apartment during the day by myself—which left an effect on me, because I was always afraid of being alone afterwards.

It was just a matter of survival. Everybody had to pull together. Lots of little odd jobs that we would do that would help us bring in a little bit of money. Running errands and that type of thing for people, too. During the First World War, I can remember my mother taking a blanket and going and standing in line at the commissary and laying down on the blanket. And in the morning there would be nothing left, she couldn't bring food home. There were many beggars that would come right to the apartment. Mother always shared whatever crust we had. There were a lot of people that were going through miserable, miserable times.

I can remember vividly saving our öre, which is like your penny, so that once in a great while we could stand in line for hours and get way,

way up at the top to see an opera. Or maybe saving a little bit so we could go to the bakery and get a big bun full of whipped cream. That was part of our scrimping, to be able to do things that other children had every day. I remember the royalty coming to Malmö one time and we lining up the street to see the coach go by—to see the king and queen, which was a big thing for us.

My mother was a great baker. I can remember her making coffee cakes, braiding them. Kåldolmar, it's meat and rice wrapped in cabbage leaves. And filbunke—when we had a little extra, my mother would clabber milk, make it like soured milk; it was smooth like yogurt. And, of course, Christmas time back there. We would always have lingonberries and rice. You would have before Christmas and you would have after Christmas and you would have so many days. And, of course, herring and lutfisk.* Then they'd have this candy that was on a string, rock candy. You'd go in and buy and they'd break off a little piece of that.

I started school there but we didn't go very long, just a very short time. Growing up the way we grew up, we had to find out ways for ourselves, how to make things go. I just picked it up. That's why it's a bit amusing to me today that we have to have all these classes, because I had to learn on my own.

We did get out into the country. The government would ask people who were of means to take the children into their homes for holidays. And I can remember one time going to a very wealthy family at Christmas time; it really made a big impression on me. The maid brought me a doll for Christmas. It didn't have its head sewed on, it was tied on with a piece of cloth because the people were busy. They did this as a thing they should do, but that's all it meant to them. They were away partying. My brother got to go out on a farm for awhile. Otherwise, our life was pretty drab.

My mother had an aunt and uncle in Porter, Indiana, that's by Chicago. They had a big mercantile store and they had written to her and

*Lutfisk is codfish that has been treated in a lye-like solution and then cooked. In parts of Sweden and Norway, it is a traditional Christmas dish. In addition, as noted in the interview with Torvald Opsal earlier, it is often featured at Scandinavian-American festivities.

asked if she'd like to come over here and work for them. They said they would send a ticket for myself and her, and she said she would not come without my brother. So she doubled up on her job. When she had enough saved, that's when we came to this country, 1919, in February. I was only nine.

This is the passport photo before we left. My brother had borrowed somebody's chain, it looked like he had a watch fob. This was a friend of mine's dress. We put on the best clothes for the passport. But mother was very unhappy to go. And in that picture it shows her face was swollen from crying. I can remember her crying so. It was her life back there and we didn't know what we were getting into. We didn't know a word of English. We thought this country was going to be a country of Indians, cowboys, shooting—we didn't know. My mother, the little bit of money she had, she sewed inside of her undergarments to protect.

I remember when we landed, squirming through all the grown-up people to see the Statue of Liberty. I had [bought] my first pair of shoes and they were button-up high shoes and somebody stepped on them and I spit on my shoes. I wanted them to be so shiny. I remember when we were met at the station at Porter, Indiana. It was my first car, a touring car with icicle glass [isinglass] in it. I leaned out, I wanted everybody to see me. I thought, "Are you looking at me? I'm in a car!" And I had a funny little round hat, a little tweed hat, and my long braids. I don't think anyone realizes the excitement of a new country. Today, of course, I'm very thankful; it's been my country.

Mother wasn't very well and we didn't realize how ill she really was. We were in Porter fifteen months and we came west to Portland [Oregon]. My mother married and then she became very ill. They diagnosed it as quick consumption—tuberculosis. She died then in June of 1920.

I was cut off by my mother passing away; no contact back to Sweden. I can't speak Swedish anymore because I didn't keep up that contact. But it's a very dear thing to me. I remember so well. I remember those streets, and what went on there.

Bergljot DeRosa

"Up in the north, they believe in trolls."

The daughter of a sea captain, Bergljot Oliver DeRosa enjoyed an urban childhood with many amenities. Then death and hardship touched the family, and individual members began emigrating. Bergljot came to Tacoma in 1922, at the age of twenty. In Tacoma, she worked as a domestic, raised three children, and taught Norwegian folk dancing.

We had our home in Trondheim, Norway.[*] In the summer-time, my mother took us children out in the country, where we could be by the water and live a healthy life. I happened to be born in Melhus. You could get out there by horse and buggy from Trondheim and I was born there in August, 1902. There was already three children; I was a little bit different from the rest of them. They were more red and robust and I was a very delicate, fair-looking baby. "Oh," they said, "she'll never live."

My father, Olav Moxness, was a sea captain. He used to run big English freighters, some of them had a hundred men on them. He could be gone a year at a time. He was in China and all over the world. When he came home, I could smell it—the whole house, engine smell. All the kids got in bed with him and had our morning coffee. My dad always had a big box with gifts and clothes for us. He bought most of our clothing in England—Scotch wool, tall long-button shoes that felt like gloves on our feet. He used to bring home beautiful stuff.

The Moxness family came from Verdalen in Trøndelag, Norway. They moved into Trondheim. My grandfather Moxness was *overlærer* [princi-

---

[*]Since the Middle Ages, Trondheim has been an important religious and cultural center. The third largest city in Norway, it had a population of 57,000 in 1910.

Bergljot Moxness DeRosa (youngest child) with her family in Trondheim, ca. 1903

pal] at Bakklandet School in Trondheim and they lived right there in the big apartment in the school. It had seven grades and A, B, and C [classes in each grade]. When I started school, we lived across the street from Bakklandet School.

When grandfather died, we moved up by the university, Norges Tekniske Høyskole. There was what they call "professor town," villas and private houses. We lived in a big, big wooden apartment house with veranda on each side. We had seven rooms and a balcony. There used to be a lot of students living there. There was a widow upstairs and she used to have kind of a *pension* for students to have their dinner. We had a bread and milk seller and a shoemaker underneath in the basement. All the houses there, my, they build them so good, tile roofs and everything. This one was just made out of wood. They said it was built by an American, so it would never hold up!

My mother was Sara Kristensen Moxness. She was born in Sortland [northern Norway], 1875. Her father used to have a store and the fishermen used to come there and load up their wares for their trips. When my mother was fifteen years old, her mother died. Then my mother went to live with her aunt and her grandmother Wiklum in Trondheim.

My mother's grandmother was a great woman. Her name was Sara Wiklum and she had what they call a saloon in Trondheim. Well, it wasn't rough or anything. She had a grocery and bakery in Lower Bakklandet 25 and beer and wine in Brandsalen, a little more west in the street where they lived. Every year she sailed with her old boat, or yacht they call it there, to Bjørnsmarkedet in Stokmarknes and sold her wares. She was eighty years old the last time she went up there, all by herself in a little boat. So she was really, really strong.

Mother met my father when she was about eighteen years old. He wanted to marry her. They thought she was a little bit too young, so they sent her to an aunt in America for two years, so she would be a little older and make up her mind if this is the way she wanted it. After two years, she went back to Trondheim and married my father. And had six children. Of course she had help when my father was gone. When we were small, we always had housekeepers. And when she went to England to meet my dad, we always had two to take care of us children while she was gone.

We didn't work at home, but when I was ten years old, my mother asked another captain's wife if she would have the patience to teach me how to bake and cook and clean and take care of her little girl. My mother wanted us to learn. In Norway, they send their girls to husmorsskole [home economics school] to learn domestic work; but instead of doing that, I got it for nothing. After school, I went there and helped. In the summer vacation I stayed all the time. The lady really was wonderful to me. For some reason, I always liked domestic work and children, so it didn't bother me at all.

Christmas Eve, we had just for ourself. We had spareribs. In different parts of the country, they used different kind of food. In cities, seems like it was altogether different than out in the country. When you live in town, you have to buy it in the stores.

My mother had the most children, and my father's relatives always chose to come to us for Christmas Day. How they took interest in us children! We got handmade gifts, little fur collars and little mittens, and stuff like that. And we sang around the Christmas tree, and they all took part in it. That's when we had our big dinner. We had reindeer roast. Mother ran strips of pork, they call it spekk, into the meat, because there's no fat in there, see. There they don't roast meat in the oven, because it shrinks too much, and they don't fry meat. They roast it in a big pot. You brown it and then you cook it in milk or cream; and that gravy was, I believe, the best thing. Then we had tyttebær [lingonberries] and multekrem [cloudberry cream].

Then, of course, there was Christmas parties afterwards. I counted ten we went to one year. I remember I went to Glassmaker Petersen where they had a ballroom and we even had [dance] cards that we carried. At Christmas, we got to put fine little patent leather shoes on and we felt like we didn't touch the ground. We felt so light, because we always had to have heavy shoes on. Oh, it was so good to dress up for Christmas!

When I took care of that little girl, they gave me enough money so I could take dancing lessons. The boys sat in one end of the room and the girls in the other. And the boys came and bowed like in the military and the girls curtsied. You had your card where they wrote who they want to dance with. This was ballroom dancing and I enjoyed that.

My mother went to church, but she didn't think it was fair that we should sit in church, because it was a little deep to understand. But we children had to go to Sunday School every Sunday. When we left for Sunday School, my mother said, "Now, when you come back, I want you to tell me what you learned today." I remember I did go to church a couple of times with my sister and we got so tired we started to get hysterical. We couldn't grasp it, when he stood up there and used all those big words. Now, in Sunday School, they made it more like a story. And we had religion in school—catechism, explanation, Bible history. We said our prayer and sang our hymn when we entered the school-room. At home, never had a meal without saying the Lord's Prayer or table prayer. We took turns. We had really a good foundation that could last us through life.

I think my mother was a very smart woman in many things, because she had six children and we never have a mark on our name. She had so many good ways about her. When she was fun, she was fun; but when she was strict, she was strict. When she called us in at night for dinner, she just called us once. And we were supposed to be in hearing reach. She would not call us again. I remember once, I was going to have herring for dinner. My mother filleted it and put it on the plate with potatoes and soup. I didn't like it and I tried to get away from it. And when I came in at night and wanted something to eat, there's the dinner. There was no way, ever, that you can get out of doing what she told you. She never had to spank us or use her loud voice. There was no loud voice in that family, but, boy, when she said something, we went by her word. She never changed "yes," when she said "yes" and never changed "no." The children knew what "no" meant. When you get out in the world, you have to accept "no."

When you live in an apartment, there's a lot of complaints about children being noisy; but we had the best reputation because we put slippers on when we came in, so there was no noise. Then we had a big dining-room table where we sat around and drew and played games, and there was a nice stove kept us warm. It was a great life. I'm glad I lived in those days.

On Thursdays, we got to choose our dessert and it was always gooseberry pudding. That was my favorite. I don't know how many varieties they have. They have big huge red ones, green ones, yellow ones, little ones, big ones, and sweet as honey. I've never seen any of them like that here. And there was black currants and red currants and blueberries and tyttebær and something we call krekling [crowberry]. The bushes look like heather; they get berries on them, very little, about the size of huckleberries here, but they weren't much good for anything but for us kids to eat.

In the laundry room there was a big round stove. We used to have a big iron pot in that stove, where they used to boil the clothes. Then you took the pot off and it was a big plate there where they baked potato cakes and *lefse.*[*] We hired a woman to come and sit down there and make big piles of it. Otherwise we had to buy most things like that.

Up in Nordland, the north, they believe in trolls. They used to tell us, the horses come trotting down the road and once of a sudden they'll stop. And there was nothing there. They said, it was a troll there. They [horses] didn't dare step over it. This is a true story: My uncle's farm had fifty cows and in one little booth you couldn't keep a cow. She stood and stamped all day long and all night long. She kicked and she stamped and you had to take her out of there. And they said, those little men, we call them *småkaller*, that's their home and nobody gets in there. They couldn't keep a cow in there. That was the truth.

I remember there was a big party at my uncle's farm and all the guests was down in the barn looking at the cows. I was just a little girl then. My father had just bought me a beautiful little linen sailor suit from England. So I came out of that big barn. Right in the corner was some geese lying there with little babies and there was a big gosling. I ran and he chased me. He knocked me down in the puddle, and he hit me with his wings, and he pulled my hairs out. I thought I was going to have no more hair left, till they came out and caught me and took me in.

During the war [WWI], we all had to pitch in and help. We children was getting pretty big and my father was out at sea. We really had to scrounge around to get food for six. We used egg flours for eggs, when we made pancakes and stuff. We had to sit for hours and hours to get just a kilo of margarine. And we had whale fat for butter. It kinda stuck to the roof of your mouth when you ate it, but that was the only thing you can get. And cocoa shells for cocoa, for chocolate in the mornings. We ate a lot of whale meat. We had coupons—rationing. We just could get so much, and you had to stretch it as far as you could. I wouldn't say we suffered too much.[†]

---

*[*]*Lefse* is a flat, unleavened bread which is fried or baked from rolled dough and often served with butter and sugar; there are many regional variations.

[†]Norway remained neutral throughout World War I. During the early part of the war, 1914–1915, the country experienced a period of prosperity. Later, continued inflation created a serious problem and a lack of imported raw materials caused

Mother rented out two rooms, the front room and another little room there that we didn't need, to a student. He was a handsome man, very well dressed. He was just like one of the family. He played piano. We had a piano in the dining room.

My father was over in New York waiting for a new boat, that was in 1918. And a captain got sick, so he asked my father if, while he was waiting, he couldn't take his boat down to Australia. My father said he would. And the boat disappeared completely. There wasn't a sliver or a man to live to tell what happened to that boat.

That year was a very hard year, because my sister died, too. Spanish flu just went all over the country. Families died out.* We were lucky, because my mother used common sense. My sister died, because she was kind of weak anyway. And then this student that lived with us, he died. My mother said she could have saved him, if they wouldn't have taken him outside and taken him to the hospital and thrown him in the bath. If he could have lain here, she said, in the bed, he would have still lived.

Another thing when we were children was tuberculosis. Whole families around us died. We were not allowed to go in the houses there. My mother was very strict, that we didn't go in, no matter how clean the houses were. It was sad, but there was nothing you can do. They called it "galloping"; you just went to bed and you never got up. They were so sure there was no hope. That's why my mother was terribly strict that we were outside. Why, when I was fifteen, I still was out in the street playing with the kids, running around, because she wouldn't let us stay in the house. My father believed that we should raise our chest so we could have room for our lungs and heart. My, he used to hit us in the back, "Come on, straighten up." He was so proud to have a big chest cavity.

I was a skier. In the wintertime, after school, I walked [on skis] seven

---

manufacturing to suffer. Rationing of selected consumer products, including flour, sugar, and coffee, was introduced in January, 1918.

*Spanish influenza swept the globe in 1918. The Norwegian population was affected starting in April of that year.

miles up the mountain to Fjellseter. I got up there and then we sat around the fire. Oh, it was beautiful! And the same night, we made it down all by foot, over lakes and all. I did that every winter till the last snow at Easter. I was on top of that mountain and it was a paradise to me. Then in the summertime there was hiking. I used to hike out in the country; I could walk alone and just look around and be perfectly at ease and peace.

Then my mother started getting us ready. Being she was alone, she thought we'll do better over here. My sister Gunvor came in 1914 and I came in 1922. And then the following year my sister came and in 1925, my younger brother and my mother came. I didn't feel anything, because whatever mother said was to be done. It was no arguing. We went and I don't think we realized what we were going into, that we were leaving everything and everybody. I never got homesick really, except for the mountains.

Else Goodwin

"I have such good memories of Christmas Eve."

Born in 1913, Else Goodwin left Denmark in 1930 to visit
family friends in New York. On the return trip to Denmark
she met her first husband; they settled in Seattle in 1932.
Else cared for a stepson and two daughters and worked in
restaurants for many years. Following her second marriage,
she expanded her involvement in ethnic organizations like the
Danish Sisterhood, where she served as district president.

My father was Laurits Theodor Hammerbak. He was born out
in the country north of Slagelse, Denmark, in a little *hus-
mandshus* [crofter's house]. *Husmand* was generally somebody
that didn't have a farm, that worked for somebody else. My grandfather
was thatching roofs, he went out and used his manual labor. They had a
great big yard where they grew all their vegetables and had their chickens and so on. Father was the youngest of twelve children. They were
raised out in the country, but most of them drifted into Copenhagen.

My mother, Valborg Kristine Christiansen, was the middle of five
girls. Mother was born in Copenhagen. But she was the first one in her
family born there, because her father and mother and the older sisters
came from the northern part of Jutland. Hjørring is the major town in
the area where they came from; it's in the center of the tip of Jutland,
above Ålborg. I don't know what made them come to Copenhagen.
Grandfather Christiansen was a streetcar operator. When he first came
to Copenhagen, they had horse-drawn streetcars; then, of course, he
got on the electric ones.

One of my mother's sisters had married my father's brother, which
is probably why my dad and mother got together. When they were first

The Hammerbak beer wagon in Copenhagen, 1915. Else is on pony at right

married, my dad got beer from the breweries in kegs. The breweries didn't bottle their own beer, they sent it out in kegs to places where they tapped it off into bottles. And my father had one of those businesses. He had a small horse and a little wagon, and he would put all of the boxes with beer bottles on that and then he had his business route, his customers. He'd go around to all the different stores and deliver the beer. My mother helped him to tap the beer from the kegs. He did that until I was about five, and then the breweries took over that part of the business. It was just cut out from under them; all of a sudden they had no business anymore.

It was 1918, the middle of the war [World War I], and my father and two of his brothers went out north of Copenhagen. They had some big peat bogs and the three of them cut peat there for a whole summer. My mother was the housekeeper for the three men and we kids were

Part One / HOMELAND

along, my brother and I. I remember earning my first øre [penny]. They cut the peat and laid it out in the sod, and then they had to be turned so they could get dried on the other side. And I got I think two øre for each row that I turned. So, I started early making my own living!

That fall my father took an exam to work as a prison guard. He got into the Vestre fængsel, a prison in Copenhagen where they mostly hold people that have committed slight offenses or are waiting to have their case come up in court. He worked there for many years and during the Second World War he was in the main police yard in Copenhagen. He was the one who had to go down and open the door for the Germans when they came and banged on the door.*

When we came back from the peat experience, there was a shortage of apartments in Copenhagen. One of my father's brothers owned an old tenement. We got two apartments in there, because the apartments were two little rooms and a small kitchen. That's when we had the Spanish flu and that was terrible. In those tenements, it went right through the building. And nobody dared take care of you, because they were afraid of getting it themselves. My mother had just had her third child and was so sick. The doctor said, "Keep on nursing the baby, it's the only thing that's going to save her." She did, and the baby never got sick. My little brother never got sick, but my father and my mother and I were really in a bad way for a while.

After a couple of years there, we managed to get a nice apartment out in Østerbro, which is in a nice area of town. My parents bought a store where they mangled clothes. They had these big electric mangles. When it was time to do the dinners, mother would go in the kitchen and cook and I'd take over from her. I learned to run that mangle machine when I was very young. We lived in a very convenient neighborhood. School was right next to it. Church was about five minutes away. I was very active in the church. I went to Sunday School and then I went into the youth group after I was confirmed. My father and mother went to church once in a while, but they were not strong church goers.

*The German army invaded Denmark on 9 April 1940 and occupied the country for the remainder of World War II. The invasion of Norway also began on that date.

I have such good memories of Christmas Eve. The stores always closed at four o'clock and the church had service at five. You'd hear church bells all over the place, and frequently it started snowing about that time. After church, we would go home to the big dinner—roast goose stuffed with prunes and apples, little candied potatoes, and red cabbage. After the dinner, dad would go into the living room by himself and light all the candles on the Christmas tree. And then they would open the doors, and here it was, in all its splendor! The little nisser [elves] decorated the tree the day before. How you knew that was, you put out cookies for them and the cookies were always gone in the morning.

My father and mother and us three kids, we were enough of us so that we could reach around the Christmas tree. We would dance around the tree and sing. We kind of hoped they didn't pick the longest songs, because we wanted to get at those packages under the tree. The presents were wrapped the way they come from the store, in brown paper. I remember one year I got a beautiful doll and my mother had named it Olga and I wasn't the least bit pleased with the name.

Christmas Day, people would drop in on each other; always some of the family visited. We made a lot of cookies and during Christmas they were always on hand. Mother started about three weeks ahead of time to lay the dough for the brunekager [brown cookies], the ones that are brown with the almond in the middle. They're very crisp and very thin and they've got syrup and ginger in them. And then klejner [Christmas crullers] and jødekager, and why they were called Jewish cakes, I'll be darned if I know. But they had baking ammonia in them; it made them real crisp. So those three for sure. And then we had the little peppernuts and the little vaniljekranser, the little wreaths.

I have often thought about how we do things over there that they do here too, but we did them at different times. For instance, the children here go around to the houses to get goodies at Halloween. We did that at fastelavn. It's like the Mardi Gras, pre-Lent. We got a little bunch of branches that we used to knock on the door with. My dad always bought those branches for us. There would be little candies tied to them and little tiny toys and ribbons and they would be beautiful.

We went to the homes, knocked on the doors, and got goodies. And at *fastelavn* they had this big barrel that they hung up on a special evening. You hit it to go to pieces and you got goodies; adults and everybody were in on that.

You know the witch at Halloween, well, we had the witch at Midsummer. That's when we burned the witch and sent her off to Bloksbjerget. Down in southern Germany there is a mountain that's called Bloksbjerget, so we sent all the witches down there. That was far enough away not to bother us! They fixed a very lifelike witch, and they had taken a line of rope and tied it to the ground and it went way, way up in a real tall tree. And then they put fire on this witch and she went shooting off on a broom.

In Copenhagen especially, but around other big cities, they had areas of land set aside by the state that you could lease for a very nominal sum. It was like fifteen, twenty minutes on the bicycle to go out there. You got in through a gate and then you had to walk from there; you weren't allowed to ride your bicycles, you had to pull them. There were all these plots of land where you put up a little summer house and have your garden. It was not a place where you were allowed to live, but you could stay overnight or for a summer vacation. On the outskirts of Copenhagen there was a number of these colonies, as they called them.

It was such fun to see what people did with them. Now my dad being a farmer at heart had his vegetables and berries and fruit trees and he kept some rabbits; and my mother had a little section with flowers. Someone else's yard might have a great big lawn, that's what they liked to have. Everybody used it the way they wanted. Even the houses were different. My father built a one-room house and then he attached a little kitchen. But you had to go outside to get into the kitchen. And then they had made an open eating area with a table and benches. We had some big parties out there. My dad had his birthday in August and it was always celebrated out in the garden and all the family came.

That was the idea, that people had a chance to get out. Anyhow, every colony of gardens had a little center where there was a little store where you could buy things that you needed—bread, flour, milk, things like

The garden colony on the outskirts of Copenhagen used by Else Goodwin's family

that. Then they had a square for everybody to use and for Midsummer, they'd have a big party there for all the people that belonged to that colony of gardens.

Every summer vacation when I was growing up, I was out on the farm in the area where my father had grown up. I stayed with my grandfather for several weeks. I would get on a bicycle and go up to these other places where they had kids. I had a wonderful time with these kids. When you went on a school vacation like that, the state paid for your trip. You got the ticket.

I went to the public school. But when we got through the fifth grade, they separated us, that is, it was your choice. If you wanted to go the schooling that eventually might lead to university, you went what they called middle school. Otherwise you just continued through the grade school. I went into the middle school, and so I got English. They emphasized languages a lot and mathematics, so I had three or four years of English and a couple of German before I quit school.

They really wanted me to be a schoolteacher, but I wasn't interested in that, no ways. I thought I'd go into library work actually. But I never really had too much of a choice. My mother got so sick that I was needed at home. I stayed home then and helped her. For one whole winter I was in charge of the shop. I couldn't handle going to school and that, too. So that was it. I remember there was a shop for sale some place and I wanted the worst way to have my father buy that for me. I figured I could run that place. I was about sixteen and I thought, heck, I've been running this one here all by myself, why can't I do the other one?

Then these people came from America and visited us. What happened first was, my father's sister lived down in Oakland [California] and one of her young friends was going to Denmark and, of course, she got the chore to look up my father and mother and bring greetings. And I got the job of showing her around Copenhagen. I was showing her all that I could in Copenhagen, and she was filling me full of America. This galfriend got me all hot on going to America.

The following year, when I was seventeen, my father and mother had some friends from New York came home on a visit. I was around them all the time. I hung on every word and tried to use my English. He was telling me about his lovely home, this car he had waiting for him in New York, and this, that, and the other thing. And the funny part was that at one time my mother and he had sort of been sweet on each other. So there was a little rivalry between those two men. And Emil says, "Wouldn't you like to go to America? You could certainly go back with us, if you want to, because you could help my wife a little. We'd even pay you something if you'd like to try it out." So my dad says, "Well, if my daughter wants to go to America, of course she's going to go to America. I'll buy her ticket." I thought that was so cute. They were both going to show that they had done well.

Well, we were comfortable, but there wasn't any luxuries. In the old times, if father thought it was worthwhile, then we got it. He was the one that decided really. After my father got me the ticket, and I actually was going to go, it wasn't so good. You know, his big girl was going so far away. But, of course, it was only going to be for six months.

When the six months was close to being up, they said, why didn't I stay a little longer? And so I thought to get the visa extended, and when those six months were up, I got it extended for another six months again. I even starting going to business school. But then, all of a sudden, I really got homesick. I thought, I got to go home. It was getting towards Christmas again, the second Christmas. There was no Christmas Eve, everything was Christmas morning. The children got up in the morning and tore into all the stuff that was there for them. The paper was all over the place. Everybody was in their robes, and everything was sort of disorganized. And that bothered me. Christmas, I really missed home. So in November of 1931 I took the boat home.

Anyhow, I met my first husband on the *Leviathan*. He was a dairyman in Seattle, a widower, and he was going to stay in Jutland with his family. He really courted me and got me talked into the fact that I was in love and wanted to go back [to the United States] again. We had a very nice, typical Danish wedding.

By that time my father and mother had gotten another apartment, a nice-sized apartment, and we had the whole family there. The minister that confirmed me also married us. We were married in church in the afternoon, about four o'clock. Afterwards we took a ride, so that we would be the last ones to arrive home. I had a pink gown; it was very pretty, ruffles. I was practical. I felt if I had a pink dress, I might use it again.

We got home and everybody was there. Mother had written a song for us and at least two more songs had been written for us, which was very much the thing they did in Denmark. We had a fantastic dinner. They started with soup, and then they had a fish course, and then a meat course. I remember also that we had a little side dish, which was leeks that were boiled and served with butter that had been stirred. That was supposed to be quite a delicacy. Then we had a fancy ice cream for dessert. You had your white wine glass with the fish course, and you had your red wine glass with the meat course, and you had your Madeira glass with your dessert. Then there was all the speeches, everybody making a speech for you. And telegrams would arrive and they would be read out. And the dinner lasted like three and a half hours, and then the speeches in between.

After that, we went into the living room and had the wedding cake and coffee and liqueurs. The wedding cake is a wreath cake—*kransekage*. Then they cleared the dining room and we danced. Then, of course, after we had danced, we disappeared. My husband had rented a hotel room while there was so much going on at home.

On the day of the wedding, people would be dropping in all day long. People that haven't been invited to the party will feel free to drop in and greet you. And they always get served cookies and a glass of wine. That's part of the treatment. Then the next day about fifteen or twenty people came for lunch and there was about a dozen for dinner that night. And the next day again there was a group of people. These things lasted three days. So it was quite a party!

We left Denmark the end of May in 1932 and finally came to Seattle in June.

Magnhild Johnsen

"When peace broke out . . ."

Magnhild Johnsen emigrated in 1929 at the age of twenty, planning to do housework for a year. She returned to Norway with her husband and two children in 1939. The family experienced the German occupation of Norway from 1940–1945 and was active in the underground resistance. The Johnsens emigrated for a second time to the United States in 1948 and settled in Washington.

My father was a manager of one of the bigger lumberyards in southern Norway. My mother worked as a teacher for many years, until just before she died. She loved teaching; she liked to work with the small kids, from first to seventh grade. She was not very well and she couldn't do the housework. We had a grandfather living with us and he was nursemaid, and you couldn't get a better one!

My mother died when I was twelve; my older sister was seventeen. She was going to telegraph school in Arendal at the time, so we had a housekeeper for a while and then my older sister took over. And after a while, when I graduated from high school, I took over, kept house for my father.

And then I decided I was going to go to America. There was one reason. It's seems kind of silly to me now, but it was a reason. I wanted to go to Stabekk husmorskole [home economics school], in Oslo. That's training as a home economics teacher. But to get in there, I had to have one year as a houseworker in one place continuously. And I couldn't see doing housework in Norway; you were not anything if you were working for wages. So I decided I was going to go to America and get a year in here.

Magnhild Torsvik Johnsen (youngest child) with mother and siblings, ca. 1909

My father, he wasn't too happy about it, but he agreed that it would be a good idea. His oldest brother was living in Brooklyn and so I came to him. And, of course, I met my husband and we married.

He's from the same hometown as I. I'd never seen him there. My old boyfriend introduced me to him on the dock before I left. That's how I met my husband, Olaf Johnsen. He had been in this country [since 1923] and he went back to see his family and then it just happened that I came over on the same boat [1929]. Lucky me! He came back to his old job up in Scarsdale outside of New York. And then he said, "How about not living in Brooklyn? How about coming out and work in Scarsdale?" He was chauffeur and caretaker of a big place, real nice people.

So I get in there. We were five people working together. I was the cook. I stayed there until I got married and till I got pregnant with my first child. A beautiful room, private bathroom and everything else.

I felt like I was in seventh heaven. I ended up with ninety dollars a month. And all my girlfriends were envious, because none of them had that kind of wages.

My baby, my oldest girl, was born. Then Olaf got another job in New York. We lived in Bronx and then we moved to Brooklyn where we had friends. My second girl was born in Brooklyn. Then my father-in-law got to be alone in Norway. He had his daughter living with him, but she got a job as a teacher in the northern part of Norway; so we decided we would go home and take care of him.

So we went to Norway in 1938. I had two children then. Of course, we got home—I don't say in right time or wrong time—just before war. We were there during World War II, from the start to the finish. Nine and one-half years before we came back. I had my boy there.

My brother was one of the leaders of the underground [in Kristian-sand].* We all worked as we could. We had a radio in the basement, hidden. Olaf and I usually went down and copied the English programs and translated to Norwegian, from Churchill and everyone else talking. And sometimes I wonder how I could do it, but I did. My oldest girl went to school. They had a little rucksack to carry their books in and I put underground papers in the sack and her teacher took them out. I don't know what would happen if she was caught, but you didn't think about those things. You just did what you could.

Then after Stalingrad, we got a lot of Russian soldiers, eighteen thousand of them. And I've never seen people treated as bad as that. They lived outside town, not so very far from where we lived at the time. And they practically had nothing to eat. So everybody who could spare one crust of bread, we'd try to give it to them. I was caught once. I had half a loaf of bread and I dropped it. We tried to drop it so they didn't see us, but this German soldier saw me. He didn't do anything to me. He just told me, "Pick it up and don't do it again!" But we did, all

*Norway was invaded by the Germans on 9 April 1940. After some weeks of fighting, the Norwegian government was compelled to take exile in Britain. The country remained under German occupation until May of 1945. During these years, an active underground resistance performed sabotage, published newspapers, and otherwise attempted to thwart the Nazi authorities and their sympathizers.

Magnhild Johnsen wearing ethnic dress

through the war, whenever we could. We tried to help them. We didn't have much, but they had less. For shoes, they had newspapers and tied them, in the middle of the winter. And '43 was one of the coldest winters they ever had in Norway. The Russian prisoners, they suffered an awful lot.

After the war, the Russian soldiers tried to repay. They made little rings of metal they picked up on the ground and stuff like that, and gave to the kids. When peace broke out—that's the expression we use in Norway, peace broke out—we had a big celebration in a park outside of Kristiansand and the Russian soldiers were the pampered main guests. Most of us had stored, hoarded a little bit. When I was pregnant with Harald, I was supposed to get white flour, not much, but a little bit. We saved that until peace broke out, so we could have white cake.

I've got good memories from the war, and some terrible ones. Because my brother was killed in '41. One of the squealers, a boy from my hometown, schoolmate of mine, gave him up. We had them there, too, you know. My brother and my second cousin and another second cousin and an uncle, I had seven people killed, executed by the Germans. And I had one cousin who was supposed to be killed May 9, 1945. Peace came just barely in time [May 7]. They suffered an awful lot. His wife was pregnant and they couldn't make my cousin talk. He was sending cables to England; he was a *telegrafist*. She was pregnant, and to make him talk, one German woman—the German woman guards were worse than anyone else—beat her until she lost the baby, right in front of my cousin. You wouldn't think people could treat people like that.

I hated the Germans for a long time. Now I feel more sorry for them, because they got to live with it. I have German friends, still got German friends here in Seattle. We don't talk about it at all; I never tell them about it. But we had friends in Brooklyn that we used to go around with a lot. When we came back in '48, we went to look them up. And Fred and Frieda, the Germans, they said, "No, I can't even talk to you, because you'll hate us." We tried to tell them we didn't, but we never saw them again.

My father-in-law was dead and we thought we would come back here. My daughters were both born in this country and they wanted to come back. Too many sad memories from the war, I think, and I can see that. We thought, we are not going to split up the family. So we went back.

First we came to Lakewood [New Jersey] to my sister-in-law. Then a friend of Olaf's, an electrician out here in Hoquiam [Washington], called him up and told him, we got a job for you. So we drove out here fall of 1948. We had a grand time. I say, my son is the only kid that ever stood up all across America. He was too small to sit on a seat, so he stood up in front.

Olaf was a citizen before we went back to Norway. I had just my first papers out. Of course, you can't stay out of the country for more than five years. We lost it. So we had to start [over]. We were on what you call a preferred list, so we became citizen again pretty soon.

There's a lot of history in your life, isn't there?

Part Two / **New Land**

En route to their North American destinations, the Scandinavian immigrants encountered a host of exotic impressions and experiences. Riding on a train for the first time, observing different nationalities and persons of color, tasting tomatoes or bananas or other strange foods—such incidents sparked personal reactions ranging from curiosity to fright.

Most of these early twentieth-century travelers crossed the ocean on third-class tickets. As such, they enjoyed greater comfort than those who were massed into the steerage compartments, but they did not benefit from the special privileges of first- and second-class passengers.[1] Ida Apalseth reports: "We had the lower deck full of eastern Europeans. They were just like they were packed in. I don't know where they slept. We could stay on our deck and look down. We happened to have a little better; we had cabins."

Often passage was booked via England. Because large steamship companies like the Cunard and White Star lines left from Liverpool, the immigrants would first sail from the closest Scandinavian port to Hull or Newcastle and then cross England by train in order to board the ship bound for America. Direct service to North America from Scandinavian harbors was provided by companies like the Scandinavian-American Line, successor in 1898 to the Danish Thingvalla Line, established already in 1879, the Norwegian America Line, which inaugurated its routes in 1913, and the Swedish-American Line, founded in 1914.

Among the multiple ports of entry, New York with its massive immigrant receiving center—Ellis Island—stood out as the most significant. Criticized by some arriving immigrants as crowded and dirty, the Ellis Island facility operated under heavy pressure to process thousands of persons daily, inspecting them for health problems and verifying

Slind family passport picture (see p. 249)

records and financial resources. Those lacking the proper documentation were detained until relatives or friends could wire the necessary funds or guarantees. Agents directed the immigrants' paths. Esther Rinne notes, "They put slip on my chest and they always escorted."

As the newly cleared arrivals left Ellis Island to catch the train to the destinations in the Midwest or the Pacific Northwest, they could equip themselves with packed lunches for about a dollar. Ole Blindheim enjoyed the apple pie packed in his box, but Esther Rinne was disgusted to find "mildewed cheese" in hers. Some were helped with food purchases and the strange currency by train personnel and fellow passengers; others relied on their own ingenuity. Hans Fahl employed a list he copied from a dictionary: "I just checked my list over what kind of a food I thought I wanted. I just ordered that and I didn't say much more than just to order." Still others were too timid to negotiate meals and sat fasting through the long trip across country.

In unfamiliar settings and circumstances, all immigrants were vulnerable to deception and humiliation, but women traveling alone faced the special threat of white slavery. Having read and heard that they must be alert and not trust strangers, some women reacted with suspicion to offers of assistance. Esther Rinne was afraid of the black railroad employees who monitored her movements during the cross-country train ride and by the officials who attempted to help her during a stopover in San Francisco. Yet she did accept assurance from an anonymous Finnish voice over the telephone. Likewise, Ida Apalseth decided to put her faith in a Swedish man: "You just had to trust somebody, and being that he spoke our language—I understood Swedish and he understood Norwegian." An apparatus for aiding and monitoring immigrants developed through religious and civic circles in the United States. The YWCA, for example, provided a network of representatives to shepherd immigrant women through the maze of railroad transfers. Traveling alone in 1930, Astrid Lovestrand was grateful for the YWCA's help. She was met in New York, Chicago, and St. Paul: "And one of them met me in Yakima. They all spoke Swedish. They were notified ahead of time that we were coming."

The immigrant journey could be a dismal experience, marred by seasickness and loneliness, or it could evoke pleasant and exciting memories of new experiences. Seeing Yakima, Washington, for the first time, with the fruit orchards all in bloom, Hans Fahl believed that he had arrived in "paradise." Ten-year-old Elsie Odmark and her siblings looked out the train window, "and to us everything looked beautiful and wonderful."

Having reached their destinations safely, the immigrants had to negotiate the transition into American society. Alongside survival concerns like housing, employment, and language ability, there were important social needs like friends and a sense of belonging. The initial point of contact was usually a relative who had emigrated some years earlier; but only rarely did the adult Scandinavian immigrants remain with relatives on a long-term basis. As Ida Apalseth states, "I didn't want to be beholden to anyone. I wanted to earn my own money and I felt I was imposing on them." Astrid Lovestrand also felt obliged to carve out an independent existence: "When I was living with my aunt and uncle, I felt like I should be earning my living and paying for my room and board." Ted Kofoed got a "sinking feeling" when he saw the poor state of his uncle's farm: "There was no money in it for anybody. I stayed with him for three months. Then I broke away."

The language barrier had to be overcome, although strategies for meeting that challenge varied. Laura Foss, who arrived in Seattle at the age of fifteen, entered a special class for foreign-born pupils. She acquired a less formal education as well, namely through her aunt's "hard school" of experience. "She would expect us to be able to do a lot of things," according to Laura, including grasping foreign expressions and finding their way about the city.

"Eighteen years old that winter and start in the first grade!"—Goodman Norwick did not relish the scenario, even though he was anxious for more schooling. Instead, Goodman hired out to do farm chores and acquired English from his employers and from reading Western novels. In retrospect, he regrets passing up the chance to go to school, since another young Norwegian was able to obtain a high school diploma after only two years of study. Domestic servants like Astrid Lovestrand had an advantage in living and working with American families: "They had three small children and it seems like it was easier for me to make a mistake in front of the children than in front of grown-ups. They would say, 'Astrid, that's not correct,' and they would correct me."

Becoming an American citizen was important to most immigrants. Hans Fahl was particularly anxious: "Within just a few days after I got here, I applied for my citizen papers. It takes you five years before you can get your citizenship. I became a citizen right away, as soon as I had been here for five years." Alli Benson, who was twelve years old when she immigrated, received her citizenship through her father. Goodman Norwick assumed a similar procedure would apply to him, but discovered that his father lacked the necessary final papers. When Goodman later enlisted in the United States Army to serve in World War I, he became an American citizen on the spot.

As part of the formal naturalization process, or even earlier as a by-product of passage through Ellis Island, the immigrants frequently acquired a new name, or at least a new spelling of their name. Much depended on how well the government officials interpreted the Scandinavian pronunciation or how forcefully they proposed a ready American substitute. Anders became Andrew, Gjertine became Gertie, and Gudmund became Goodman. Even if the old-country name was officially retained, an informal American nickname was inevitable. Sigvald was called "Steve" and Thorvald "Ted."

Feelings of inferiority could hinder integration and upward mobility. Astrid Lovestrand acknowledges her own tendency toward self-effacement and traces it to the social distinctions of her youth: "There is a certain class in Sweden and lots of things I felt like I didn't belong to, that maybe I wasn't good enough." Thorvald Kofoed says about his three-year stint in the Army during World War II: "I got on a more equal basis with men, and I found out that some of them guys wasn't any smarter than I was."

In his Swedish-American church, Andrew Johnson (Part One) discovered that young people born in the United States "kind of looked down on you, as what they call a greenhorn." By and large, however, the ethnic community stretched out welcoming arms to the newcomers. Laura Foss attended a Danish folk school in California. This proved an enjoyable learning experience and reinforced bonds with fellow Danish immigrants, one of whom she soon married. The Swedish colony near Yakima, Washington, became the focal point for Astrid Lovestrand's social network. She married a Swedish American and established her home there. Coming from the only Swedish family in a rural German settlement, Elsie Odmark felt isolated among her peers in school and depended upon an ethnic newspaper to stay connected with her roots. These dynamics and circumstances are considered in more detail under "New Lives" (Part Five).

In times of national crisis, the immigrant population experienced special difficulties. Two historical events require mention in any consideration of early twentieth-century immigration, namely the First World War and the Great Depression. During the First World War, the United States was gripped by a wave of intense patriotism that cast into doubt the intentions and loyalty of the country's foreign-born. As a result, pressure mounted for the widespread use of the English language and other signs of assimilation. The Selective Service Act required military service of all young men who were, or wished to become, full American citizens. A few Scandinavians exempted themselves from wartime service by turning in their citizenship papers, but most did not.[2] It may be seen as somewhat ironic that young Scandinavians who had emigrated from neutral homelands intent upon improving their personal lot in life found themselves back in Europe, fighting for their adopted country. Goodman Norwick's narrative offers one example of such an immigrant saga. He spent considerable combat time in France and returned to the United States in 1919, luckily "without a scratch," one of only six from an original group of 253 to remain physically unharmed.

Those who immigrated around 1930 faced a different crisis. The onset of the Depression meant that there was little or no work to be had and that anti-foreign sentiment was once again running high. When Sigvald Stenersen joined his cousin in New York in 1930, he found the cousin out of work and living on his meagre savings and judged that the prospect for employment on the east coast was "absolutely nothing." Eventually, Stenersen was able to enroll in the Civilian Conservation Corps (CCC), the job corps started as part of the Roosevelt administration's New Deal: "That was the best thing that ever happened to me. I learned a lot of things and it was a good morale builder, too." Prior to joining the CCC, Stenersen experienced "tough days" on a farm in eastern Washington, including one miserable Christmas Day spent hauling manure. His participation in the CCC not only smoothed the way for a future career in the construction industry, it also offered a yardstick for measuring his own difficulties: "I thought I had it tough, but to hear some of those boys that came from [Ohio] tell about lying in bed, because they were afraid they were going to get more hungry if they got up!"

When the hard times hit the Upper Midwest, Thorvald Kofoed saw his wages drop from thirty to five dollars a month: "Many of them just closed the farms and took off. There was young guys, they was roaming around looking for work and looking for places where they could just eat and sleep, room and board." Rather than "freeze for five dollars a month in Minnesota," Kofoed decided to try his luck on the west coast.

Both Stenersen and Kofoed tapped the ethnic network in an attempt to counter the limitations of the Depression job market. The hard-nosed farmer for whom Stenersen worked in Spokane county, Washington, was a fellow Norwegian to whom he was referred by an aunt's neighbor. Kofoed relied upon a Danish-language newspaper to locate a job—"I didn't know it was a doggone German that was advertising"—and then later to establish Danish contacts in Seattle. With perseverance, Stenersen and Kofoed managed to survive the early 1930s without extreme hardship. Not all immigrants were as fortunate, as we learn from Alli Benson's description of a return voyage to Sweden in 1931. On the ship were several young Swedes who had been deported, including one who "had been in America for three years and hadn't worked one day."

Hans Fahl, who grew up near the sea in Sweden, made an easy transition to the novel environment of central Washington. He "forgot about" missing the ocean, because the inland climate impressed him so favorably. When he did visit the Puget Sound area it was, he admits, "just like coming home." Still, Fahl developed a fierce loyalty to the Yakima Valley, his "paradise." For Gustav Simonson, on the other hand, the longing for the sea could not be stifled or redirected: "That was probably the hardest thing for us to take, to be removed from the water. That was horrible." He sailed one summer on the Great Lakes; otherwise he worked his way west as a farmhand, logger, and laborer. The Depression finally spurred him on to Alaska, where he resumed the work pattern from his island home in Norway. As a fisherman, he found his "Jerusalem."

Eventually both Hans Fahl and Gustav Simonson discovered an American paradise. But for Simonson, joyful adaptation to the new world environment entailed approximating the rhythm and emphases of life in the homeland. In this he was not alone. The transfer of occupational skills was a strategy adopted by many immigrants to smooth the transition and bolster self-confidence. Over time, the hurdles and insecurities of the early years faded. As the selections in "New Lives" will illustrate more directly, work, family life, community involvement, and awareness of their heritage defined the contours of the immigrants' lives in the new land.

The narratives here are arranged in chronological order according to the date of arrival in the United States.

NOTES

1. In *The Distant Magnet* (New York, 1971), Philip Taylor describes the quality of the steamship accommodations and the institution around the turn of the century of a third class, which in the course of the next decade or so totally eliminated steerage.

2. For a detailed discussion, see the chapter on World War I in Sture Lindmark, *Swedish America, 1914–1932* (Uppsala, Sweden, 1971).

Ole Blindheim

*"We were thinking America in high tones
when we saw that Statue of Liberty."*

An emigrant from western Norway who traveled to America
in 1908, Ole Blindheim experienced Ellis Island, the Southern
Pacific Railroad, and gold mining in Alaska before settling in
Seattle in 1913. There he and a partner developed a successful
dairy business. Ole helped found the Norwegian Commercial
Club of Seattle and he and his wife Anna raised two children.

My full name is Ole Andreas Rasmussen Blindheim. The owners of the big ranch where our *husmannsplass* [cotter's farm] came from, his name was Ole and her name was Anne, so that's where I get the Ole Andreas. Rasmussen, that's my father's name; his name was Rasmus Mikkalsen. Blindheim, that's a larger area that takes in the big farm and three other large farms besides that. The *husmannsplass* where I was born was Reitebakken.*

My maternal grandfather's name was Nikolai. Nikolai was the originator of Reitebakken, which was inherited by my mother and her husband. She was the only child. I was unfortunate; I was only six years old when she died. They used to sleep on straw, *halm* we call it. I remember when they were burning the *halm* from her deathbed out in the field. Oh, how I cried! My father was a carpenter and a handyman. He was

---

*Traditional Scandinavian naming customs included the frequent use of patronymics, for example, the son of Rasmus becoming Rasmussen. It was also typical for people to take the name of the farm or place from which they came. Ole refers to the farmwife at Løset as "Løset Marie."

Like a tenant farmer, a cotter had to pay in labor or cash for the use of the land. The cotter was attached to a larger farm; often there would be several cotters under the same farmer. See the interview with Andrew Johnson in Part One for another reference to cotters.

The Blindheim dairy cart, Seattle, ca. 1914

well established at a woolen mill. We had the pleasure every Saturday night to go out to the steamboat and meet him; Sunday evening he had to get back.

Although we lived in the same house, the grandparents lived in the back of the building. They left the front room to the younger ones. I was born in the front room April 17, 1891. It's a long building with a grass roof on it. My boss was my grandmother Olava. She used to tell me, "Be frugal, my boy, save your money, put it in the bank." Grandfather Nikolai took care of Reitebakken and whatever time I had, I learned all the trade from grandfather, to cut hay with a scythe.

Early in my life I had to leave home and earn a living. Two years [1904–1906], I was hired out as a *dreng* [hired hand] to a place where they had about twenty goats. All that goat milk make me strong and make me grow. I was confirmed in 1906. Next I go to the farm Løset, nearer the fjord. They had a similar kind of work there. Anything that needed to be done on the farm I was able to pick it out and do it, and that's why they like me, I think. I was in demand really, all the time.

I remember when I came to America and the last time I visited Løset. Løset Marie went out to *stabbur* [storehouse] and got me a great big *spekelår*, leg of lamb all cured. And I took it along and I made a lot of friends with it after I came to America. That was just about the only thing I brought along, except change of socks. I knew that everything else I needed, I would be able to buy here.

It so happened that by our place, right by my grandfather's boathouse, a man from Slesvig-Holstein set up a cement block factory. There was quite a lot of activity there, so after I got through as a *dreng*, I got a job there, to make these cement blocks. I had to compete with grownup husky guys, so I had something to learn, to see that I earned my way. I was lucky enough to finally do so; I could manufacture as many bricks as anybody else, so I became in demand there, too. At lunchtime, my friend and chum Lars Olsen Vik—which later became Louis Vik here in America—we were sitting up in the hillside eating our lunch and talking about the America trip. And the more we talked about it, the more this America loomed up; it was America first and last. So finally we decided that we were gonna be on the way.

We checked up on some of the ships to Bergen and we decided to leave Ålesund on the 4th of July, 1908, which we accomplished.* That was decided and no matter how sad or bad we felt, we had to go through with it. One of the worst things I had to do was to shake hands with grandfather Nikolai, because I knew how he would feel and how helpless I was to do anything about it. I just had to make him realize that this was part of me and I had to take care of it someway. I promised that I would write often, which I sure tried to do. I remember I told them, "I'll be back in five years or so."

My own brother had been gone a year or two. Already I had a letter from him from Alaska from this mine where he was working. Then,

---

*Ålesund was the nearest urban center to Ole's home and a port of call for the coastal ships.

of course, Louis—that was the greatest inspiration really—Louis had an older brother being five, six years over here and spent most of that time up in the Yukon—Klondike. He was able to bring home five or six thousand dollars and that was a lot of money in Norwegian money. He got married pretty soon and built a house over in Norway and settled down. Louis was telling me when we were eating lunch up there where we were working, "Ole, you don't need to worry about the English. I have learned enough already from Klaus"—that was his brother that came home from the Klondike—"that I'm sure we're gonna get along." So I took him on his word.

We left Ålesund on Jotunheim, it used to be a fjord boat. As soon as we went through Statland, which is halfway between Bergen and Ålesund, I had to feed the fish overboard—seasick. At Bergen, we got aboard the steamship Hera. We stopped at Stavanger and from Stavanger to Newcastle, England. We were going on a journey on the train from there to Liverpool. That was the first time I was on a train. I remember my friend Peter Tomas, who emigrated a year earlier. He used to send me postcards and letters and he told me, over England the train was traveling so fast that the telephone poles stood like a solid wall. That was some impression!

We came to Liverpool and boy that was an odd thing too—all those different people. Then finally the ship came to take us to America. The ship was so big that it really changed the landscape of Liverpool. It took a big ship to haul us passengers over to the side of Mauretania and get aboard. Louis and I paid each forty-seven crowns extra to travel on that ship. We had read about the record of Lusitania—that Lusitania had crossed the Atlantic in less than five days; and here was this Mauretania, built as a sister ship, and there must have been some special reason for charging extra. Anyway, Louis and I was satisfied to pay those forty-seven crowns. Everything was new, classy. The only thing bad about it—those English waitresses was too demanding; they wanted too many tips; they were out begging all the time; they almost kept us broke. The deck was bigger than two ball fields. We were walking around up there and saw that big ship vibrating and we were wondering what they were doing. They were making a record on that trip. They came across the Atlantic in something a little more than four and a half days, anyway, beat the Lusitania record.*

We came to Ellis Island. We were thinking America in high tones when we saw that Statue of Liberty. Our order was to roll up our sleeves, which we both did. Outside of that, we were just ordered to go right on. On both arms, I had three big marks of being vaccinated. They saw that, that was enough. As we were waiting there, here came a fellow with a horse and wagon and he had packages about a foot and a half long and a foot wide and that was loaded with lunch stuff—sandwiches. He came there and was yelling, "One dollar, one dollar, one dollar!" So that's what we each got, a box of those.

We got on the train, the Southern Pacific. Louis had opened his box and in there was a raspberry pie and we didn't know what that was. We had raspberries, but we never made any pies. So Louis said, "Oh, my, this is good bread!" I hadn't opened mine yet, but I was lucky. I wasn't so crazy about raspberry, but they had given me apple pie, which I liked better. So there we were with our lunch and pretty soon we were riding by the White House; we could see the White House from the train. We were going down through Georgia, south to Louisiana and Texas.

In Texas, we saw those great big watermelons laying out there in the fields. I didn't see how pigs could thrive together so close! Pretty soon the darkies came up with watermelon slices. I had so much watermelon; boy, it was really something. We never forgot Texas. Our heads was out the windows, and up above the sun was straight up. Awfully hot, awfully hot. Louis had looked out the window so much that he had lost his hat. We were lucky to have a Swede returning from Sweden to this country and he, of course, could speak English and when we came to New Mexico, Louis got him to go with him to a store and he

*These sister ships were owned by the Cunard Line. The Mauretania made its maiden voyage in 1907 and came to be known as the Grand Old Lady of the Atlantic. Challenged only by the Lusitania, she held the Atlantic speed record until 1929. During World War I, the Lusitania was of course sunk by a German submarine with a great loss of life.

came back with a real crisp hat. It was turned up and Louis didn't do nothing to turn it down either! It was really crisp. To me, it was sitting rather loosely on Louis' head.

It took seven days to ride across on that Southern Pacific. Just think, we made a record across the ocean, and here we was seven days across America. I was sitting on the train with my shoelaces tied up tight. Never be as foolish as I was, to sit in one place on the train and sleep sitting up and with your shoes tied tight. When I was supposed to get on the job, my feet was swelling up and I had to wait three or four days before I was able to take on a job.

On the Pacific, we are now coming into San Francisco. Just as we got off the train, here came a guy with a team of horses and he wanted to know, "Where are you going and where can I take you?" As we started off, I was sitting in the driver's seat with the driver and Louis was standing, holding on on back. I happened to look back, "Why, my God, where is Louis?" And he is way back in the alley someplace trying to pick up his hat. We had gone over the cobblestones and his hat jarred off. Naturally I busted out and said, "Brrr, brrr, brrr." That's the way we stop the horses in Norway. The only thing that stops them is a big, loud "R." And this driver thought, what the heck am I into here, what kind of a problem, are you crazy or something? He stared at me like I never saw anybody stare at me before. Then we look back and by golly, here was Louis. He was back in the wagon and he had his hat. I never saw Louis move so fast in all the life I was with him. So I said to the guy, "O.K., everything O.K., see, Louis, hat."

We had a ride all the way across San Francisco. Louis and I were getting kinda hungry by now and we went into a restaurant. Up to now we had just short snacks and far apart, and here on the counter this guy had some lamb chops that I could tell was really lamb. I told Louis, "We need some meat." Louis couldn't order, so I told him, "For God's sake Louis, you got a hand, you got fingers, point at it." Louis was too bashful to do that, so it took me to get over there and order our eats. No problem. The guy was glad that I came over there and pointed; and I could tell "coffee," you know, so everything went all right.

Pretty soon we found out about the steamer that was supposed to go to Albion. We had some friends, some Sykkylvings,* in Albion, a lumber town in Mendocino county. They had a job and they was telling us that they were able to work as much as they wanted to. We got to Albion overnight on a lumber steamer. We were hoisted onshore by one of those lumber hoists. Some experience!

First we got a job on the railroad, loading ties. Oh, that was a tough job. I put those ties on my shoulder and got raw meat almost right away. They called them sinker ties, because they were made out of a certain lumber that is watersoaked. Then they were gonna build a new water supply for the mill, so Louis and I got a job digging ditches and we enjoyed that very much. Believe me, we gave it all we had, too. We didn't want to get fired.

We came there in the beginning of September. We were getting now close to March. We went to the boss and told him that we were on our way north. He didn't like that and he told us that we were making a mistake. He thought that we had a better future in his country right there than we would in Alaska. We told him how much thanks we owed him, but said that something was already lined up. My brother knew that we were on our way.

We arrived in Valdez and there we saw more snow than I had seen piled up even in Norway, because the snow was over the roofs and we had to go through steps in the snow to get into the bunkhouse where we was gonna sleep. The next morning we got on our way over the Thompson Pass which is right back of Valdez. We had a pair of ordinary rubber shoes with rubber bottom and leather top that we could lace, and they were real comfortable. Beside that, I had socks and a pair of felt shoes along. There had been somebody going over that trail already, but it was slow going. We even chipped in five dollars apiece for some fellas to buy a horse for twenty-five dollars. I don't see how they could get a horse over the pass, but they did. Louis more or less took company with those fellas.

This fella Jack Vigen wanted to go with me, so he became my partner. We got to the next boarding house long before anybody else, and

*People from their home district of Sykkylven in western Norway.

Ole Blindheim   99 we had a chance to doze off and rest. Those people finally got there and they had some *spekelår* along, too, from the old country. They lost it leaving it on the sleigh overnight; some dogs or wolves got it. So that was shortsightedness. Now we were getting interior and the snow is getting drier and there is where my felt shoes came in. I could wear cloth shoes and never get wet and we really made time. Jack Vigen and I, we got to Fairbanks a day before the other guys did. Jack Vigen was working on Ester Creek, too, in the same mine my brother did.

We were probably a hundred men mining at Ester Creek. I spent all season as bell boy. That meant that I had to ring the bell to make those buckets go up and down. The buckets went up to be dumped into the sluice box and that's where the gold dust was sluiced out. The agreement was that we were to be fed and there was a lady that was running this restaurant and fed everybody. I presume we had done our stuff; otherwise, if it wasn't satisfactory, quite often your check would be underneath the dinner plate or lunch plate, that you were through. We was lucky not to get any of those.

Next we went to work at Three Below Ester Creek. My brother and I was together sinking the shaft, which is eight feet by eight feet in a square and all the way down 125 feet. We worked frozen ground. We had ten-foot points, just plain pipes with a steel head on them so that we could hammer them with a sledge hammer. Brother and I worked eighteen months straight on that job without missing a shift. Naturally brother was very happy, because he was intending to go back to the old country and take over Reitebakken. Regular pay up there in those days was five dollars a day and board, and they fed you well, although you didn't have the fresh food you have here. We got paid better when we was on those points; we held a responsible position.

Grandmother told me, "Be frugal, my boy, and save your money, put your money in the bank." Well, the first money I had saved up after I paid for my ticket, around eight or nine hundred dollars, was in the Washington Alaska Bank. One Christmastime when I came there to buy my bacon and more grub for the winter, why the bank was closed and I come to inquire about the manager, he had gone on to Mexico to buy

Mining camp mess hall, Alaska, ca. 1910

a banana ranch and left that bank to go broke. My brother was lucky, because he had sent all his money home to Reitebakken.

I stayed two years more [in Alaska] after he had gone home. I stayed there and "bached." I remember one Christmas Eve. I was alone at Ester Creek, but I thought I'd better go into town to see what's going on. Ten miles to Fairbanks. Finally I arrive in the saloon—saloon was the only meeting places those days. Here I come in the door, I felt like somebody had a match to each side of the face. I was frozen. And I looked outside and it was 58 below zero. To me, it didn't seem that cold. It was a calm night, no breeze or nothing. I had to walk fast in order to keep warm, that was the only thing. But I didn't have a complete parka that I usually had. That was carelessness. So in order to relieve my pain, I excuse myself and went to the hotel. I begged for a bucket filled with ice and took it up to my room and the pain was gone as long as I kept ice on there. I had to do that all night. I didn't have no sleep.

Never at any time can I remember that I was lonesome, because there was a purpose in my mind and that purpose was stronger than anything. The purpose was to gain some independence—to earn a few dollars and save them and go into something that would be interesting.

Goodman Norwick

"I never got into any hand-to-hand fighting
and I was glad of it."

*He was born in January, 1892, in Frosta, Norway, and
baptized Gudmund Joakim Naavik. He emigrated with family
members in 1909. Goodman worked as a hired hand in South
Dakota before enlisting in the United States Army and serving
overseas during World War I. Poor harvests drove Goodman
and his wife Anna out of farming in the 1930s; he later joined
a construction crew to support his family of six children.*

When my dad came to this country, he was carrying the
Kristian Olsen name. It was so many Olsens in the community where he come to that he took the name of the farm
of Naavik, where he was born and raised, same as I was. My father and
mother was never married. They were engaged to be married, but they
decided to wait until he established a home in this country. I came to
the world after he left and she lost all interest in coming to this country.
She almost died during birth, and my dad's parents decided, which dad
wanted them to do, to take and raise me. So I was raised by my grandparents, Ole and Marine. We lived neighborly like. As soon as I was able
to walk between places, I spent every weekend with my mother and
her family; she got married three, four years afterwards.

I only missed two days of school in the seven years I went. I hated to
miss them. I liked it all; I always got along. My grandfather died when
I was fifteen, just before confirmation. Of course my own ambition
was to get more education, but I couldn't get it because no money.
So I took work on my own and worked for two years. I could get in
the military academy for nothing; that was five years, from eighteen to
twenty-three. By going through this academy you have military train-

Goodman Norwick, 1983

ing, but you have also other education along with it. By the time you get those five years in, you have the rating of a commissioned officer. That was the best future I figured I had.

The requirements are that you have to be past your eighteenth birthday. Well, in September, 1909, I'd be short about three, four months; but my teacher said, "Let's try. I'll give you a good recommendation. Won't cost nothing to try." I had to have good marks in school, have athletic recommendations, had to be up to par. All right, they accepted me, even though I was too young, because my credentials was so good.

In the meantime, my uncle Haakon come back from America just before Christmas of 1908. The intention of his was to remain and take care of his mother, my grandmother; she was kind of a sickly woman. But then Haakon wanted to go back here. He arranged quarters for grandma, and her boys—my dad and his brothers—would pay for everything; it wouldn't be no load on the community. Well, she couldn't see that was necessary, "Why can't I come along over there? Ain't got nobody here anyhow, except Goodman, and we don't know where he'll be going." "Well," I says, "if you gonna get tickets for grandma, I'll have to have one, too. Where grandma goes, I go." That's it.

We come by train from Trondheim to Oslo and on boat from there to New York. Nice trip, very nice weather, enjoyed it very much and so did grandma. She was seventy-three and after she come to this country she got to feeling better and she lived until eighty-six. Of course Haakon, he had the papers and everything; we just followed his lead. By train from Chicago, stayed overnight in Chicago, and then from there on to Brandt, South Dakota, on the train all the way. Got to Brandt the first of July [1909]. That heat struck me rough during July and August; I wasn't used to that.

Where dad lived was a Norwegian settlement and there was no use to stay there, because I never heard hardly an English word spoken when I go to town on Saturday evenings. Dad only lived a mile from town. Of course I helped him with the haying and threshing, to pay off my ticket and get some clothes. And when that time was done, he says, "Well, Goodman, I haven't got no work for you this winter, so what do you want to do? Do you want to go to school or go out and do chores for somebody?" Well, that sounded good to me, that school. But you know, eighteen years old that winter and start in the first grade! I don't know why I didn't do it; I had a chance to, but I didn't. In place of that, I went out and done chores, worked from six o'clock to ten o'clock at night for ten dollars a month.

I was sorry I didn't go to school. They had high school and everything in that town. The following year, there was a young fellow come over and he done what I should have done. He went to school and he wasn't any smarter than I was, but he went through all the grades in the first year and high school the second, and had a high school diploma in two years.

So then I helped dad put in the crop the following spring, and again for the haying. Then this Joe Bryan come along, he wanted a man all year round. They lived at the edge of a big German settlement. I got away from all these Norwegians. His mother-in-law, she owned the farm they lived on. He came from Chicago; he was a Norwegian, but he couldn't talk it. But his wife and the old lady—she come right from Norway, they were good Norwegian speakers. That wasn't all. The old lady was a great lady to read. She had books of all kinds. Of course, that was my weakness, too. I was nuts over books.

She had a library right there in the house. I could help myself whenever I had time. The real good part about it was that I had this lady for explanation if I got stuck. After I got kind of the base of the story, then I pick up quite fast. Especially the western novels, I would pick up faster. Between the books and the women and working with him, I could handle English fairly well in one year. I looked at that place—Bryan farm—as my home. They were, tell the truth, closer to me than anybody except grandma.

In the fall of 1917, I enlisted. So, of course, the question came round, are you a citizen? "I think I am," I said. "Dad's been here long enough and I was here before I was twenty-one." "Well, you'd better check on that," he said, "because we've got to know." At that time, regulation was a little bit different. You get a paper in the first year, they called it a first paper; but then in order to be a complete citizen, you have to get a second one in five years. Dad had the first one; he didn't have the second one. So naturally I wasn't. Well, that was all right, but I had to take the oath of allegiance to the country when I enlisted. Then, actually, I become a citizen there and then.

I didn't get in until pretty near Christmas, because I had to wait till the Fourth Division come in before they called us. We was at Camp Green, North Carolina, about a month. I never had no field maneuvers or military training whatsoever. They had English officers training American officers in bayonet practice and, of course, they was using dummies for jab practice, and they had to have somebody out there to get them repaired. That's the job I and two other guys got, so we never got a chance to do any right and left or nothing before we started on the move.

We landed in Brest, France, and went across northern France to Calais. When we landed in Calais, there was soldiers off the front. They got into a fight that night and one of the guards was killed. Anyway, the next morning, the bulletin come out—if you Americans want to fight, we put you where there is fighting to be done. So they sent us right down to Paris.

I spent about eight, nine months [in combat]. Each division had their own objective to reach; whenever they went in and reached their objective, you stayed there until somebody else took over and then you move on. We spent about four weeks at Château-Thierry. The next move we made was to St. Mihiel. We wasn't there very long, only about a week. It's a major battle, but it was a short engagement. Then we move out to the Argonne. We were in there for about thirty days. That was an awful rough one; lot of fighting there. Then we landed in Metz, but we didn't get no chance to get into any action there, because it happened the armistice was signed then, the 11th of November. We were on the move all the time. Wore out two gas masks. Fought in the open. I never got into any hand-to-hand fighting and I was glad of it.

I spent eight months in Germany afterwards. The last three months I spent right in Koblenz. They picked out two from our company to be sent back to France for special training to become commissioned officer, and I was picked for one. But I didn't want to go, because there was also rumors of going back, and I had been with the company from start to finish, same company, Company M, 47th Regiment. There was very few boys left that came over with us, but at the same time I wanted to go back with them. Probably there is another point in my life that I made a mistake, I don't know. I didn't go; but they was back and had their commission before we left, so I could just as well have done that. A stripe on the sleeve was as good as a bar on the shoulder, to me, as far as that goes.

When we was going to leave, they approached me again. They wanted recruits to stay in the occupation of the army; they offered me, we'll give it [the commission] to you if you serve one more year. Well, if I had done that, I think I would have stayed in. But I was discharged August of 1919.

There was 253 in the company when we left. Out of them, there was six that come back without a scratch. Me and my pal from the same town, that's two of them. Just lucky. I call it that anyway.

Elsie Odmark

"Did we get to heaven?"

In May, 1915, ten-year-old Elsie and five of her sisters and brothers made the journey from Sweden to Nebraska, where they joined their father and their other siblings. She married a Swedish immigrant in 1928 and their four children were born in Michigan. In later years, the family relocated in Tacoma. Elsie Odmark ran a catering business and was an active member of the Swedish Vasa Lodge.

In Sweden, my name was Elsa Karlsson and I wish they would have kept it that way when we came over here, but they didn't. I was born the first of June, 1904, in Töreboda in Västergötland, Sweden. It was a small farming community in the heartland of Sweden. There were twelve children in the family; I was the youngest girl. Both my father and my mother were born on pretty big farms. They started farming after they were married, but before they were through, we were very poor and my father was out working on the railroad. He left Sweden in 1911. Five of my brothers and sisters had already left for over here before my father left. They all settled in Nebraska.

In Sweden, I have to say this, we didn't have much. My sister and older brothers were out working. We were living in a little rented house, two rooms—big living room with an open fireplace and a big kitchen with two beds in it. When I was eight years old, I went out and worked for this lady, cleaning up the house and making the beds and feeding the chickens and going to school. My father sent home his check every month, the money he earned on the farm. But if it missed the boat, which came every two weeks, then it was bad.

My mother always seemed to manage so we were not hungry. But after mother died—she died when I was going on ten—then my sister that was eighteen came home and took care of us. One time the check missed the boat and we didn't have anything to eat. We got down to where we had just a couple of pieces of sugar left in the house. I was so hungry, oh, it hurt so bad, and I wanted a piece of that sugar and my sister said, "No, you can't have that, you have to save that for the two little ones." Of course I cried, and she said I was too big to cry. My mother's brother was quite well-to-do, had a big farm with several people working on it. He came down to ask us lots of times if we wanted anything. But my sister was too proud, "Oh, no, we didn't need anything. We were doing just fine, we didn't need anything."

But the night that I cried, two of the hired people came down to visit with my sister. I had been crying and they could tell it and so they said, "What's wrong with Elsie?" And my sister said, "Oh, she's hungry. We haven't got much in the house to eat." And they said, "Well, we will go up and ask your Uncle John if we can have something for you until the money comes." But my sister said, "Oh, no! No way! We can't do that. We don't ask for charity. That's not to be done." So they said, "Well, what if we go up and just take some stuff out of the cellar and not tell him?" That was fine. The lie was fine and the stealing was fine you might say, but not the asking.

So they went back home and they had these big aprons on. I can still see those. And they came down with them *loaded* with food. And then, of course, I could eat and I was so happy. But I never have forgotten that hungriness and I have never been hungry in this country and that's why I love America so, because I have never been hungry here. I have had to work hard; I don't mind that. It was the hungriness that I did not like.

Then they got us all ready to come to this country. Of course, the idea that we had in Sweden about America was that we were going to have plenty of money. There was going to be no poverty and plenty of money. I don't think we thought that we would ever have to work as hard as we had to do. I was very happy to leave Sweden. I had no regrets about it at all. My older sister did; she did not want to go. But you know when you are a child, a ten-year-old, you just think about the fun of going.

We left from Oslo. The *United States* was the name of the boat, of course we called it Oon-ee-tets Stah-tus. I can remember when they played the song *Amerikabåten lägger ut* [The America Boat Is Sailing].* It always made me feel so bad when they played that. Most everyone was seasick. One of my brothers was so sick he didn't think he was going to make it. We were on third class, the lowest we could get. Everyone was very nice to us, I think because of the fact that we were a bunch of "orphans." Everything went fine except that my two brothers were forever fighting with a bunch of Finlanders. They were taking care of themselves and they weren't going to let no Finlanders tell them what to do!

I can remember when we saw the Statue of Liberty. We were just elated. We thought that just meant everything. And then we got to Ellis Island and they examined us. I can remember how they went through our hair. I felt just terrible about that, to see if we had any bugs, I guess. They must have talked Swedish to us, but I can't remember that. And we were very, very excited and thought that we could go right away. When they said we couldn't go, we couldn't understand that. I can remember those fences, kind of like a barbed wire fence, and us just roaming around like lost sheep, wanting to know when can we go, why do we have to stay here? We were too young to understand. It was just like a prison, but they were not mean to us or anything.

They had to send a telegram to my dad, telling him that they had to get three signers, good signers, or we could not come in. We were healthy and we had the twenty-five dollars that was required to land in this country and our tickets to Omaha were already paid for; but because we were under eighteen, underage, they did not want to take us in without signers. My oldest brother, who always took care of our business, he got Mr. O'Keefe, a big real-estate broker who my dad rented the farm from, Mr. Swanson, the president of Nebraska Clothing Company, and some lawyer that my sister was working for. They signed for us. I want you to know that we went through with flying

---

*The song is titled "Emigrantvalsen" or the emigrant waltz. The text may be found in Monica Lantz, ed., *Emigrantvisor* (Stockholm, 1981), 73–74.

colors when we got that. Later, my dad took us down to Omaha and showed us where these people lived, and [said] for us to always behave ourselves, because they had signed us in and if it wasn't for them, we would not be there. So that was pumped into our head that we had to be good.

I'll always remember the train trip from New York to Omaha. The six of us were sitting there, talking Swedish. An old conductor that was on the train kept teasing me all the while. He would sit down by me and I would move over, [until] I couldn't move any farther. He pestered and teased me all the way into Omaha. Of course, I couldn't understand a word he said. I can just imagine how scared I looked, and he thought it was funny. We looked out the window and to us everything looked beautiful and wonderful. That's how I found America.

When we came into Union Station [in Omaha] nobody was there to meet us. We were dumbfounded; we expected the family to be there. We'd run up and down the steps to see if somebody would come and claim us. Nobody came. Finally a lady came up to us, dressed just beautiful, beautiful hat and tall and slender and she asked us in Swedish, "Are you Swedish? Isn't there anyone here to meet you?" We said, "Well, there was supposed to be somebody." "Where are you going?" she said. My sister showed her the slip. The lady said, "That's right by Loveland Farm. I'll take care of you." But we had been frightened to death in Sweden before we left, because we were told that so many children got kidnapped and stuff, and we were not to go with anyone. So we said, nope, no way, she couldn't help us. So she said, "Well, if I go get a policeman that's outside here, doing the beat, would you listen to him?" My sister said that would be O.K.

She went out and got this tall policeman. He was a Swede and he talked Swedish. And he came in and talked to us and she stayed there, too, while he was talking to us. He said, "I am going to call a taxi for you and send you out to McCartel's store which is only a little ways away from where your dad lives and then they can call from there. He has a Swedish girl working there and she will take care of it, I'm sure." So he got a taxicab and we all piled into this taxicab a little bit frightened and a little bit scared, wondering what are they going to do with us.

We got to this McCartel's store and they did have a Swedish girl and they were all very, very nice. Of course, they called over to Loveland farm to go tell my brother that we were at McCartel's store. In the meantime, Mr. McCartel, who was a very nice man, he gave us all a banana. I had never had a banana in my life before. I didn't like it. And I had a brand new coat on that I had had made before I left Sweden, navy-blue; thought I was really dressed up. And I half-peeled the banana and didn't like it and stuck it in my navy-blue coat and forgot about it until the next fall; and the coat and the banana and the whole works was ruined!

Then my brother came with a big lumber wagon and two horses. And we were so excited. There's no way I could explain to you how excited we were. I can remember myself running around looking at all the furniture and the different stuff that they had, especially the stove. I was amazed at that stove. It had a heating oven up above, a hot water tank on the side. I had never seen anything like that in Sweden. We had a brick oven built into the wall, so this was all new. That was May of 1915.

The next day we were out running round, playing and having a good time in the yard, looking at the chickens and the pigs and the horses and everything was big and new to us. And my sister called us to come in for supper and, of course, we thought that was soup, because in Sweden we call it *soppa*. We came running in and we sat down at our table and it was all set up nice—bread and butter, all the milk we wanted to drink, chicken on the big plate and vegetables and mashed potatoes. I just could've almost flipped. I looked at my brother and I poked him and I said, "Swan, did we get to heaven?" And he said, "No, I don't think we did, Elsie. It's not heaven. But it's got to be the next thing to it." And I have always felt that way about America, and I always will.

In the fall, we started school. It was rough. I specifically remember trying to pronounce "pencil." The first time I thought I could say it, I said "pencile" and they all laughed. But my first teacher was just marvelous. She'd keep me after school and show me pictures and name them and try to get me to talk. [Later] we moved four miles away and rented a farm. This was a German community. The Germans didn't like us; they treated us like dirt. We were the only Swedes in this school. This was at the start of the [First] World War, so the authorities came to check out if the kids were talking German in school; and I said, yes, they were. So that was put a stop to; they couldn't talk German anymore.

I was fourteen when I graduated. All the schooling we got was an eighth-grade education. I did get a two-year scholarship from the Swedish Consulate in Omaha to go to business college, but I couldn't use it, I had to stay home and work. I kept house for my brothers and dad. What made me feel different through my years as I grew older was the fact that I only had an eighth-grade education. That inferiority complex was with me, up until the time I was twenty-six and went to Sweden. I'm glad I got over it. Now I'm just the other way around, almost too much. I'm just as good as anybody, you know.

Of course, my father talked Swedish all the time, so we never heard anything but Swedish from him at home. Us children always talked Swedish to him; I did it all through my years. I left Sweden when I was so young and everybody in Sweden thought that I would not be able to remember all those things. But I give a lot of credit to the Swedish newspaper that my father got —*Svenska Amerikanaren.** I read that from the time I came over. It was printed out of Chicago and it had stories and a lot of good articles. After dad died and I got married, then we started taking it and I read up about all what was going on over in Sweden.

My children cannot talk Swedish and that is too bad. I'll tell you what, I was so disgusted with those children when I went to the German school that I always said, "I don't care if my kids can talk one word of Swedish as long as they become good Americans." I guess I always felt that way; I wanted them to become good Americans. My children learned a Swedish prayer when they were little; that's the only thing they learned.

If I had to take my choice, I don't suppose I would want to be any-

*Svenska Amerikanaren (The Swedish American), founded in 1896, had a circulation of more than 75,000 in 1915. Over the years, it merged with a number of other Swedish-language newspapers; in 1936, the name became Svenska Amerikanaren Tribunen.

thing but a Swede. I always said I was very, very proud to be a Swede, because I feel this way, that the Swedish people are a very ambitious, and most of them very good, people. But I also very much love America. When I first came here, I thought it was the greatest place on earth.

We were taught as children to be very dependent upon ourselves, not to ask for anything, never be afraid to work, and everything will come out all right. And always trust in God and everything would be all right. That was the attitude my mother had. She was a very religious woman. So we were always told never to accept charity but to take care of ourselves. I think it was a good lesson, because we kept it when we came to this country. We took care of ourselves, no matter how hard we had to work.

Ida Apalseth

"You just had to trust somebody."

*Ida Apalseth grew up on an island in northern Norway. Born
in 1896, she emigrated in 1916, during the First World War.
Although originally bound for Alaska, she settled in Seattle,
where she enjoyed the ethnic community and met her husband-
to-be at Norway Hall. Following their marriage in 1920, the
Apalseths moved to Tacoma. Ida worked outside the home for
a brief period during the Depression.*

My dad was a businessman. He bought and sold fish; he had a
grocery store; he was also the mailman. He also had a little
bakery for the fishermen. They used to come there and fish
in the spring; some of the best codfish was around there, in Vesterålen.
He was called *neskongen* Ole Pedersen. That means that he lives on the
point and has a little bit more than the rest of them.*

We had quite a bit of help. We had one that took care of the barn, we
had a cook, and my cousin kept house. In the summertime, we had to
have help to do the haying. That's all handwork, no machinery—cutting the grass, drying it, and bringing it into the barn. We had usually
eight cows and twenty-five sheep. With sheep and eight cows you need
lots of hay.

When I grew up, we were eight neighbors, and the lighthouse had
three families. We had school for three weeks and then we'd be off. We
had one teacher and he had two, three places to go during the year.
In the summer, we'd row in the boat, morning and afternoon. In the
wintertime, we boarded over to the other island. It wasn't very far, but

---

*Neskonge literally means king of the promontory. Vesterålen is an island group off the
coast of northern Norway, near exceptionally rich fishing banks.

in rough weather people drowned and those on shore could not go out and help them. Like a friend of mine, her dad drowned right out so we stood and watched. Sometimes the wave flooded our island on two sides and would wash out the potato acre on both sides of the house. In nice weather it was smooth. We used to go out and fish; I had a little rowboat that had my name.

I'm not sorry that I grew up there. You got a nice home life. It was just after we were confirmed, and grew up kind of, that we felt like we want to get out somewheres. So my sister and I left for Trondheim and that was in 1913. We had aunties and cousins in Trondheim, so we had family. I worked as a baby-sitter. I liked it very much there, but still I wasn't quite satisfied. I thought, "My goodness, there must be something different than just baby-sitting. I want to do something!" So I then decided to go to America.

I had an older sister—my dad was married three times. She was grown up and away from home when I came along. She left Norway and went to Alaska and got married and she had three little boys. I wrote home to dad and said that I wasn't very satisfied, maybe I'll go to America if I knew that my half-sister would care to have me. Dad had written to her and she said, fine, she needed help. So I was going to Petersburg, Alaska. Well, I didn't get there.

This was 1916 and the war had already been going real big over in Europe. We came out from Bergen on Bergensfjord, the first ship the Norwegian line had.* I was all alone, didn't know a single person. I was nineteen years old. This is in the late fall, in November. We had icebergs all around. We had to go the real northern passage because of the U-boats. They were all around England and it was all mined, so you went in the middle of the mines. We had to go into Kirkwall in Scotland and stay overnight.† The government came; they were looking

*The Bergensfjord was placed in service in September, 1913, just a few months after the Kristianiafjord inaugurated the trans-Atlantic passenger routes of the Norwegian America Line.
†During World War I, Norway remained a neutral state and the British Navy required that all Norwegian America Line ships submit to inspection en route.

for spies or something. And they picked someone out and took him ashore from the ship. Whoever they were, we never found out.

We had the lower deck full of eastern Europeans. They were just like they were packed in. I don't know where they slept. We could stay on our deck and look down. We happened to have a little better; we had cabins. We were lots of Norwegians. We had bad weather on the Atlantic, so it took us eleven days to get across. We were happy. They played music and we danced on the deck. We didn't think about anything. It didn't seem to bother any of the young people. I got acquainted with a girl from Stavanger that was going to a sister in Seattle. We have been good friends ever since. Her name was Sigrid Dahl.

Anyway, we came into New York on a Sunday and Ellis Island is closed on a Sunday. You don't get through there. Then on Monday you get a big piece of paper that tells who you are and where you came from and that you are an immigrant and that should get pinned on your coat. So then we were going to have a bite to eat and you got the ham sandwich with no butter on and you get sugar in your coffee and no cream. We thought to pay a dollar for that was terrible.

But it didn't take too long to get through. So I got a chance to send a telegram. We were about six, seven together and we went and sent telegrams. This Sigrid and I were going to Seattle and some was going to Everett and two sisters was going to Tacoma. Well, they told us we would arrive in Seattle Saturday morning at eight o'clock. Well, fine, that's what the telegram said. So we took off and went on the train and we went through the United States so fast I don't know how it happened. We were in Seattle on Friday night. Well, here I came to Seattle and nobody to meet me.

I had better backtrack and say that a neighbor left our island and one of the girls that I called Aunt Molly after I came here babysit for me until I was about four years old. Then they left for America, the father with seven or eight children, and they went to Grantsburg, Wisconsin. She was married and living in Seattle. So my sister had contacted her and I knew she was going to meet me and see that I got on the ship. Then she isn't there. What am I going to do? I don't know how to speak English, in the dark, on the November night.

So Sigrid's sister came down. She lived on a houseboat on Lake Union. There used to be an awful lot of houseboats there in those days, more so than now. Anyway, she didn't have room. Sigrid was gonna sleep on the davenport. I thought, well, gee, I wouldn't mind, with a blanket, to sleep on the floor instead of sit down here all night until in the morning Aunt Molly comes down. Well, we were talking back and forth.

Then there was this Swedish fellow we got acquainted with. He knew we couldn't talk English, and he helped us to buy fruit on the train. Then we'd sit and play cards and he talk to us and tell us about things. He had been to get married, but the one that was supposed to be his wife had passed away in Montana somewheres. That's where he came on. Just an awfully nice man. So he came over and talked to us and said, what was the trouble? And we said, "Well, the gal that was gonna meet me isn't here. And Sigrid, they haven't room for me. What am I gonna do?" He said, "Sigrid, if you go with me, we'll take her to a hotel and I'll come and get you and we'll get her and we'll find her place in the morning." He seemed to be a nice fellow. So long as he had Sigrid with him, I was O.K. You just had to trust somebody, and being that he spoke our language—I understood Swedish and he understood Norwegian.

So they took me to the N.P. Hotel. That's down by the King Station in Seattle. I didn't sleep that night, and the chair was in front of the doorknob. In the morning, they come pick me up with the taxi and took me driving. Went out to South Seattle. That wasn't the place. We were clear out to Alki Point and they couldn't find that address—217—so the chauffeur called evidently in to the office to find out where it was. It was up by Woodland Park. So we come there on Saturday morning and a little boy, about eight years old, meet us by the door, "My mother is down to the station to meet the girl that's coming from Norway." "Well," he [the Swede] said, "Here she is." So, we went in and we sat there and waited and waited. And pretty soon Molly come with tears in her eyes and she seen me and she said, "What?" And I said, "Yes, I came last night. They were mixed-up with the train. They were just glad to get rid of us, so they put us fast through the country and here I am." "I was just crying," she said, "and thinking, what am I going to write your sister, up in Alaska, when I didn't find you?"

I was there one week and I got work and stayed. We contacted my sister and she said, "Well, it is kind of nasty weather up here and maybe she just as well stay there if she have a good job." And it was a pretty good job. I didn't want to be beholden to anyone. I wanted to earn my own money and I felt I was imposing on them [Aunt Molly's family]. I think my dad was nice to them when they left Norway, but I just wanted to be on my own.

So many from my part of Norway, from off the mainland, were fishermen in Ballard.* Some of them had their own boats. I got more in with different people than I did at home, or even in Trondheim. [There] it was all your family; you didn't get acquainted with strangers. I thought Seattle was pretty big. It was funny; when I left Seattle after I got married, I was homesick for Seattle.

*A community northwest of downtown Seattle, Ballard was annexed into the city in 1907. After the turn of the century it attracted a strong Scandinavian community and became the hub of ethnic activity.

Esther Rinne

"Finland those days, you never see any black people."

*Having lost her mother when she was two years old and
having been raised in foster homes, Esther Rinne emigrated
from Finland in 1920 to join sisters in California. She was
nineteen at the time and her trip across the United States
proved to be quite frustrating and frightening. Esther later
settled in Oregon, where she met her husband, also a Finnish
immigrant; together, they cleared a farm.*

My father's name was Antti Wiirre. He was carpenter and contractor; he build houses. He was a very good father. He tried
to take good care of me. But he always had to hire a place to
put me in and so he didn't know how they took care of me. He came
to see me very often, but I don't know, I was so funny, I didn't dare to
complain. And some place was so cruel; they make me work so hard
and I was just a little kid. Then when I was fourteen, I found real good
place to stay—a farm in Pyhajoki. They took real good care of me. I
stayed there until I was seventeen.

I had brothers and sisters: Heikki, Jenny, Hilda, Anne, Helmi, and I
was the youngest. Brother was twenty-two years older and older sister was twenty-one years older and so forth. They were here when I
was born. They settled Eureka, California. That's where I came, too.
Everybody came to Eureka.

My older sister came from this country and she got married, so she
called me to come to Rauma, southern part of Finland. I was there,
when another sister sent my ticket to come to America. I was nineteen
when I came here. Those days it was hard to get passport from Finland;
that was 1920.

The ship was all right. It was real big ship when I crossed the Atlantic.

Then I landed at Ellis Island. That was terrible; it was the dirtiest place I ever seen. My sister wrote to me and said, "Don't take any money with you." They gonna send that $25 what a person had to have—they gonna send that to Nelson Lumber Company and I can get from there. All right. When I got there, Nelson Lumber Company was in New York and Ellis Island is Ellis Island. So finally the Finnish agent said, "Well, you have to telegram." So I had to send telegram for my sister to send another money. I had to wait two days. It was the filthiest place you can imagine. They had all kinds of bugs. We stayed in the dining room, we Finnish girls. We waited there; almost everyone has the same trouble. There was five girls from Finland.

Finally, I got the money and then I started to go and they give the lunch bag. It cost three dollars and there was—oohh—bread and cheese, mildewed cheese. They put slip on my chest and they always escorted. So I got the train all right. But then the "nigger" boy. I never seen before. Finland those days, you never see any black people.

Every time when they stopped the train, they put me in some room and they locked the door so I can't go anywhere. Then when the time came, they came and took me out to the train. I don't know if they changed the train or what. I never understood. Soon as I get to the train, there was that black man again; of course it was different guy, but the blackest you can imagine. I wanted to get orange. I wanted so badly the orange, because the train stopped and it [fruit stand?] was outside. Well, I went to the step there, the "nigger" boy pulled me back. He wouldn't let me go. I had to go back to my seat. He escorted me to the seat and ordered me to sit there.

Let's see, I think it was nine days before I get [to California]. I came to San Francisco first and I thought, well, now I can get rid of that "nigger" boy, and boy, I went fast. You know, when you are young, you are not afraid, so I thought, well, now I can get away.

I got away from him and I was so dirty, so I went to wash myself a little bit. And I left my suitcase on a bench and there was two ladies came and they looked at that suitcase. There was a sign—Finland—and all kinds of stamps. So when I came, they grabbed me and I thought, gee whiz, what's going on now. They took me and they took the suitcase and we went to the streetcar and then we changed another streetcar. Finally we went to the hotel way up the sixth floor and it was just a little room and they start looking for my purse and I start fighting because I thought that twenty-five dollars. They didn't speak any Finnish or anything.

Finally, the other lady went to the little hallway and there was a telephone, so she pointed me to come to the telephone and there was a Finnish voice said, "Don't be afraid. They are lady policewomen." And they just want to know if I had a dollar and a half to pay the room overnight. Well, so it was all right. And that was fine after that. They took that dollar fifty; I didn't understood that American money.

Then they took me about two blocks from the hotel and showed me where to go in the morning. And then they pointed the clock what time I supposed to be there. Naturally, I thought I'll be careful so I won't oversleep and I was there about 5:30. Well, the bellboy didn't let me go. He stopped me. He wouldn't let me go anywhere. And I thought, gee whiz, this is terrible. Then finally he had to go with the elevator, so I took my suitcase and I went to that place what they showed to me. Here I find the place and oh, I got so scared. When I went there, there was ocean in front of me instead of train. And I thought, well, gee whiz, where I going now? Because if you don't understand, you don't understand.

Well, those two ladies came again and they give me a letter and they said to give it to the conductor. I understood that "conductor." And they escorted me and that was a ferry. So I crossed the bay with the ferry. I went to the other side so there was a policeman and he escorted me to the train. When the conductor came, I give the letter and he looked and he kinda smiled and that was bothering me the whole day.

It took a whole day to go from San Francisco to Eureka by train. That was eight in the evening when I get there and my sisters, they had been waiting and waiting there and they was wondering where in the world I have been, because they have been coming almost two weeks every evening. I say, "Go ahead, go ahead and find out what the letter said." Anne didn't know anything about the letter, "What letter?" I said, "Well, the conductor has a letter so I want to know what was it."

She went and she said, "Did you try to get away?" I said, no. "Well, the letter was not to let you go anywhere." Because, those days, there's a lot of girls, they just disappear, to those road houses and—. My sisters, they wanted to make sure I get safely in Eureka. That's why they had protection everywhere.

I was really home right away. I wasn't lonesome at all. I was a little bit lonesome when I left Hangö. Hangö, that's where the ship started. It was beautiful evening when I looked at the city and I thought, well, I wonder if I ever see that city again. But when I get to England, then it was over and I meet other Finnish girls, so it was all right.

When I came to California, Anne, my older sister, said she'd try to keep a job for me. So I only had two days to fix up my clothes and go to work. My sister said, "Don't bring anything with you, because they are old style and we can get here." And I had suits and nice dresses and they had the same style there as here and I felt so bad, because I left such good dresses and here they was so expensive. I have to pay seventeen dollars for the dress and I only got fifty dollars a month for wages, and I owed the sister for the ticket and the money, the twenty-five dollars. I feel so bad about the dresses.

I went to work for cookhouse. I was dishwasher first, and then I start waiting tables and wash the dishes. I lived at the cookhouse. There was four girls. The cook was German and the second cook was Swedish-Finnish and then Mrs. Curry is the American. They was so nice to me, even if I make so many mistake. When you don't understand, you don't understand. What was the worst—cabbage and lettuce. If the cook wanted me to go and get from the vegetable room, either one, cabbage why I bring lettuce. I had to learn English because there wasn't any-body who speak Finnish around there. Only every fourth week I get to go to Eureka and then I speak Finnish with my sisters and Finnish people in Eureka.

I was there for two years. After that, they gave me two weeks vacation and I came here to Astoria [Oregon]. I had one sister here in Gearhart [Oregon], but I never seen before so I was anxious to get to know her. I came by boat.

Then they start coaxing and coaxing me to get job here instead of go back to Eureka. I get more wages here and so I thought, I wonder. Sure enough, I got job right away. I went to work at the restaurant as a waiter. And here I am. I got married here. We had one boy, but he died in the service. We moved to our own farm near Gearhart. It was a stump farm first, but we cleared and we worked like the dickens and day and night.

Alli Benson

"I got infested with lice."

A Swede-Finn, Alli Benson grew up speaking the Swedish language and eventually married a Swedish immigrant. She left Finland in 1920, together with her sister, to join family members in Seattle. Alli finished school in the United States and worked prior to her marriage in 1930. During the Second World War, she resumed her career as an office worker. She gives a poignant account of immigrants forced to return to their native country.

I was born near Pargas, Finland, June 1, 1908. Out where I came from, it was nothing but islands. Beautiful country, something like the San Juan Islands [Washington]. My dad had a general store and bakery. There were about thirty or forty families on the island. The mail was delivered to our home, maybe three times a week. People had to come to our home and pick it up. We thought that was just great; we had a lot of company.

My dad had been in America—he was in Seattle in 1889, at the time of the fire—and had always wanted to [go] back. So dad and my oldest brother, Arthur, came to America in 1913. My younger brother came in 1916. They were to earn enough money so they could send for my mother, my sister, and I. They fished up in Bristol Bay, Alaska. The First World War broke out and then we had a civil war in Finland and we were not able to contact anyone in America. My mother became ill and died of cancer in 1918, and here my sister and I were all by ourselves.

First thing after my mother died, we had to get my neighbor lady home; she had to come in and wash the body. I remember she put a coin on each eyelid to keep them closed. Then, of course, she laid "in state" for two-three days and we invited everyone to come and see

Alli Benson and her mother, ca. 1916

her. Then we took her to Pargas to be buried. There was snow eight-
ten feet high and we met a truck that said "dynamite" on it. That was
the Bolsheviks or whatever. On Sunday, her funeral. The ground was so
frozen. They had to dig two graves. One of the Bolsheviks had died and
my mother was buried next to her. We thought that was the worst thing
that could have happened, that she had to be buried next to someone
like that.*

*When the Bolshevik government headed by Lenin came to power in Russia in
November of 1917, Finland's independence from Russia was formally recognized. At

In Finland, it was awfully hard times.

In December, 1920, we came over. Dad sent the tickets. I didn't want to leave Finland. We had an old neighbor lady; she had heard how bad it was in America. If she would only have let me stay with her until I was confirmed! But, of course, I had to come. My sister Gunhild wanted to leave. She had to work hard to maintain our little place. I was twelve and she was eighteen.

We took a boat to Åbo [Turku]; we stayed there overnight and took a boat from Åbo to Stockholm, which takes twelve hours. We no more had gotten on the boat but what my sister got seasick; but I didn't. I guess the sailors and the captain took a liking to me, the only child on board. So the captain invited me up to his quarters to have coffee and coffee bread and I thought that was great. We landed in Stockholm the next morning and took a train across Sweden to Gothenburg.

Our ship was to leave the following day, but there was something that detained the ship, so we were not able to leave before another day. All right, so we got aboard; the name of the boat was *Stockholm*. My sister sat up on deck all day long, sick. She was sick the whole way coming across the ocean. You know, aboard that ship the rats were as big as cats. We had lots of rats. We traveled third class.

We finally arrived in New York harbor. They came and took all the bedding away from us, because we were to land that afternoon. Apparently the Swedish-American Line used the same dock as the Italians and there were two-three ships ahead of us, so we couldn't land. So we anchored and laid in New York harbor for a couple of days. Those days they didn't have the facilities to wash clothes like they would have now, so they handed us somebody else's dirty blankets and pillows. How we hated that, we were so afraid to go to bed!

We landed and were sent to Ellis Island. We slept in a room with

---

the same time, however, Bolshevik revolutionaries sought to overthrow the Finnish government and civil war broke out. The early months of 1918 saw bloody battles pitting Red Guards and Russian soldiers against Finnish civilians and government troops under the command of General Carl Gustaf Emil Mannerheim.

Alli Benson (right) and her sister Gunhild, 1911

thirty-five other people. They were all Catholics. We had never seen a Catholic, although we had heard of the Russian Catholics. They felt sorry for us and tried to pray for us. We knew that, but still we were scared to death. Finally, they had roll call and we were called up— "Gunhild and sister Alli." We understood that and boy, were we happy to leave.

In the meantime, we had bought four or five lunch boxes that we were going to eat on the train. We left one evening and about three o'clock that morning we had a head-on collision with another train.

There were a lot of people in the car where we were sitting that were hurt. All the windows were broken. Neither my sister nor I had a scratch on us. But we had to get off the train and it was cold!

I can't remember how long we had to wait. Instead of going into Chicago, they routed us through St. Louis. My dad had written that when we came to Chicago, we should get a Pullman. Well, we never did come to Chicago and they didn't understand us, so we just sat up all the way to Seattle. There were a lot of soldiers on the train and they were not very clean any of those people. I got infested with lice. My dad and brothers didn't know we were delayed—in Sweden, on Ellis Island, because of this collision—so they had to take turns to meet each train. One morning about six-thirty we arrived in Seattle.

My brother took a look at all those lunch boxes, which we had never opened. All we really ate as far as I remember—the porter came through with some candy and we put all the money in our hand and he picked out whatever he needed, so we ate some candy and I think some apples. My brother looked at those boxes and he said, "What in the name of goodness have you got here?" And he dumped the whole thing into the garbage can. When we were in Finland, we didn't throw away a crumb! So then we arrived and my sister-in-law took one look at me and she put me in the bathtub and washed my hair in real hot water and I don't know what else. She gave me a couple baths a day and I finally got rid of them [lice].

I had to start school right after New Year's and I did not like that. I was twelve years old and started in the first grade. My brother took me up to school, it was North Queen Anne. During recess, every child in that school came and looked at me through the window! The second or third day I got acquainted with some very nice girls who understood Swedish, so after that I got along pretty well. But they didn't live in the same direction as I did, so I had to walk home by myself through Seattle Pacific College and there was a little girl there about my age and she'd throw rocks at me every day. I knew she didn't like me.

I told my brother, "I'm never going to go back to school again, I'm afraid of her." So he said, "The first day I have available, I'm going to go with you and see what it's all about." You know what it was, she thought I was German. But after she found out that I wasn't German, she and I became the best little pals. Children can be so cruel. It took me about four years to go through grammar school. I must have been fifteen or sixteen when I graduated from eighth grade. Then I went two years to high school and then I graduated from business college after that.

I was confirmed in 1923 in the Swedish-Finn Lutheran Church. We were only twelve, and I was the only one confirmed in Swedish. I knew everything in Swedish from home—the Bible history, the catechism, so it was a lot easier for me to be confirmed in Swedish. I knew the minute he asked a question in Swedish, I'd better be prepared and answer it. You couldn't slide down into your chair so they couldn't see you!

In 1930, my husband Gust and I got married. I met him through a friend. We used to go to Scandinavian dances and have a wonderful time. We went together for about four years before we married. He came from Värmland in Sweden. He first worked in a boiler shop, then he bought his own milk route. We just had a small wedding at my sister's home. I had a pretty white dress, not a long dress. We didn't go anywhere on our honeymoon. We had rented an apartment on Capitol Hill and moved into the apartment. My sister-in-law cooked a chicken dinner, which in those days was quite a treat.

Nineteen thirty-one, he wanted to go to Sweden and visit his parents, so he sold his milk route and we went to Sweden. We hadn't heard of a depression on the west coast at that time. When we came to New York, we saw all these people standing in the soup lines and wondered what had happened. Then we found out that no one was working.

Gust had a friend who had become sick in this country and been in an insane asylum. He heard that Gust was going to Sweden and he wrote to him and asked if he could help him home. So we did all we could. On the ship, he had to be watched twenty-four hours a day. There were two-three Swedish boys who were working their way across; they had been deported. Here was this young Swedish boy who had been in America for three years and hadn't worked one day. He didn't have any clothes, so Gust lent him his overcoat at night, because he had to stand outside the cabin [of the sick man] and watch that this fellow didn't get out. We let him have some underwear and such, because the poor man was real cold, and he appreciated that.

When we came to Gothenburg, then my husband was in full charge of him [the friend] and we got to Värmland and got into a cab and delivered him to his parents. That was a pathetic sight, to have a fellow come home who had left them perfectly all right. He became ill and it affected his mind. He was in Idaho in the logging camps. It was terrible to have to deliver him to his old parents. He was probably not more than forty.

I became an American citizen through my father, I don't know which year. I wasn't yet sixteen, so I came under his application. Later on, I was a witness for Swedish boys and girls who had taken their citizenship. In 1941, I was to be a witness and the judge said that while I was a citizen, I had to get my own derivative citizen papers. This was a time when it was again difficult to get information from Finland. [So] I had to get my school records, which wasn't difficult, and then I had to get someone who could remember that I had been born and that I was a child of my father and my mother. My brother was eleven years older than I and he remembered distinctly that I was born, because he was told he couldn't stay in the house, something was going to happen. And he saw the midwife rowing across the sound and he said, "Oh, no, not another baby!" He had an affidavit sworn out to that effect. So then I got my citizenship papers. I have three sets now, so I must be an American citizen!

Laura Foss

"We had to start all over again,
writing A's and B's."

Born in Copenhagen, Denmark, on July 1, 1905, Laura
traveled to Seattle in 1921 to visit her aunt. She attended
school, worked as a domestic servant, and participated in
the Danish community. In 1925, she married a fellow Dane;
they had two children, Paul and Norma, and spoke Danish in
the home. A second marriage, also to a Danish immigrant,
followed the death of her first husband.

We were six children growing up, all born in Copenhagen.
We had a nice home, not too much money but always
enough to eat. The six of us could all sing and we had lots
of singing and music and laughter. My father had a good sense of
humor and was extremely proud of his kids. When all the stores and
streets were decorated for Christmas, he would take us into downtown
Copenhagen. We would stand outside the store windows and look at
all the wonderful, wonderful things. We knew we couldn't have any of
it and we never went in the store, but we would stand outside and look.
And he would stand patiently waiting, until we had our fill and went
on to the next window. It was one of the highlights of my childhood.

After confirmation, I worked for this family for a year. I lived at home
and walked there. Then I decided that America, here's where I'm going.
I had an aunt and uncle in Seattle. My uncle was a well-known contractor and my aunt was my father's sister. I just thought it would be
interesting to come over here and see some of the world and go back
home again. So I did come when I was fifteen. Of course, I couldn't just
travel alone, but a family was going home on a visit and they had been
asked to look after me on the way back.

Laura Foss (far left) with her family, 1909

Aunt Marie was quite well-to-do and she always had money standing in the bank in Copenhagen in case her father, my grandfather, needed anything. And she said, "You can take the money out of the bank." So they took the money out of the bank for my ticket. At age fifteen, you are all excited; I never stopped to analyze how my mother felt. But when the day came for departure, she said, "I'm going to say good-bye here because I am not going down there and see that ship sail." And she didn't. This was in January, 1921.

The last minute, it was decided that my cousin from Germany was to come along. It was sort of an afterthought. Greta was exactly a year older than me, just sixteen. We sailed on *Frederick VII*; it was a Danish ship. We sailed on second class because this family, their name was Nielsen, had tickets on second class and, of course, we were with them. We weren't used to afternoon coffee with homemade pastry every day. It was quite elegant.

We came to Chicago and we had a couple of hours or more between trains and they took us into a drugstore and we sat at the counter and I was served my first ice cream soda. I had never tasted anything like it and I thought—ice cream, in a drugstore! A drugstore in Denmark is strictly a pharmacy. That was one of the biggest surprises and I promptly wrote home. On the train, I was introduced to my first baked potato. It was enormous. I looked at it and my eyes must have popped out. I had never seen or heard of a baked potato. I ate it and I thought it was good.

I remember we got to Ogden, Utah, and we must have had quite a layover, because they took us to a show. The name was just plain "Love." Of course, this was a silent picture. We couldn't read what it said, but I remember the movie. We got to Seattle on the 25th of January and it was raining. My uncle had white hair and he never wore a hat and he came running down to the depot to pick us up.

My aunt and uncle had a nice house on Broadway. We stayed there with them. Then we had to be sent to school. The neighborhood school, the ordinary grade school, wouldn't take us because we couldn't speak [English]. They told my aunt that we would have to go to Pacific School; it was a regular school, but they had a class for foreigners. It was on lower Broadway, out Jefferson Street. We were enrolled in this class with Chinamen and Russian girls and Greek and you name it.

My aunt told the teacher, "Don't let them sit behind each other, because they'll just sit and giggle and won't pay any attention." So we were separated by one Russian girl. But we could communicate without anyone ever finding out; we had a system of mimics and our hands. We were closely knit, because we were in a strange country—strange people, everything. We felt we just had one another.

We had a good schooling, I in Copenhagen and she in Germany, but we had to start all over again, writing A's and B's. Of course the Chinese had to learn our letters. We caught on very fast and the teacher was so proud of us when we had done something, she would send us in to the principal with our papers and he would pat us on the back.

Like I told you, my home in Denmark was a lively one, with lots of singing and lots of laughter and lots of young people. My aunt and uncle, they had lots of friends and she had a lot of dinner parties, but they were all their ages. As soon as we were through serving dinner and washing dishes, well then, we could go up and go to bed. There wasn't any life, any laughter, any fun. But I will say this as far as my aunt goes, she was a good cook and when it came to food, the sky was the limit. She bought the best and plentiful. And, of course, all the fresh fruit and all the goodies we were not used to. We could have all we wanted. But she had no patience. She would expect us to be able to do a lot of things, not being able to talk.

One experience I never forgot was, once she told me to go to the butcher shop. Now I had been there with her; it was a few blocks from home up on Broadway. I knew the butcher and he knew me. So one day she told me to go up there and buy twelve loin pork chops. She wouldn't let me write it down, because I had to memorize it, I had to learn. If she had told me in Danish what a loin pork chop was, I knew what it was; but she didn't. I had no idea if I was going to buy pigs' feet or if I was going to buy round steak. Twelve loin pork chops, that's a mouthful when you don't know what it is. I just knew I had to go to the butcher and I got the money.

All the way from home I said, "twelve loin pork chops, twelve pork loin chops, chop loin pork chops." By the time I got there I was so muddled, I didn't know. So the butcher, of course he knew who I was and he knew Aunt Marie, she was one of his best customers. And I stood there and if I had come home with the wrong thing, I tell you, that would never do. She didn't mince her words then. But I stood there and I don't know what I jabbered. And he tried and he tried and finally he got to loin pork chops and I lit up—ju, that was it! And he knew that she always bought plenty and when he got to twelve—ja! I got them. But then coming home, she takes it for granted.

There was an old couple that lived down below Broadway, an old family friend. When there was a lot of food left over, bring it down to Mrs. D. So one day we had had a party and there was a basketful of food and she said, "You go down to Mrs. D." Well, I had never been down there by myself. She said, "You just go down such and such and then you take the steps down to Eastlake and then you can find it." I found it all right and I delivered my basket and we sat and talked—that is, they did; I couldn't talk. Pretty soon it was time for me to go back. I got my empty basket and she took me as far as up to Eastlake and then I knew I had to go this way to find that long stairway that would lead up towards Broadway.

So she said goodbye, and I started and you know, somebody had moved those steps! They were not there. I walked and I walked and I walked and I couldn't find the steps. I knew I had to get up. It's straight up like this. So then I thought, I have got to get up there somehow. So I found another street, a steep one, and I started to climb up and I didn't know where I was, but I knew I was in the right direction. Well, I thought, if I meet somebody, I'll ask. So I met a lady and I said, "Broadway, here" and pointed and then she said, yes, so I kept on going. Once I was up on Broadway, I was on familiar ground and I found it. But I didn't say anything to Aunt. She wouldn't understand that I couldn't find those steps. It was a hard school in a way, but it didn't hurt us any.

Then I had jobs. All of us young girls, we all were working in homes as domestics and we had Thursdays off. So Thursday afternoon, we would meet at the church. Then we got acquainted with young people our own age and it was all clean fun like picnics and basket socials and little plays and entertainment evenings and what have you. That's where all the young people met. The fellows after work would come in the evening and we played croquet in the evening out on the church lawn and we would have some kind of little entertainment in the community hall and we would have coffee and do a lot of singing. All clean, innocent fun. It was nothing that would interest the young people today. We were a big group of young people, all Danish.

Then we heard about this Danish folk school in Solvang [California]. Greta and I decided maybe that should be O.K. So we wrote to Pastor Kristensen who was in charge, he and his wife.* It was decided that we

*The Solvang school opened in 1911, the fifth Danish folk high school in the United States. It became known as Atterdag College and provided adult education courses until 1936. (The folk high school tradition is discussed in some detail by Frederik

could come down for half price. It was two hundred dollars for the school year from October to some time in March, room and board, but we could get it for one hundred dollars if we could help out in the kitchen and so on. We soon found out that this was all work and no play, because we had to get up early and get all the halls and steps cleaned and washed and tables set for breakfast and all that before the rest of them arrived. Then when they went to classes and what have you, then we were left with the dishes.

After two weeks, Greta took the lead; she just decided, we're paying a hundred dollars for this? So then she said to Mrs. Kristensen, "How long is this going to go on?" "What do you mean?" "Well, I mean this, we are working all the time; we never take part in anything." "Well, you better speak to my husband about that." So we did. And he was a peach of a man, so he said, "Why don't you just forget about working; we'll hire a full-time girl." Then I said, "What about the money?" "Oh, you can always pay me whenever you get the money." Then they hired a girl that was to work for wages, and so from that time on, we had a ball.

It was lectures and it was gymnastics and it was folk dancing and reading and it was handiwork. It was wonderful. That's where I met my first husband, Harald Christiansen. He had attended school the winter before, but this year he was working as a carpenter for a contractor in town. They had some little cottages in the back of the school and some of these young men were living there and boarding at the school. So then, of course, I saw him in the evenings and on Saturdays and Sundays.

When school was out in March, Harald knew that I would eventually be heading back to Seattle, so he went to Seattle to find work. We were not engaged. We had some kind of an understanding, but it wasn't just one hundred percent. But I wasn't going to come back to Seattle before I had earned money to pay what I owed at the school. Greta and I got jobs in Santa Barbara, in homes, and saved every penny. Never had five

---

Madsen in Part Five. Evald Kristensen headed the Solvang school between 1921 and 1931.)

Laura Foss and her first husband, Harald, 1925

cents for an ice cream cone; everything was saved and paid back. We
worked there all summer; came back in August.

When we left for the school, my aunt said, "Your uncle will pay the
hundred dollars." And we were to work for the second hundred dollars. But my aunt was all for working and when she found out that we
weren't working any more, I guess she decided that we weren't going
to get the hundred dollars. So we owed two hundred dollars. That was
a lot of money. I always thought it was a bit unfair after they had promised. I got fifty or fifty-five dollars a month in homes. So I had paid

back, [but] I still owed seventy-five dollars. Then we had to earn money for our fare home. So we got back to Seattle and we got up to my aunt's apartment and after she greeted us, the first thing she said was, "Have you paid your school? Have you paid up what you owe?" And I told her a lie; I said, "Yes." I didn't tell her I still owed seventy-five dollars.

Then Harald and I became engaged and Harald paid the seventy-five dollars. I got a job and I said, "I'm not going to get married until I have that seventy-five dollars in my hand." And I did. Before we got married, I bought bedding for that seventy-five dollars, so I felt that I had taken care of it myself.

We were married the 8th of April, 1925; that was my parents' silver anniversary. The church on Spruce Street wasn't built yet, but we had had services all these years in the parsonage basement and it was real cosy. Our friends decorated it with wild cherry blossoms. There were a lot of cherry trees on empty lots in the neighborhood. Our friends had gathered armfuls and it was just beautiful, and it didn't cost anything. I had a nice white dress that my aunt gave me; she was wonderful in so many ways and very generous. We had a big wedding cake. Greta was engaged and she got married in August that same year. She and her husband-to-be were the attendants. She married the gym teacher at Solvang; he was eighteen years older than she. She had a very happy marriage, so did I. Harald was a wonderful, wonderful guy.

I went to school and got my citizenship papers in 1930, because I was going back to Denmark on a visit. Paul was at that time two years old. Paul and I were gone five months. I remember coming home, in that area [of Copenhagen] where my home is. Everybody had the flag up [to welcome them]. It was wonderful.

Hans Fahl

*"The fruit trees were in blossoming white
and I thought it was like paradise."*

*Hans Fahl came to central Washington in 1923 to assist his
aunt and uncle on their fruit orchard. The farming community
of Selah, near Yakima, was predominately Swedish, and Hans
was impressed with the warm inland climate and the fertile
volcanic soil. From the outset, he was prepared to settle down
and become an American citizen. Hans took over the family
orchard and later married a woman of Swedish descent.*

Hans Johan Fredrik Fahl. It's a long name. I was born in Karlskrona, in the province of Blekinge, southeastern Sweden, November 28, 1901. The city of Karlskrona is a naval base.

I went through the regular school and something similar to what you call high school here. Then I went into the Navy and I was in there until the time when I left for America. I was stationed all the time in Karlskrona. I was a torpedo man. Sometime I just wonder, maybe I'd been better off being a retired torpedo man now, than to be still struggling along as a farmer!

My dad sang in a church choir for fifty years. I grew up in the church that way. He went to church every Sunday and it was customary I would go along with him. Then I was also interested in the young people's work within the church. By the time I was going to leave, why they sprung a nice big party on me and they presented me with a Swedish flag, an ornamental deal on a silver pole. I still have it.

I emigrated to the United States. That was sixty years ago, in 1923. I recall so vividly. It was a frosty morning, little frost on the ground as we left, and as we came further west and further west, why it got warmer and warmer. Of course, coming to Yakima [Washington], it was just all

Hans Fahl, 1983

spring here and I thought it was a wonderful thing. I was traveling all by myself. I wanted to see what it looked like on the other side of the horizon and, of course, everytime you came to the horizon, there was another horizon. When I got here, I was very much impressed with the climate and that made me stay.

As I went to the train in Karlskrona, they gave me a lot of flowers and stuff to wish me bon voyage and I said to myself, by golly, this is my own funeral! I had a lot of friends, so it was a hard thing to come over here. And not knowing the language at all—more than just a few phrases that I had for emergency, that I could use in traveling.

I went to a library and got hold of an English-Swedish dictionary and the most phrases that you need for traveling was to be found in it, so I took and copied them off. And by writing all that stuff down, it imprinted on me much more, so that right now I write pretty good English. I had that [list] with me and if there was a phrase I wanted to say, I just read that thing over; and then it was also how to pronounce it, so I tried to pronounce it just about as close as that. I didn't have any difficulty at all.

I came on the motorship *Stockholm* and there was one incident on that trip which I'll never forget. It happened to be the anniversary of the sinking of *Titanic*. And we came to the very spot where this *Titanic* sank and the ship stops there for twenty minutes. And they had a beautiful memorial service for those 1,500 people that disappeared in the water, and then they threw a big wreath of flowers down in the ocean. It was, I think, the eleventh anniversary of the sinking of *Titanic*. A day or so before, why somebody said, "There's an iceberg over there!" And you know, the iceberg was far away, but it cooled the temperature down to thirty-two degrees.

When we landed in New York, we were hoarded alphabetically in different sections of this big building, and then they checked our passports, and then checked if we had any money. I remember when I arrived in Yakima, I had my ticket paid for and I had sixty-five dollars left. And I still got the sixty-five dollars! Not exactly the same, of course!

I traveled on a train to Chicago just by sitting up, and then from Chicago and on to Yakima I had a sleeper. I went to the restaurant in the train car. I just checked my list over what kind of a food I thought I wanted. I just ordered that and I didn't say much more than just to order. He took the order and came with it. He put a slip and I just paid him up and that was it. I didn't say anything, so nobody knew anything about me.

It seems like it took four days from New York to Yakima at that time, continuous traveling. It surprised me the immenseness of it. It was beginning to be springtime and the further west we came the warmer it got. Came to Spokane, boy, I thought it was a regular summer compared to the Swedish climate. I remember we came through Montana

Hans Fahl   143

and there was a woman, a well-dressed lady, and the train stopped on just a very small place. And golly, I sit there looking and that lady she got off and walked out in that dusty country. She hiked over across by the depot and somebody took her in a coach. And I thought, gee whillikins, such a godforsaken place and somebody like that come walking out! It was really cowboy country.

My aunt and her husband, Kjerstin and Anton Fahlquist, came and met me at the train. They knew what time I would be coming. She was a sister to my mother. She came over here in about 1890. She was the only one of her family that came and I was the only one of my family that came.

They had a fruit orchard and as they died, I took over the operation of it. They had twenty-three acres. They were growing apples, mostly. Then I planted pears in with them. When the trees got to a certain age, I took the old trees out and I replanted, so my orchard right now is the second growth of apple trees. The acreage is the same but the type of planting they're doing nowadays is a tighter type, so that you are growing more fruit on an acre. It isn't quite so much handwork now as it was. Before, you handled the boxes and stacked them up, whereas you have now a mechanized lift.

When I first saw the fruit trees here, they were in blossoming white and I thought it was like paradise. I said, well, it's just like a Navy man got grounded on dry land. I would probably compare Karlskrona with Bremerton.* The warmth here, it was just so comfortable here all the time, you forgot about it [missing the sea]. Every now and then I took a trip over to Seattle and it was just like coming home.

I was the only Lutheran in the whole community [Selah, Washington] at the time. They were all Covenant people.† There was a minister in St. Paul [Minnesota] and he got interested in real estate and he found out there was land for sale out west and he went to investigate it and he bought a certain block of land. So he came back to his parishioners

---

*A Navy port in western Washington.
†Members of the Mission Covenant Church. See Andrew Johnson interview in Part One for background on this denomination.

and said, "Well, here's the future for you." So they all bought five acres apiece and they moved out here. They grubbed the sagebrush out and then they planted trees. That was 1910. My aunt and uncle moved out in that same group.

These people were all belonging to the Covenant Church in St. Paul and then they formed a Covenant church in Selah. They were the mainstays. They were the mayor and they were the cop and they were everything in town. They had Swedish in their church and anyplace you went, you could just buy everything in Swedish. Now, of course, other people move in, so the Swedish influx in Selah is just a part of history.

When I first came to the bank, I was going to cash some money I had. It's a custom in Sweden, you always take your hat off when you come to the bank. So I took my hat off and laid it on the side. And the cashier says, "Hey, it's high to the ceiling here, keep your hat on!" I never forget that.

Within just a few days after I got here, I applied for my citizen papers. It takes you five years before you can get your citizenship. I became a citizen right away, as soon as I had been here for five years. It was the time when Coolidge was president. I remember when I came to the judge, he asked me my name. "Well," he said, "here's your chance; you can cut out all those extra names." "Well," I said, "I was baptized with those and they'll stay." So he respected me for respecting my parents.

Gustav Simonson

"The sea is where you have to look for a livelihood."

Gustav Simonson spent two years in the Midwest before working his way to Washington state in 1925. His love of the sea drew him to halibut fishing in Alaska. Eventually, he became skipper of his own boat and enjoyed this occupation until retirement. While Gustav fished, his wife and seven children maintained a rural home east of Tacoma. For certain immigrants, like Gustav, it was extremely important to settle in a familiar natural environment.

I was born December 3, 1905, in southwestern Norway. Every kid on the island learned to row and fish. You more or less grew up with an idea that the sea is where you have to look for a livelihood in one form or another, whether you want to engage in fisheries or go sailing in the commercial fleet. To own your own boat was the ultimate. That give you a little more leverage as far as making a living, and at the same time you didn't have to go around and ask your neighbor if he was full-handed or if he needed another man.

I finished schooling in 1920. This was right after the First World War. I was fifteen and the first winter I fished, we never made one dime. There was fish, but there was no price. The export market collapsed. Whereas two years before you got a hundred crowns for a hectoliter of herring, in 1920 it sold for one crown! There was absolutely no way you could make a living. So consequently, you started to think, shall I migrate or shall I go sailing?

I went for weeks, trying to get a chance to go sailing. I had an opening, if I wanted to sign up for three years in the tropics. Well, I never had much liking for the tropics; I like cold weather. So I said, "No, I am not going to sign up for three years, because that's too long to be in the tropics for me. I'll go to America."

Many others on the island migrated at that time. I came with my school chum Vilhelm, or Bill, Larsen. I had a cousin that was married to a farmer in Minnesota and I came to Sandstone. At that time there was a large number of people that wanted to migrate and the Norwegian quota was practically filled. But if you would migrate as a farmer, you had a little better chance of being accepted.

I left Bergen the 15th of September, 1923, and arrived in New York the 26th of September. We went over England. *Olympic* was one of the largest vessels afloat at that time. There was emigrants from every nation in Europe—Scandinavian, Italian, French, Spanish, Polish. And I tell you, it was a Babel. I am not positive now how many we had on that boat, but I think it was a little short of five thousand. I had no complaint about the steerage accommodations; I wouldn't hesitate to make the same trip today. Lice was one problem that was prevalent.*

We came into New York harbor in the evening. We docked, but we could not go ashore. The next day, we got into some smaller boats and was taken out to Ellis Island. That was quite an interesting experience. You were supposed to have twenty-five dollars in cash. Well, my partner didn't have, so I had to lend him. And when I lent him enough so he'd get in, then I had only twenty-three dollars and, of course, that kind of worried me.

But nobody inquired what we had, because we were young and healthy and apparently they judged us more physically than anything else. I went through the line—a big, long line, twenty side-by-side. They ask a few question and we answer whatever we thought it was. I got some rash on the trip over and the doctor told me to go with him into a cubbyhole and he looked at this rash. Of course, it was nothing but heat rash and so, go ahead and go. When enough of us got out, we went aboard the ferry and was taken up to the railroad. You had to kind

*The *Olympic* was considered a luxury vessel and had third-class cabins for up to six persons rather than open steerage compartments. Simonson was probably a third-class passenger on the ship.

of look after yourself, although there was an agent. I had a ticket right to Sandstone. I had to go over Minneapolis and then get a local train.

When you are born on an island, you are removed from anything that you call a crowd. I have always had an aversion—even today, I don't want to live in the city. All we thought was to get away from the cities and get out to God's country. You can't imagine what the cities was at that time. You burned coal and the garbage can was standing on the sidewalk and they stood there all day. The sanitation wasn't what it is today.

Sandstone is sixty miles north of Minneapolis. The only industry was a sand quarry and outside of that, it was farming. I stayed with my cousin only two weeks. I worked for a farmer picking potatoes and I have hated that occupation ever since. I saw more potatoes in two weeks than I could shake a stick at. I took the train up to Duluth and I was lucky, I got to work for the city on a road project. We worked there till it froze up, that was only a matter of six weeks. Then we went in the woods. That was more or less standard procedure for any greenhorn. Winter come, you either have to go in the woods or you could go out and work for a farmer for little or nothing, board and room.

In the summertime, we went sailing. That's the first thing I looked for. Even when I was working for the city, it was up on a ridge and we could stand and look out over Lake Superior and see the boats coming and going. That made us homesick. So next spring come around, I gonna be on a boat. Probably the hardest thing for us to take was to be removed from the water. That was horrible.

I was a deckhand. The first month I was aboard that boat, I hadn't had my stomach full of fish since I left the old country and I eat fish for one month. And after that month was over, I couldn't look at it. That lake trout was just like eating pork—fat. In the old country, we would have salted it. We were raised on salt fish. That salt, hard to get away from.

All the way back of my mind was Alaska—go to Alaska. We had not the slightest idea how big the country was. The cost was one thing and, of course, we had the Dakotas between us. At that time you could get a harvest ticket and go anyplace you wanted to go in the Midwest— the railroad had a policy to help the farmers getting help up in the fields. So when that time came around in 1925, I bought a harvest ticket for five dollars. I got off the train in Youngstown, North Dakota, and I inquired around there, if there was any farmers that needed me. No, there wasn't, so I went right back on the train and took it to Wiley City, that wasn't very far. And next morning I inquired around what would be the best place to go. "If you go south, go down to Litchfield," one of them told me. I did. I had picked up the information that a Mr. Sortland came from the same island, but I didn't know him.

I went into an implement store and asked if he knew Sortland. "Sure, that's my father." "I'm looking for work on a farm, harvest hand." "Stay right here. My father was in here just a few minutes ago, and I'm gonna go out and get him." It wasn't long before he was back with old man Sortland. "Ja, sure," he said. They were glad to have a greenhorn, because they knew he would work hard. I never been anyplace in my life where I was treated better than I was by Sortland. If I had been son in the house, I couldn't have been treated better.

After the harvest was over, I bought an old automobile and started north, going to drive to the Pacific Coast with another harvest hand that I met when I worked for Sortland, Chris Eriksen, he came from the same island, too. I bought a 1916 Overland, an old touring coupe. It rained that week and good gravy, the roads up in North Dakota—it was just like you were driving through a bowl of mush! But anyway, we got up to Crosby and we knew there was a family living there that came from about the same island as we did. We found them and stayed there overnight. It snowed that night. The harvest was pretty well over there, so we decided we'd better go west into Montana.

We took off for Montana. The shift was outside on the gearbox and anytime we was gonna go from low to high, you had to go underneath and change it into gear. We had no brakes. My partner had to jump out before we come to a dead stop and put a rock back of the wheel so we didn't roll. We crossed the Missouri River and when we got on top of that ridge, it was a long hill and we had no idea it was that long going down. The car got to go faster and faster and the road was as crooked as a snake's back. Couldn't stop! Well, we finally came to stop down by the city and everybody was alive yet!

Well, there was nothing doing around there. The harvest was over, and we kept on going west because we had all intention of driving to the coast. But when we came to Glasgow, it snowed, about four inches I think, so we decided that we had better abandon the car and take the train. We sold the car for fifteen dollars and bought a ticket to Spokane. We went out in Spokane and went out to a camp up at Priest River, Idaho, and worked there for three weeks. Then we went to Tacoma, Washington, on the train.

I tell you the first thing I did, I went into a restaurant and ordered a boiled salt mackerel. Salt mackerel in the old country was a delicacy, but that mackerel I got I wouldn't feed it to a dog! So salty I couldn't eat it. There were Norwegians wherever you went. I don't know whether you smelled them or what, but you always ran into them and you had an affinity for looking up another Norwegian.

I was engaged in heavy construction for eight years, but then the Depression came and everything went haywire. So then I decided that this here will not do, so I took the steamer to Juneau, Alaska. Middle of the winter, with a chunk of salt pork and a few potatoes. Very few dollars, I think I had twenty-some dollars when I took off. When I started fishing, we got two and a half cents a pound for halibut. You know that you wasn't gonna get rich in a hurry, but anyway you were going to make a living. I've been fishing ever since.

Halibut boats were relatively small boats, three men, four men; that was what they call a mosquito fleet. We in the Juneau fleet hardly ever fished outside the island at that time, mostly inside the island. You were out ten days. Every ten days or two weeks, you were back in again. You bait and you haul and you dress and you ice. You have a line that is three hundred fathoms long and at that time, you have probably 115–120 hooks. You set them down on the bottom, anchor on each end in a buoy. We would leave it out for many hours, overnight. You haul that back up again. Sometimes you got lots of fish, sometimes you didn't get so many.

I was accustomed to that. I had no problem there. I was right at home. That felt good. It felt just like I been back in Jerusalem!

Sigvald Stenersen

"My first Christmas,
I hauled manure on Christmas Day."

*In 1930, Sigvald Stenersen returned to the United States,
the country of his birth. The Depression made it difficult
for him to find employment, and working conditions on the
farm in eastern Washington were miserable. The Civilian
Conservation Corps provided a welcome training environment
for the Norwegian, who later made his living in the
construction industry around Spokane, Washington.*

All of them around here call me "Steve." That's the nickname I've been stuck with for most of my life. I was born in Sand Point, Idaho, March 15, 1912. My father's name was Søren; they called him "Sam" when he was here. My father was a yard foreman for Humboldt Lumber Company in Sand Point. He spent about sixteen-seventeen years here; he was a citizen of this country, too. He made two trips back to the old country and then on the third trip, my mother came along with a lot of other emigrants. She was young, only sixteen years old; and she worked two years as a housekeeper and then they got married.

They were from the southern part of Norway, not too far from Farsund. It was hard times for most families in Norway. They couldn't stay home; most of them had to go to town or someplace and find some kind of work. My dad had two brothers that were working for this same Humboldt Lumber Company and my mother had three sisters beside herself that came, but they went on to California. My grandfather on my dad's side was also working in the United States for a time; he was a carpenter.

My dad was a hard worker and he was strong. Piling lumber and handling lumber took a lot of power and in those days they took contracts, instead of getting paid by the hour. The harder you work, the more you made. Dad wasn't wealthy or anything like that, but for a working man he had a good job. I think my dad would have stayed, but my mother didn't like it here, even though conditions was much better for her. In the fall of 1914 they went back with the idea that maybe that was just gonna be a visit. But then World War I broke out and that put a stop to that. They bought the farm where my mother was born and raised. Dad and my neighbor built a small sawmill that they operated part-time, so between that and the little farm they made a go of it.

We had to work from the time we could walk. I shouldn't say walk, but even before we went to school we had chores to do. I thought many times when I was a child that it was an awful thing you couldn't play. But one thing I know I profited from, I never been afraid of work and never been fired in my life. I learned how to work and carry responsibility.

I went seven years to grade school, till I was fourteen and confirmed, and then I went two winters to continuing school. There was about probably eight hundred people in that small community and very few went on to any more schooling. Most of them just started working when they were confirmed. My dad wanted me to have more education; he had seen that the more education I could get the better I would be off. I didn't have a hard time with studies; I had a real easy time of it. In fact, my grade school teacher, he had some money, and he offered to give me money to send me to college. He says, "I'll borrow you the money to go to college." But no, I was gonna dig gold!

I was an American citizen, so there was a certain pride I carried. In high school we had debates once in a while, the advantages and disadvantages of emigrating to the United States. I remember I led a debate for going to the United States; I even got hot under the collar. There was a kind of a pride that you knew the big country of the United States, that was your country. The dream was, everything was so much better in the United States, that if you want to apply yourself, you could really do so. In the '20s there was literally hundreds of men and women that went from the district; most of them went over to New York and Brooklyn, some to Chicago, and would work and come home. Some of them had some money and some of them—we didn't know how much they had, they used to do a lot of bragging. Being a young fella, you kinda fall for that. But dad told me the truth, that conditions weren't just as rosy as they were pictured to be. Not that I ever heard him being dissatisfied or anything like that, he just put the record straight.

The only thing I had to do was get my birth certificate from Idaho. I had to come before I was twenty-one. Five years was the limit I was gonna stay. I was only going to New York; I wasn't figuring on coming out here. There was three other men from the community that went at the same time; two had been here before, and there was another boy the same age as me. We went on a coastal steamer from Kristiansand to Oslo and there you boarded the big ocean liner *Stavangerfjord*.* That was April, 1930.

I had a cousin that lived in Brooklyn; I came to him. There was absolutely nothing to get any kind of a job there. He was a carpenter by trade and a good one, but he had been out of work for I don't know how long, and what little money he had saved, he had to dip into pretty heavy just to exist. I was pretty desperate. We went to several hiring places. The only thing I could have got—I could have gone on a tramp steamer as a deck boy and I was willing to go, but my cousin says, no. If it had been a Norwegian ship, O.K., but not on a French tramp steamer.

I had two aunts, my father's sisters, that lived in Spokane and one of them I knew from childhood. So I wrote to her and asked if there was work to be gotten out here. She wrote back right away and said, well, it wasn't very good, but she sure thought I'd find something. So I borrowed money from my cousin for train fare out to Spokane and I got to Spokane and it was just as bad. In the time it took to get out to Spokane, the Depression hit out here. Idle by the thousands.

A neighbor of my aunt knew this Norwegian farmer that lived about forty miles from Spokane. So I wrote to him and he said, "O.K., come on out." So I started working there just about the middle of the summer. He was probably the richest farmer in Spokane county. During the Depression, I remember one day he came home and had lost five

*A mainstay vessel of the Norwegian America Line. It first saw service in 1918.

thousand dollars in the bank and still survived, so he had money. He drove the first Cadillac car, I believe, this side of the Mississippi. He was about seventy years old then and he was not very well liked. He had gobbled up all the farms around there, small farms that couldn't make it.

I worked out there, thirty dollars a month; that was "digging gold." First thing he told me I had to do was milk the cows. I had never milked a cow. Back home, that was always the women that milked the cows. I told him I didn't know how. Well, I'd have to learn. Well, they were wild cows. Big pastures they were running in and I had to round up the cows after supper with a saddle horse and get them in. Didn't have a barn really for the cows, just more like a shed. I got through it. I made it. But those were tough days.

He had an old farmhouse. He had two of his nephews from Norway and another hired man besides myself and a cook. He was not married. One of the things I had to do that summer was pick up wheat sacks. I was eighteen years old; I weighed 135 pounds. And I had to pick up those sacks, every sack weighed over 150 pounds, and throw them up in a wagon. Somebody jabbed a knife in my back, it wouldn't have hurt any more. But I lived through it. The saddest day I had on the farm was my first Christmas, when I hauled manure on Christmas Day. If I could have cried, I would have cried that Christmas. There was no such thing as having a Sunday off; you might get a few hours off. He'd always find something to do.

There was a summer day, we had been out cutting grain. At lunch, the old farmer says, "It's too hot for the horses, better not go out with the horses in the afternoon; but you boys can shuck around the hill." So you can understand I was pretty sour on the farm. I spent two and a half years out there. I stayed long enough till I had money enough to pay back what I had borrowed. Then another boy from Idaho came out to work there a little bit, and he got disgusted and said, "Let's go to town." And I said O.K.

This boy said we could make some money going down to Lewiston picking cherries. So we went down there and we couldn't find anything to do there either. That's the time they started the CCC.* You were supposed to be a resident down there, of course we said we were. One thing that helped me—I didn't lie about that—I was born in Idaho. But I hadn't lived in Lewiston more than about two weeks. Anyway, we got in.

That was the best thing that ever happened to me. I learned a lot of things and it was a good morale builder, too. You want to apply yourself, you get promotion. I got to be a crew leader and made more money. We were building roads down in southern Idaho. I got to be what they call a powder man, too, set out blasting and things like that. I had seven-eight guys in the crew. You had more free time than you know what to do with, really. You worked your eight hours, but that was it. We had barracks and it was like an army in a way, except you didn't have a gun. You had army clothes and you stood inspections and roll call for this and roll call for that and pay call and what have you. That was the period I really enjoyed myself, enjoyed what I was doing.

When I first came in, we were working in the woods and we got a whole trainload of people from Toledo and Cincinnati and it was pitiful to see some of these. I thought I had it tough, but to hear some of those boys that came from there tell about lying in bed because they were afraid they were going to get more hungry if they got up! Didn't have anything to eat. Most of them from Toledo were Polish. Of course coming out to the wilderness in Idaho was quite an experience. We filled them up with all kinds of bear stories and what have you.

I learned about compressors and about blasting and learned how to read grade stakes on construction and things like that. Which put me in good stead. When I left the CCC, the head ranger—it was the Forest Service that was overseeing it—said, "If you want to stay on, in three years I'll make you head powder man over three states. But I won't try

*The Civilian Conservation Corps (CCC) was part of the New Deal program. Established in 1933, the corps was providing training for over 500,000 young men by 1935. The CCC camps had a military flavor, but corps members were not under formal military control.

to keep you, because I know you can get a job on construction wherever you want to." I thought, well, I'd worked for little or nothing for so long, I'd better make a little money some way, so I left. I worked on a dam right in Spokane. There the skills came in that I had learned.

Thorvald Kofoed

"I'm not going to freeze
for five dollars a month in Minnesota."

*When Thorvald Kofoed came to America in 1930, he was
disappointed to find primitive farming conditions and low
wages. He moved to the Pacific Northwest the following year
and took various jobs in dairy farms, sawmills, and gold
mines. Following service in the United States Army in World
War II, he earned his living as a carpenter. Ted, as he was
called, married in 1949 at the age of forty-two and had one
son. In later years, he edited the newsletter for the Danish
lodge in Seattle.*

I was born on August 18, 1907, in the little town of Allinge on the
island of Bornholm in Denmark. That's the easternmost part of
Denmark, out in the Baltic Sea. It takes about eight hours with the
ferry from Copenhagen to sail over there.

Before I was confirmed, I used to have different jobs after school. I
worked in bakeries, in sheet metal shops, in cabinet shops, and one
thing and another. My mother being a widow, she could not afford
to send me to school and give me any special training. She couldn't
even afford to have me go through an apprenticeship, because the first
four years you serve an apprenticeship you don't make any money. So I
didn't have much of a choice except to go right straight to work and get
a job when I was fourteen years old. And I went to work on the farms
there. I learned to milk cows and to harness the horses up and plow
and everything like that. My mother died in 1926 and then I worked on
jobs in town and up in a stone quarry.

My dad had a brother and he lived in Minnesota. His name was
Andreas Kofoed, they called him Andrew. My uncle from America

Thorvald Kofoed at the age of fifteen

came home to visit in Denmark and he hadn't been home for thirty years and nobody had heard from him either in thirty years. And he came home with the idea that he was going to surprise his mother and my mother. This was 1926 and here he come home the day after my mother was buried. That made him feel rather strange. After he came to visit, I got the idea maybe I should come over here to America, too.

I come over to America in 1930. I knew it was hard times all over the world in 1930; I realized that. But I thought, maybe if I came over to a big country like United States, maybe there would be bigger opportunities here. I had to make a special trip over to the consulate in Copenhagen and have my physical and all that, but I got a visa. I was twenty-three years old; I had a birthday aboard the ship.

I came on a boat by the name *Hellig Olaf*, that was the Scandinavian-American Line. After we left Copenhagen, we went up to Oslo and then from there out in the North Sea and Atlantic. They went to Halifax first and let off passengers for Canada. All the newspaper boys climbed aboard and sold newspapers there. They picked up the anchor again and we proceeded down towards New York.

I was always told that when you approach New York harbor, one of the first things that you see is the Statue of Liberty. Well, the first thing my eyes caught sight of there was a giant neon sign—"Wrigley's Chewing Gum." Well, I look at it and I know I must be in America now! I had an old wooden trunk that I had tied together with ropes and I had to open that up in the customs. They didn't pay much attention and finally passed me through. A Swedish pastor was there and he was receiving the immigrants. He helped me to the train. First we went into a restaurant and had a snack, and then he went and bought a great big bag of doughnuts that I could take with me on the train. I let him have the money for that. That was something new.

I was a little bit perplexed when I got on that train, because everything was so new to me. As the train made stops here and there, it made me so perplexed because there were so many colored people coming aboard. All these colored women come with great big hats and loud-colored clothes and they was blacker than the ace of spades and I shone white and I felt that they was looking at me all the time. I was really perplexed.

From St. Paul [Minnesota], I came on "Galloping Ghost"—small mobile cars that used to run on rails. I got up to Shevlin, that's a town between Bemidji and Bagley, just a small farm town with an elevator. I got a sinking feeling when I stood off there and there was nobody to meet me. I found a fella, a Norwegian, he was a blacksmith by trade, but also he was the preacher in the Lutheran church there. He got out the small T-Ford and took me out to my uncle. That's another sinking feeling I got out there on my uncle's farm. He was a bachelor and he had a little one-room shack with a kitchen and a lean-to. And the barn was just a log stable where he kept the cows. He had 120 acres and about half of it he had under plow; the rest of it hadn't been cleared yet.

He had been over for a good many years; as a matter of fact, this was his second homestead. He was married, but his wife had died on him, and he had a couple sons and they had died, too, so he was all alone.

Thorvald Kofoed

Thorvald Kofoed and fellow emigrants en route to America, 1930

He went through the rough way there. I wasn't used to that kind of farming. Anybody that think that they are old-fashioned over in Denmark, they have another guess coming when it comes to farming. We was way ahead in Denmark of anything he had—in the way we took care of domestic animals and everything.

He wanted me to take over half the farm. But in 1930 you couldn't make anything. Potatoes sold for four-five cents a bushel or ten cents for a bushel of oats or barley. There was no money in it for anybody. I stayed with him for three months. Then I broke away and I think I must have had about twelve–fifteen dollars to my name.

I ran into a Swede and he said, "I know a farmer south of Crookston, and he might need a fellow for the winter there, so I give you a letter and you walk out there." I got out to this farm and there was some Swedes by the name Anderson. Well, they said they did need a man, but they had already hired one. But he hasn't come yet, if I want to stay there for a couple days and help them out, I could. It was going toward Thanksgiving and I remember I helped them kill off a bunch of geese and we picked them and took them into town and sold them. Then I had Thanksgiving there. We had turkey, a beautiful Thanksgiving. They made an arrangement for me; they found another place close by there, another Swede, Olson was his name. I come in there as a hired hand.

I was making ten dollars a month the first winter and my room and board. During the summer months, he raised me to thirty dollars a month and I thought I was really in the money. But then came the fall of 1931 and they had some awful times back there. Things was getting real tough and then they had all them big dust storms and crop failures in North Dakota. Many of them just closed the farms and took off.

There was young guys, they was roaming around looking for work and looking for places where they could just eat and sleep, room and board. They even come into the place where I was working and the farmer said, "Well, I got a man here and he's been with me for a year and I'd kinda like to keep him." Nothing was said what he wanted to pay me. So one day I asked him, "Hey, Jake, you say you'd like to keep me here this winter, what do you think you can pay me?" "Well, you know, I haven't made a thing myself this summer. You see how I can get all kinds of guys for just room and board. But being that you have been with me for a year now and I'd like to keep you, I'll pay you five dollars a month this winter." I thought, five dollars a month, I can't even buy my winter clothes for that.

I had met an old Dane in Crookston. He was a widower and a character. He was police judge in town there. I used to meet up with him sometimes when I was in town on Sunday. In the pool hall, he'll be coming in and he'll have a great big sombrero on and he'll have a suit coat from one suit and a vest coat from another and a pair of pants from another! And he always carried some hard candies in his pocket, loose, and they'd be full of tobacco crumbs. He said, "What about we go up to my office and read the Sunday paper?" The first time, I didn't know what he meant by his office, but I found out that the entire courtroom was his office. He'd hand me the funnies and he'll climb up on the judge bench and sit there and read the paper and I'd sit down there in the courtroom and read the funnies on Sunday afternoon.

Anyway, he had a subscription to this Danish paper *The Pioneer*, and in *The Pioneer* I found an ad.[*] Somebody out in the West was advertising for a hired man. And I answered that. I didn't know it was a doggone German that was advertising, that's what I found out later on. I decided to pick up my stuff and go west. I thought, I'm not going to go here and freeze for five dollars a month in Minnesota.

So I went west and I found that place up by Sequim [Washington]. That German was one of the worst guys I ever could have hit on to work for. I stayed with him for three months and the neighbors told me that was the longest he ever kept a man working for him. Then I come down here to Seattle. Here again, through that paper *Pioneer*, I saw this boardinghouse they advertised—Washington Hall, that used to be the Danish Hall. I found that address and it cost eight dollars a week for board and room. It was pretty nice.[†] I stayed there two-three weeks, then I found a job on a dairy farm. That was in 1932 I came to Seattle. The same year I became a member of the Danish Brotherhood.

I went in the service in 1942. I was thirty-five years old, and I was thirty-eight when I got out. I never did get to go overseas. I was quartermaster sergeant at a hospital in California. Well, that's doing pretty good for an old country boy—about ten-twelve years after you come over here to go in the service and become a sergeant in the American Army! Actually, it helped me an awful lot to go in the service, because I found myself. Before I went in the service, I used to be a little bit perplexed and timid with certain people. I used to look up to people, for instance, who wore white collars and ties and worked in office. But after I got in the service, I got on a more equal basis with men, and I found out that

[*]*Den Danske Pioneer* reached a peak circulation of 40,000 in 1914. Founded in 1872, the newspaper was published weekly in Omaha, Nebraska, until 1958; now it appears biweekly from Hoffman Estates, Illinois. See Marion Marzolf, *The Danish-Language Press in America* (New York, 1979).

[†]See the interview with Grethe Petersen in Part Three for further information about this Danish boardinghouse.

some of them guys wasn't any smarter than I was. Some of them could probably run a typewriter, that's one thing I never have mastered yet, but as far as reading and writing, I can do that just as well as they can. As a matter of fact, I always been pretty good at that and right now I read and write Danish and I read and write English.

Astrid Lovestrand

"A lady from the YWCA met us and she talked Swedish."

*A YWCA network aided Astrid Lovestrand on her journey
across the country to Yakima, Washington, in 1930. A single
woman of twenty-three, Astrid left Sweden to join relatives
whom she had never met. They provided a warm welcome and
matched her with an eligible bachelor of Swedish descent.
Astrid and her husband Emil managed a fruit orchard and
raised eight children. In later years, she worked as a practical
nurse and taught community enrichment classes.*

My grandparents on my mother's side came here in approximately 1907. Grandpa and grandma came to St. Paul, Minnesota, first, or was it Omaha, Nebraska? They stayed there until my aunt and uncle, Nels and Sophia Nystrom, moved out here to Yakima. They decided to come to Yakima, because they had heard so much advertising about the new land out here. It was just raw land then, nothing but sagebrush, and they had heard that it was gonna be under water [irrigation]. So they all came out here—my aunt and my uncle and grandpa and grandma and an Uncle Axel and an Uncle Albin.

My own mother had married my dad when grandpa and grandma left with their family, and so she did not want to go to America. So that's how come I was born and raised in Sweden. I was born in Dömle, Deje, Värmland, April 4, 1906. Dömle *Herrgård* was a big estate and my dad was a *rättare* [foreman] on this big estate. I was born on that place and I also went to school there and was confirmed in the Lutheran church in Deje. Our nearest biggest town was Karlstad.

My mother died when I was only two and a half. She died in childbirth. I lost my father when I was fourteen. I was confirmed 1920 in the summer and he died in November. After my dad died, I took on housework for different people. It took a long time for me to decide to come over here because, after all, I didn't know any of my aunts and uncles. It was a big decision to make. But then when I was twenty-three years old, I decided, well, the times was not too good in Sweden. And when I came over here, why, the Depression was just as bad here.

I left Sweden, my home place, on a winter morning in 1930 and it was cold. I called a taxi and it took me to the depot and I rode the train to Gothenburg and that's where I took the boat. It took us twenty-two days to come over and let me tell you, I got seasick. It was stormy, terribly stormy, and the boat had to stop in the middle of the ocean and wait for an iceberg to pass.

I arrived in New York and a lady from the YWCA met us and she talked Swedish. We were just herding around; there were lots of immigrants. We had our name on our lapel. Well, she took care of us and put us on the train. We rode the train to Chicago and in Chicago, we changed train to go to St. Paul. When I got to St. Paul, there was a man at the train depot that called my name, "Fröken Rehn! Miss Rehn!" And he took a hold of me on my back and I ran to beat the band to talk to this YWCA lady. I said, "It's a man that's coming and he wants me." She said, "Well, don't be afraid. He knows your name, he must know you." He came up to the lady. He didn't talk very good Swedish, so I couldn't understand him. He was my mother's uncle and a free missionary minister. He told this lady from the YWCA, "Astrid has an aunt that lives here in St. Paul and we would like to have her come and eat dinner there before she leaves." We had a two and one half hour stopover, so thank goodness I got to go over there and take a bath and clean up and put on clean clothes. I hadn't changed clothes since I left the boat. Oh, I was terrible looking.

There was a lady from YWCA in New York, one in Chicago, and one in St. Paul. And one of them met me in Yakima. They all spoke Swedish. They were notified ahead of time that we were coming. I also had my uncle and aunt meeting me here.

I loved it from the first time I came here. It was spring and it was frogs in the ponds and I have never heard so much noise from frogs before. And then I had such a nice feeling with my relations here; it was just like I had known them all my life, really. They lived on a farm up on Wiley Heights. It's about fifteen and a half miles out of Yakima and it's a Swedish colony, what is now called Swede Hill. It's at least twenty or thirty families.

It was a store in Wiley City that was run by a man, he didn't come from Sweden, but his wife did. I can remember my aunt sent me down to the store to buy butter. It was just terrible hard for me to say "butter," so I asked him if he knew what I wanted, I said smör, and he said, "Oh, ja, I understand." His wife was always in there with him, and she helped him along.

I made up my mind that I was going to get away from the Swedish colony, otherwise I never was going to speak English and I was anxious to learn how to speak. It was through that [YWCA] lady that I got my first job. Somebody told me I could call this lady and tell her that I would like to do housework, if she could help me. Well, the first job I had was for a banker; I only worked there while their steady girl was on vacation. Then she helped me to get a job for Mr. and Mrs. A. C. Davis, the superintendent of schools in Yakima, and I stayed there until I got married. At that time I earned forty-five dollars a month.

That's when I learned to speak English. They had three small children and it seems like it was easier for me to make a mistake in front of the children than in front of grown-ups. They would say, "Astrid, that's not correct," and they would correct me. So that's really how I learned to speak, from those girls. I think in three months I learned the English language. If you really put your heart into it and you want to learn, it don't take you so long.

I was responsible for all the housework. Mrs. Davis belonged to lots of clubs and she did a lot of entertaining. It was difficult for me to recognize the American food. Like squash, I had never seen squash. I had never seen pumpkin. A steak was different than a steak in Sweden. A roast in Sweden is called a steak and here we have a piece of meat that's called steak and I had never seen that before. She unthawed this big piece of meat and she told me this was what we were going to have for dinner and I said, "Well, how do I do? How do I fry it or how do I fix it?" That was all new to me.

When I met my husband, Emil Lovestrand, he had a brand new car, a Model A Ford. I had met him in church, just to be introduced; my Uncle Albin was married to his cousin. So Uncle said—he worked down in the hardware store in Wiley City—"Well, if you marry Emil, I will buy you a washtub and a scrub board!" They teased me forth and back about Emil, before I ever really had met him. Anyway, I was thinning peaches for my cousin, Clarence Nystrom, and when I came in at noon to eat lunch, his wife said, "Well, Astrid, you stay in and take care of my children, while I run down to Wiley City to the hardware store. I have to buy some paint." She came back home and said, "You can't go out and thin peaches this afternoon, because we are going to have company for supper. Somebody's coming up here that you're going to be really interested in." Here, in the evening, why Emil came up and he drove his new car. He had fifteen miles on it. After supper—oh, I can remember what a fancy supper we had prepared—why he said, "Would you like to go out and take a ride in my new car?" And I said, "Sure." So that's how our romance started.

When I was living with my aunt and uncle, I felt like I should be earning my living and paying for my room and board. And I was real anxious to make enough money so I could pay for my ticket, because that's what I had promised to do. The way it was going, why I wasn't earning money fast enough. So when I had been one year, Emil offered to pay my ticket over and we got married. He always said that he had an "imported wife" because he had to pay my ticket. It cost $150. Earning $150 at that time was a lot of money, especially when I wasn't making more than forty-five dollars a month and I had to have new clothes and this and that.

Emil was fifteen years older than I was, so he was forty when we got married in 1931 and I was twenty-five. Our first little girl was born 1931 in the fall. We raised eight children. I have six girls and two boys: Barbara, Phyllis, Rita, Bernard, Elsa, Sharon, Roland, and Becky. I was so afraid to name my children, because I was afraid people was not going to be able to pronounce them and laugh at their names. Those days, you wouldn't want to recognize that you were Swedish.

My husband had me promise that I wouldn't teach them the Swedish language. He knew Swedish, but he said that's all he knew when he started school and he was laughed at and made fun of and he said, "I don't want my children to go through that." So I kept to the promise and my children are so angry with me, because they cannot speak Swedish.

It's an altogether different living over here than it is in Sweden. Sweden goes so slow, everything goes so slow. We're so free here. There is a certain class in Sweden and lots of things I felt like I didn't belong to, that maybe I wasn't good enough. I think that's the way all the Swedish people were when they first come, they belittle themself. My children keep telling me this to this day, "Mother, don't belittle yourself. You can do that. You're good enough for that." But it's inbred in you. Because you always had to curtsy for people in Sweden and if you was walking ahead, you always open the door for somebody and let them go through first. It's a whole lot easier living here.

I could never have done as well if I had stayed in Sweden. So I'm real thankful for my aunt and uncle that sent me my ticket. And then I feel real fortunate that I met my husband the way I did.

Part Three / **New Lives: Work**

T he desire to improve one's standard of living served as a major impetus for emigration. "I come to get a little butter on top of the bread" is John Kuivala's striking phrase. Although some immigrants subscribed to the fantasy of striking it rich in America, the majority possessed a more sober understanding of how economic success would be won. As Jenny Pedersen declares, "I didn't find no gold on the streets of Seattle. I knew beforehand I have to work for it." Their upbringing prepared the Scandinavians for vigorous work lives in the new land, since most of them had combined farm chores or part-time jobs with schooling and then sought full-time employment by the age of fourteen or fifteen.

Exactly how long and hard they would work for their buttered bread, however, few foresaw in advance. The oft-stated expectation was that five years of toil in America would generate a nest egg with which to return to the old country and buy or improve a farm. In some cases this happened. Ole Blindheim's brother, for example, sent his Alaska gold-mining earnings to Norway, so he could go back and take over the family place. Immigrants who remained single were more likely to adhere to the original plan of temporary residence than were those who married and had children. The shift in attitude is explained by John Kuivala, who arrived in Astoria, Oregon, in 1910: "I didn't feel, not yet you know, it was my home or not. I was young. Then when I got married, 1915, it was different. Then I realized, this is the home place now."

Securing a job was the first priority for the newcomers, few of whom had any cash reserves. Often an ethnic connection smoothed the way for employment. Another approach was to place, or answer, a newspaper advertisement. Emmy Berg landed a position with a millionaire family in Portland, Oregon, after pursuing a classified notice. When Hanna Sippala advertised her services as a maid, she received several offers: "A lot of ladies came see me same night when they get the paper. And I take the closest one; that was minister place." Because of their reputation as exceptionally dedicated and hardworking, the Scandinavians were considered desirable employees. As Hanna remarks, "They like Finnish girls. They get a lot of work; they hard worker."

The hard-driving attitude toward work encouraged an entrepreneurial spirit among the immigrants. Anton Isaksen skipped the mandated rest periods between fishing trips so that he could fit in extra jobs and increase his income. Ralph Strom ferreted out temporary employment in order to survive the low-paying apprenticeship that represented his investment in future security. Much valued, also, was the autonomy of running one's own enterprise. Beginning as laborers, first-generation Scandinavians in the Pacific Northwest might go on to operate small businesses like those described in the interviews below—tailor shop, dairy store, restaurant, or fishing vessel. Few had, or obtained, training as white-collar professionals; a study of the 1900 census in Washington state found Scandinavian men "underconcentrated in every professional class, especially as: teachers; physicians; and lawyers."[1]

At the turn of the century, the most common female occupation in Scandinavia was that of *tjenestejente* or servant girl, as illustrated by the fact that sixty-one percent of all Norwegian working women were classified as servants in 1910.[2] Not surprisingly, domestic servants also comprised the largest single occupational group among female emigrants from Scandinavia. According to the 1900 United States census, "61.9 per cent of Scandinavian-born women worked as servants or laundresses."[3] The majority of these immigrants brought relevant work experience from the homeland, having learned how to clean and cook and do farm chores. Some had been employed at hotels or sanitariums. Many had cared for children.

Considering that they received free room and board as a condition of their employment, the immigrant servants earned good wages; in fact, the total compensation was comparable to that of the standard

Ralph Strom (center) with logging crew, Lake McMurray, Washington, 1913
(see p. 189)

male occupations.[4] In the 1920s, a Scandinavian maid could expect to make at least thirty dollars a month in Seattle or Tacoma; forty-five or fifty dollars a month was possible. Typically, wages rose as the women became familiar with the English language and with American house-keeping practices. In urban centers, domestic servants had little fear of layoffs or lack of employment; rather, they displayed a self-determined mobility, moving between households, and between types of service jobs, in search of a better working environment.

Paid household labor in the United States was dominated by black women and immigrant women and, within the wider society, carried low social prestige. The question of low status appears not to have bothered Scandinavian immigrant women, as long as they were re-spected by their individual employers. The oral history informants present their jobs as honorable and demanding, requiring long hours, stamina, and multiple skills.

A distinct advantage of work as a domestic servant was that it opened up avenues to assimilation. Daily contact with a family supplied intimate knowledge of American lifestyles and facilitated language learning. Frequently, the children of the household played a key role in helping the immigrant women to acquire English vocabulary and proper pronunciation. Still, not all women found the situation agreeable, preferring the greater freedom of outdoor work or the regular hours of restaurant or cannery employment. The interview with Margit Johnsen is revealing in this regard.

Marriage brought an end to employment as a live-in maid and, in some cases, an end to all paid employment. But catering, part-time cleaning jobs, restaurant work, selling milk and butter, and raising berries were typical income-producing strategies adopted by the immigrant wives. Others entered into partnership with their husbands and ran grocery stores, delicatessens, motels, and dry cleaning shops. The six women represented in the section on work demonstrate remarkable flexibility and adaptability as they move through the various phases of their work lives.

Drawing on skills and interests from home, Scandinavian immigrant men turned to mainstay Pacific Northwest industries like fishing, forestry, and farming. The specific job details might be new, but the general parameters of the work seemed familiar. Although Anton Isaksen had never encountered salmon trap fishing before, he was "used to making seines" and so felt comfortable rigging the trap. These employment arenas were fraught with dangers. John Kuivala was seriously injured in the woods. A series of sawmill accidents spooked Isaksen, who felt certain, "next is me"; years later, the boat he was skippering ran aground on a reef and sank. Like the women, the men would often hold a series of short-term jobs. Some of the work was seasonal, of course, but job mobility was also dictated by volatile local conditions—the boom and bust cycle prevalent in the Pacific Northwest economy.

Taken together, the Simonson, Kuivala, and Isaksen narratives provide an overview of fishing practices and innovations in the Pacific

Northwest, from gill netting on the Columbia River to the halibut fleet in Alaska. The Scandinavians dominated certain fisheries more than others. Salmon traps, salmon trollers, and halibut schooners attracted the Norwegians who fished in Puget Sound and Alaska; the Finns and Norwegians employed gill nets on the Columbia. One estimate suggests that, in the 1930s, fifty percent of the Alaska trap fishermen and twenty-five percent of the Alaska gill netters were Norwegian.[5] The halibut fishery in the 1920s appears to have been almost exclusively a Norwegian enterprise.[6] The goal of those dedicated to fishing as a livelihood was to buy their own boat or a boat share. This enabled them to operate like a "small business selling their product at the highest price that market conditions allowed."[7]

The Swedes gravitated more to agriculture and to the wood-products industry. The sawmill town of Preston in King county, Washington, was once ninety percent Swedish.[8] Logging camps could be quite cosmopolitan, but it was a rare crew that did not boast at least one Swede. Occasionally, "Scandinavian" served as the working language in the woods, owing to the large number of loggers with Nordic backgrounds. In 1900, Scandinavians made up twenty-five percent of all Washington state forestry employees.[9] Like the fishermen who became boat owners and operators, some mill workers and skilled carpenters started building houses and eventually formed successful construction companies. In Tacoma, a number of Scandinavians invested their dollars and their labor in the cooperative association known as Puget Sound Plywood, Inc., founded in 1941.[10]

East of the Cascade Mountains, the arid conditions posed special challenges for farming. Irrigation of the Yakima Valley enabled a thriving fruit orchard industry to develop, as the interviews with Hans Fahl and Astrid Lovestrand in Part Two suggest. Further to the east, in the Palouse country where Christine Emerson lived, the open country lent itself to wheat farming. Those who homesteaded farther north, like Anne Hansen, struggled to make a living on marginal land with no readily available water. The Scandinavian farmers west of the Cascades also faced monumental tasks. As Olaf Sivertson describes in detail, the thick timber had to be cleared and the stumps blasted out before any cultivation or building could get underway. (See Part Four for Emerson, Hansen, and Sivertson narratives.) Still, agriculture agreed with the immigrants, who appreciated the advantages of country living and prized farm ownership. Of foreign-born Swedes living in Washington in 1930, almost twenty percent were classified as rural-farm population.[11]

On-the-job training, through formal or informal apprenticeships, produced the expertise needed for skilled trades like tailoring and boilermaking. Neither Jenny Pedersen nor Ole Nissen, trained as needleworkers in their native Denmark, were able immediately to employ their skills in the new land. They coped by learning other things, like farmwork and waitering, until the right opportunity arose. Jenny did sewing out of her home; Ole eventually ran his own tailor shop. Ralph Strom desired a more stable and productive life than he found in the logging camps; the timing of his move into commercial boilerworks was auspicious, for World War I brought a demand for his skills.

Regardless of the venue, work was a key element in defining self-worth. Perhaps because of this, retirement came comparatively late for the first-generation Scandinavians. Ole Nissen was eighty when he visited the Social Security office and announced his intended retirement. Anton Isaksen could say, "I'm seventy-nine now and I'm still not retired." Olaf Sivertson did retire from farming at the age of seventy-two, but he stayed busy into his late nineties: "I still take care of my lawn and try to keep the place neat and clean, take care of my house, do my own housekeeping. I do this by myself." In their working lives, the Scandinavian immigrants attached greatest importance to following the dictates of an inbred work ethic and to securing a comfortable life for their families. The rhetorical accent is placed more on having lived productively and honestly than it is on specific career attainments.

NOTES

1. David L. Nicandri, "Washington's Ethnic Workingmen in 1900: A Comparative View," paper delivered at Pacific Northwest History Conference, Portland, Oregon, April 7, 1979.

2. Sidsel Vogt Moum, *Kvinnfolkarbeid. Kvinners kår og status i Norge 1875–1910* (Oslo, 1981).

3. David M. Katzman, *Seven Days a Week: Women and Domestic Service in Industrializing America* (1978; reprinted Urbana, Illinois, 1981), 49. The percentage reported here reflects Scandinavian women in the labor market, not the total female population.

4. Katzman in *Seven Days a Week* (313) states that "when the equivalent cost of room and board are added to the annual earnings of domestic servants, their wages were at the same level or exceeded those of women in shops and in un- or semiskilled factory jobs." For a comparison with male earnings and other relevant aspects of the job situation, see Carl Ross, "Servant Girls: Community Leaders," in Carl Ross and K. Marianne Wargelin Brown, eds., *Women Who Dared: The History of Finnish American Women*, (St. Paul, Minnesota, 1986), 41–54.

5. Sverre Arestad, "Norwegians in the Pacific Coast Fisheries," in *Norwegian-American Studies*, 30 (1985), 101–102.

6. Local expert A. K. Larssen projected that ninety-five percent of all halibut fishermen in 1920 were Norwegian. See Odd S. Lovoll, *The Promise of America* (Minneapolis, 1984), 161.

7. Paul George Hummasti, *Finnish Radicals in Astoria, Oregon 1904–1940* (New York, 1979), 18.

8. Helge Nelson, *The Swedes and the Swedish Settlements in North America* (1943; reprinted New York, 1979), 329–335.

9. Lovoll, *The Promise of America*, 156.

10. A privately published history of this company may be found in the Pacific Lutheran University library: *Puget Sound Plywood, Inc.: A Cooperative Association 1941–1974* (Tacoma, Washington, 1974).

11. Nelson, *The Swedes and the Swedish Settlements in North America*, 331.

John Kuivala

"Butter on the bread"

John Kuivala emigrated in 1910 at the age of eighteen. He
came to Astoria, Oregon, where the Finnish presence was
strong and where there were employment opportunities in
the fishing and lumber industries. John married a Finnish
woman, Elna, and they had a daughter and a son. The
Kuivalas spoke Finnish at home.

I was born March 18, 1892, close to Oulu, Finland. When I was a
little kid helping out, there were about fifteen cows, horses, sheep,
chickens, pigs. My father couldn't very well keep hired man, not
enough income. In the wintertime, my father went with the horse,
dragged the logs from the woods to the riverside. And then when the
spring comes, they float those logs down river. Then they make a big
raft and tow it to Raahe. There was a sawmill in Raahe. They were his
logs; they wasn't company logs. They pay so much. Get a little coffee money.

That was five hours a day you had to be in the school. I only got
through two classes, first class and second class, and I quit. Then I
worked at home some and worked for someplace else, too. Got to get
a piece of bread, you know.

My sister was over here before I. My mother's brother was over here
and my father's brother was over here, too. My sister came then. And
my sister sent me a ticket, 1910. The rest stayed over there. I come to get
a little butter on top of the bread.

It was kind of rough on me—go to places where I hadn't gone before, far from home and all that. Crying, but not much. I remember,

my father came with me about a mile from home, and then he turned back and said good-by. And that's the last time I saw him.

I take six days to come from Boston to Astoria on the train, six days. It was tough for me and I haven't got no sense to change to anything. I didn't have like a sock, and my feet were burning like heck, you know. Summertime, hot summertime. That was in August, 1910, when I came. And oh, my feet was burning. Then I took my shoes off and oh, they smelled! By gosh, enough people moved away! That was terrible. But what I could do? I could do nothing.

Two or three days it was before I went to work. There was a sawmill right there where the plywood mill [is] now. I was working there and boarding [with] Finnish people. I ate the meals; that was fifteen dollars a month. That was pretty cheap. But my wages wasn't very good either—$1.75 a day.

We had in Astoria six or seven boardinghouses or more. There was close to a hundred in every one, a hundred men. And lots of people, they have to room in family houses, because the boardinghouses were full of men already. All full of young people, mostly Finns.

I was making bundles out of the flooring. Tied them with a rope. Then I get a job on the trimming. When they come through the planer, then you take the knots off and make a good piece so there're no knots on it. It was pretty good-sized; there were two shifts. There were four sawmills in Astoria in those days. Lots of big logs in those days. No more like those, about eight-ten feet through. There were donkeys in those days, steam donkeys. Before my time, they used to have ox and horses.

I worked a little while across the river in a logging camp, but that was pretty hard. I happened to fall down and I had saw and ax when I fell down. And by God, I think there are still scars today where I put that saw tip! It went right to the bone. It was sore for a long, long time. That's the end of it, my logging days. No more logging camp for me. Sometimes it depends, if a man happened to die, they just bring him over to the nearest cemetery and bury him in it just like a dog. A single man, you know, nobody ever care.

I was fishing, too. My uncle, he had a boat with another man. And then 1911, he got this motor boat. That's the time they start to get the motor on the fishing boat; there were sails before. And I went to fish with him on the [Columbia] river. And, oh, that was a good year! I paid my bills and everything.

Fishing season started first of May and lasted four months till the 25th of August, except you'd take off the river six o'clock Saturday night and then you'd have to start fishing again on Sunday night six o'clock. Two men on the boat, twenty-six footers. They were independent fishermen. Pretty near all the canneries paid the same price. Woman worked there, lots of Finnish woman. They were filling, putting the fish in the can. They were called fillers.

I didn't feel, not yet, it was my home or not. I was young. Then when I got married, 1915, it was different. Then I realized, this is the home place now. I went to live in Warrenton [Oregon] when I get married and I worked there for some fellow to do this and that. Then I went to work for the Great Northern passenger ships. They run between Astoria and San Francisco. They were big ones, you know, steamships. But then when the First World War came, the government took them ships. I worked there quite a while. I don't remember what I done after that. Let's see, I start longshoring, that's what. I start longshoring, loading ships, you know.

Summertime, I went fishing, Bristol Bay, Alaska. First time in 1919. I fish over there in the summertime, and then wintertime I went longshoring. Nineteen thirty-two, I quit. That was the last year I was up in Alaska, 1932. Most of the time when you were fishing, you have to live on the boat, except Sunday. That was closed season on the Sunday there, too. When they open the boat, most of the time it rain and rain and rain, cold rain, and no chance to dry your clothes. Nothing. Ja, that was miserable.

You get sick, Finnish Brotherhood look after you. They look how you are and how you get treated and you get so much money a week for sick benefit, forty-seven weeks a year. It start to get a little thinner now than used to be. There were over a thousand members, but now they're over there in the cemetery. There were lots of dances and lots of people and they make pretty good money.[*]

In wintertime in Finland you get a cold, they give you oil from the pine tar. Put lump sugar in there, and then put that in your mouth, to cure a cold. And you know that inkivääri [ginger]—awful strong stuff— it comes in a chunk, from a drugstore. We scraped that and put that in a syrup and put the syrup in the spoon and heat it up. And then take that, too. That was good for colds. My father take a stick, take tobacco oil from the pipe, and put that on your teeth. And that was good stuff, fixed toothache up.

I'm glad I came over here, because I lost lots of misery this way. See, if I was there, maybe I wouldn't be here any more. They were through the two wars over there. I missed that anyway. Over here, I didn't have to go to war at all. But in a way, now is a good time over there in Finland. By God, they live better than we are over here. Pretty good houses they make, nice houses. They're just common workers; I don't know how they manage to do that. And they got plenty to eat—lots of butter on the bread!

[*]The Finnish Brotherhood was, in the words of Paul George Hummasti, "the most successful organization in bringing together the socialists and the Church Finns, and therefore the most popular organization in the Finnish community in Astoria." The Brotherhood was organized in 1886 and sponsored a wide range of social activities, in addition to providing the sick benefits of which John Kuivala speaks. See Hummasti, Finnish Radicals, 23–24.

Emmy Berg

"I worked for wealthy people, that's for sure."

Born in 1892 in the Dalarna region of Sweden, Emmy Berg
left for America when she was seventeen. She was employed
initially as a domestic servant; during the First World War
she ran a restaurant in Seattle. In 1919, she married a fellow
Swede. A son was born in 1921. Throughout her marriage,
Emmy continued to work at service jobs. She was also active
in local Swedish organizations.

Our grandmother raised us. My mother died; I don't even remember her. I had a bunch of cousins here and my older
sister Kristina was in Seattle. I lied to my father. He was never
home, but he wasn't going to let me go to America anyhow. My mother
had left us some money when she passed away and my uncle on father's
side was my guardian. So I lied to my father and told him that my uncle
has already sent for the tickets. Father says, "There's nothing I can do
about it then. I just have to let you go." So I did go, in September, 1909.
I was gonna come back inside of a year, but then I didn't.

My father's cousin sent me to school in Puyallup [Washington]. And
the kids in the schoolhouse, they made fun of me. So I says, "Everybody's laughing at me, so I'm not going there. I'm gonna start to work,
because I'm going back to Sweden anyhow. I'm gonna work and make
some money." So I got a place for a schoolteacher. She used to be a
high-school teacher and she had four kids. I did housework for her.
And she tell me, "You work for me and do all the washing and the
cleaning, and I feed you and give you all the clothes and any little thing
that you really want to spend money [on] I give you, but I won't give
you any wages." I worked for her a whole year. But I told her then, "I'm

working for money not love." I was so sorry afterwards that I went back to the lady and apologized.

She got me another job for a doctor. And he also had a bunch of kids. And the kids corrected you, every blessed time. If you said anything wrong, they didn't make fun of you, they corrected you. They were nice to work for and the kids were nice, well-behaved youngsters. Just before I left Sweden I went to cooking school, so I had no trouble at all. Monday, you did the washing. Tuesday, you did the ironing. Wednesday, what on earth, I think you did the baking. Thursday, you had off, and Friday, you clean the bedrooms. That [rest of the house] has to be cleaned every day, especially when they have kids.

My sister Anna came after I did. She was gonna get married, but they busted up, so she came. Anna and I, we decided that we were gonna see the United States. So we started in Tacoma. Then we came to Seattle and we stayed one year and in Portland we stayed one year. We did housework. We didn't get much. Let's say we got fifteen dollars a month [and room and board]. And if anybody get twenty dollars a month, that was high wages them days. We had to buy our own clothes—we had to wear black dresses and white apron and a white [hair] bow. That was the same thing all over.

In Portland, I came off the train and I bought the paper and I saw an ad [for a job] that was on one of the heights. I rang the doorbell and she asked me, the very first thing, "Have you got any reference?" And I says, "No, I just came from Seattle." She slammed the door in my face. And I got so doggone mad, I rang the doorbell again. And I said, "I think you could apologize." I had asked for many, many jobs and I said, "This is the first time that anybody's ever slammed the door in my face." She said, "Come on in," and she hired me. I worked there for almost half a year. They were millionaires. They had a bunch of helpers. She had a nurse that took care of the kids and she had a cook and she had a dishwasher. I was a pantry girl; I clean the glasses and the silver. They had a huge, big house; I had my own room. The help ate all by themself.

After I clean the glasses and the silver, I went to work in a ice cream parlor. I worked in the ice cream parlor from eight o'clock in the evening till twelve at night, just that four hours. The chauffeur they had, he brought me down and he always came and got me. It was a fun job in a way.

Nineteen fifteen my oldest sister Kristina and I went to the World's Fair in San Francisco.* I didn't do a bit of work in San Francisco, not one day. We had another funny experience when we came there. We had money in the bank in Seattle. We thought for sure that we go right to the bank in San Francisco and get the money. Couldn't get anything! They didn't telephone and they didn't telegram them days. Well, we went to the YWCA and they gave us the money. They say, "We trust you. You looks honest." Of course we paid them back after we got the money.

Kristina went back to Seattle. She worked at the Augustine N. Kyer bakery; they had a grocery store and a bakery right downtown on First Avenue. When I came back to Seattle, I had just lousy fifty cents in my pocket; it must have been at the end of 1915. Four o'clock in the morning I got up and called the bakery and I said, "I'm Kristina Erickson's sister. I'm living at the hotel; I haven't got enough money to pay for the hotel. Won't you please give me a job?" So he said, come on right down. He was a German guy. Well, they know my sister; she was a good worker, too. I put cream in the cream puffs. And Kristina, my sister, she cooked for the gang that worked there. So they call me "Cookie." I don't know why, because my sister was the cook. We were always paid by the month them days. It was either fifteen or sixteen dollars a month. Started about four o'clock in the morning, worked till twelve. Slept all day. I was there about a year.

We moved away from the hotel because it was too expensive. We had different rooming houses. I did all kinds of work. I don't know how many different unions I belong to. I worked for wealthy people, that's for sure.

And I run my own restaurant. We open up the restaurant, 1917. We rented it, a Norwegian girl and I, Marie Davis. Both she and I used to work for a restaurant downtown; we had lots of fun. In 1917, on Sunday morning, all the soldiers came from Tacoma, from Camp Lewis, and

*The Panama-Pacific International Exposition of 1915 was designed to spotlight the 1914 opening of the Panama Canal to commercial vessels from all nations.

were we forever busy!* They came to Seattle Sunday morning to see different things, just curiosity. A market was right down on University and Sixth, it was just about two blocks. Anybody who ordered a steak, we run down there and bought one. They had just teeny bit of ice boxes them days, no refrigerators. We did good in that restaurant. They walk clear from First Avenue up to our place, because we had sugar on the table. They froze the sugar. You had to have sugar stamps, during the war. You were allowed just so much sugar. We didn't have any lump sugar, because people would stick that in their pocket, so we had fine sugar on the table. The end of the war, we closed the restaurant. We were tired. We were tired of everything.

Nineteen nineteen, I got married. That's another funny story. We got married day before Christmas Eve. I was taking care of a house that belongs to the Hammerbergs. They went to Idaho and they had a dog and I stayed there all alone. So when Al came that morning, I said, "I'm never gonna stay in this house all alone another night. The dog run up and down the stairway barking all night. I was scared stiff. I didn't sleep a wink." So Albin said, "Well, I guess we'd better go and get married."

So I called Pastor Friborg, that's at the Baptist Church downtown.† "Do I know the couple that's gonna get married?" "I'm pretty sure that you know them," I said. I didn't tell him who it was. So Friborg said, "Listen, Emmy, are you coming with them so I'll know them?" "Yes," I said, "I'll be with them." So Friborg, he laughed, "Why didn't you tell me that you were gonna get married?" He was a nice guy. We went just exactly the way we were; took my sister with me. Then in the morning we were still in bed when Joe and Hilma Hammerberg came home. "Why, Emmy," Joseph says, "I never thought that of you." And I said, "No, we're all right. Don't think anything bad of me. We are married."

We bought a house in Port Angeles. I went to work in a restaurant. I was waiting on tables. I left a note for him [Albin] when he come home at night, that you better come to the restaurant. Oh, he looked awfully

---

*Camp Lewis, now known as Fort Lewis, was established as an army camp in 1917; it is located south of Tacoma on American Lake.
†Emil Friborg served as the pastor at Central Baptist Church for many years and was well known in local Swedish circles.

mad; he give me a dirty look. He wanted me to stay home and cook his own dinner for him. He don't like to eat in restaurants anyhow. Stubborn as a mule [she kept working there]. Cook breakfast before I went to work; cook dinner when I came home. That wasn't bad. We used to take the baby with us and go down to Masonic Temple and dance. We were there and when we come home, it was all gone. It burned down. Well, we were going to move to Seattle anyhow, because Al got a job at the Bank of California.

We lived on Eastlake. We stayed with Mrs. Johnson. She lived in one part of the apartment and we lived in the other, for nothing. We did all the washing and the ironing and the cleaning. We stayed there until we build this house. My sister and I owned the property and she wanted to go to Sweden, so she wanted the money. So we went to the Washington Mutual Bank and wanted to know if they would lend us any money so we could pay her. They didn't ask any question or any description, they just gave us the money! We paid them thirty dollars a month till we got it paid.

I worked in a laundry, in the starch room. They had stiff collars them days, so I made the collars stiff for the man's shirts. The forelady, she came here one morning and said, "Why don't you go to work, Emmy?" And I said, "What on earth am I gonna do with the baby?" "Take the baby with you and put him in a basket!" No, heavens, no! Albin worked at nights; I worked in the daytime. And the baby, he went on the streetcar every day. He was sitting on Second and Madison, waiting for me to come down and pick him up. Al left him there. You can't do those things now days! He didn't have to sit there very long, probably ten minutes, till I could pick him up. He was three or four years old.

I worked after Roy started school, sure I worked. The last job I had, I worked in the bank on Second Avenue. They used to feed all the employees, so they got their lunch there for forty-five cents. Them days are gone forever. I made their lunch. Nineteen fifty-two, I quit the bank. Oh yes, I worked at the Sunset Club. Old-timers in Seattle, they formed the Sunset Club. I worked there for years; waited on table. We had banquets and I used to cut the full cake. I worked there, but I haven't worked since.

Marie Berglund

"It's hard to be put down."

As a twenty-year-old woman, Marie Berglund found
employment doing housework and waiting on tables.
She spent three years in British Columbia before settling
in Tacoma. For Marie, association with other Norwegians
was an important facet of immigrant life. She became a
leader in the ethnic community and was honored by the
Norwegian king for her contributions.

I was born in Nordfjord, Norway, January 22, 1891. I left Norway, September 9, 1911. I want the excitement of traveling, of the new country, and my brother was here. I came all by myself. I came to Vancouver, British Columbia. Both my brother, Henry Torheim, and my uncle were there to meet me. My brother had gone over to Vancouver two years before. We were close pals. Mother was kind of worried about my little brother and she thought it was good if we were together. So he sent me the ticket. He was a steelworker; he had a good job.

I came by train across Canada. There was one girl from Stavanger [Norway] and there was another one, she was Swedish; they were just about the same age as I. We had a pleasant time together. There was no comfort on the seat then; there was nothing but wooden seats. We could open up the seat, so we made a kind of bed out of the two seats together. We three was laying there, on those hard boards—it wasn't so good. I was given a beautiful blanket to have on the trip, but that was too heavy. I used a plaid shawl. Everytime the train stopped, they came aboard the train to sell [food]; there was no dining car.

I never got frightened. It was exciting, of course, a big city like Vancouver. Vancouver is a beautiful city. I joined the Good Templar Lodge and met so many Norwegian young people. We had good fellowship, all the picnics in Stanley Park; we had beautiful time. The Good Templar Lodge, that means there's no drinking, no liquor—just good, clean fun. I cannot say how many was in there, but probably over a hundred young people. And you look forward to that.

My brother arranged for a room for me at a hotel where the manager was a Swedish lady. There I got a taste of tomatoes, something we did not have in Norway in those days. Uff, I didn't like them—how people could eat that! She tried to get me a job. The first job I had, I went to a family and she put me to work to sweep the floor.'Course we were not used to the big carpet, we just had rugs that you take out. And she took lots of newspaper, wet it, and crumble it up, and spread it all over the carpet. So I was to clean the carpet that way. As I sweep, the dust would gather on the newspaper. It was a smart idea, but it wasn't smart to clean it—it was heavy to sweep all that. I guess I didn't suit her very much, so two days, I was fired.

They advertised for Scandinavian girls to come in the house, for housework; there was lots of work to be had. I came to a family where they had a beautiful big four-story home. The man of the house was a banker. The first morning I came there, he took me down the basement to the kitchen: "This is stove, you say stove. This is table." I had to keep on repeating. He tried his best to get things in my mind.

I was to work in the kitchen. They cooked the meals down in the basement and they had a dumbwaiter to hoist it up to the dining room. One night, they had cooked some herring for me. And herring always made me deathly sick, both in Norway and here. They came down; they saw I hadn't touched the food. The lady of the house, she said to her sister, I could understand that much, "Probably she is just going to show off that she didn't need that." It kind of hurt me—it's hard to be put down. I was there at Christmastime and they took me up to show the beautiful table they had set. My brother and I were invited to a family from home, so they took care of their own Christmas dinner. But then I went to look for another job. She put me down and that was hard to take when you come from a home where there was love.

I got another job; it was no hardship to get work. I came to a place where they had three children. They were so nasty. They would throw the food on the floor so I could clean up and they even went up to walk on the table! Anyway, that was no good at all. I suppose I stayed there a month or so. I just couldn't take it.

I took a notion to come to Tacoma to visit, because I knew so many here and I wanted to come down and celebrate the Seventeenth of May [Norwegian Constitution Day]. But I was disappointed, because I came to relatives and they did not want to mingle with the Norwegians; no, they didn't care for the Seventeenth of May. They [the Norwegians in Tacoma] had a tremendous big celebration, but my father's cousin didn't care to go. So I couldn't go and celebrate. I was so disappointed, I lay there crying.

Then I worked as chambermaid in a hotel. They had stage plays in those days and many actresses stayed there. They broke down the beds and drinking, bottles all over, carousing; it wasn't very good. Then my brother, he said, "There's a Swedish lady, she want a waitress up in Hope [British Columbia]." I came there in the latter part of 1913. Every afternoon, we were free two to four o'clock, and we were horseback riding. I really like that. But it was hard to see all these young men from Norway—they had been out logging and they also contract to lay the railroad. They had contract for so many miles and when that was through, they got their pay and they would come in from the camp with their blanket on their back, dirty and grimy, poor fellas, and head for the saloon. They were so tired and then they head for the saloon and there they just clean them out.

I liked the Swedish lady, she was honest. Boys would come there with their money and ask her to keep that money, so they wouldn't drink it all up. Next door to the cafe there was a gambling place and they were Swedish, too, the man that ran that. I could tell every morning when he came in—if he had made lots of money out of the boys, he was smiling and he would give a nice tip. But if he hadn't, he was mean. I felt so sorry for the boys, because some of those are outstanding, fine boys from good homes. As I was waiting on them, you learn to know them and they would talk. Some of them was just so homesick, it was pitiful. That was really a rough town. I was staying at the hotel there. I had good wages and then we got the tips, so I was doing fine.

In 1914, I came down to Tacoma. My friend Kristina kept on writing. She was working in a cafe here and there was a place vacant. This restaurant, we called it coffee house, that was Henry's place, 1305 Commerce Street [she later married Henry Berglund]. There was so many Norwegians there that you could talk Norwegian all day long. Mostly men; now and then a woman would come, but very seldom. In the morning they would serve oatmeal mush, with the milk and sugar and coffee. And they had such good ham sandwiches. They sold coffee and three lumps of sugar. Underneath the counter, we had tiny little dishes for the sugar. At first it was four lumps, but then they cut it down to three. They had a good trade. I was married in 1917.

As young people in the Good Templar Lodge, we had really good entertainment. We had singing, we had folk dances, we had debating, and we had somebody writing a paper on a certain subject. It was about things going on and what we remember about home and what we should do here. We had a regular business meeting and then the entertainment was the debating or singing or folk dances. We met once a month. We were all Norwegians, nothing but Norwegians. We had a password. You had to promise not to touch liquor and to promote the welfare of our young people—to get the young people in to carry on the tradition from home.

The Daughters of Norway started 1907 [in Tacoma]. The Sons had already started.* They were interested that the women should have that group so they could go together—not meet together, but meet the same evening. At Normanna Hall, we Daughters met in the small hall and the Sons met in the big hall. I didn't join before in 1922. I was on the first bazaar committee; that's how I got going. It lasted three days between Christmas and New Year, when all these loggers came in. It was stormy and rainy and we did not even have doors into the hall; they had just some boards to keep the rain out. We done tremendous well.

At one time, the Daughters were close to four hundred members. We have a kind of feeling of the same background, that interest in keeping cultural things alive. Something to live for, to take pride in.

*Embla Lodge #2, Daughters of Norway, held its first meeting in Tacoma in April, 1907. The Tacoma Sons of Norway was constituted in 1904.

Ralph Strom

"I was with the worst—gamblers, prostitutes, everything you could think of."

Ralph Strom came to America in 1912, when he was sixteen years old. His first years in Seattle were difficult; but then he obtained a position as an apprentice boilermaker, and from the time of the First World War on he made his living as a skilled worker. Most of his working years were spent in Alaska.

I changed my name when I took out my citizen paper. It was Karl Rudolf Wikström in Sweden. In this country I changed it to Ralph Strom. I was born the 19th of March, 1896, in a farmer village outside of the city of Luleå. I was raised by my mother. My father went to this country just about the time when I was born. They were never married, you see. She was a caterer and a good one! I was eleven years old when she got married. I lived home with them till I came to this country. It was farming country, but we didn't have no farming ground, just laborers, that's all. I really didn't have more than about five years of grade school. I started to work in the sawmill when I was ten years old. I was supposed to be twelve years when I went to work, but I was pretty good size for my age. And believe me, we were working, ten hours a day. It was awful poor up there.

I went to this country when I was sixteen years old, 1912. I started to figure on that always, to better my conditions. There was an awful lot of emigrants went. But then, to get the money! Well, by golly, my mother had worked for a lady that had a wholesale grocery business. So she went to see her and borrowed the money from her for me to come over here. Six hundred crowns, and that was a lot of money them days. And this lady, after much thought, she give me the money. She says, "You're gonna pay me now, aren't you?" I says, "You can be sure I am." Well, my grandfather had learned me to handle an ax, so I was a

Ralph Strom, Christmas 1912

pretty good axman, even if I was only a kid. And I come here to Seattle
and went to work at Arlington [Washington], in the logging camp. I got
along fine. I paid that lady back the first four months I was here.

I came over on the *Lusitania*. It only took us about six or seven days.
That was an immense boat. Landed in Ellis Island, then took the train
from New York to Seattle. When we got to Dakota, a moving picture
outfit got on the train. They were gonna go into Montana and make a
Western. I had never seen them guns, oh, boy! And there was a drunken
Indian. They picked him up and laid him down alongside the stove and
he slept there till they took him when they got to Montana. That was

         Part Three / NEW LIVES: WORK

really something for me to see! They started to make fun on my clothing, you know, how we dress so different in Sweden—very narrow pants, long shoes, and kinda funny coats. I was looking at them guns!

I stayed in Seattle Friday, Saturday, and Sunday, and the following Monday I went up to the camp and went right to work. I took in at a hotel down on Washington Street, together with this fellow that took me up to the woods. He was a neighbor in the old country. The lady that run that hotel says, "Why, you ain't gonna let that kid go around dressed like that! He's got to have a suit of clothes." Well, I didn't have no money to get a suit of clothes. So by golly, she took me to Lipman's Pacific Outfit on Third Avenue and picked out a suit for me and bought me that suit right there. Gosh, she was a nice lady. I used to go in and see her when I come into town. Her name was Kitty Martin; she had been around a lot.

I stayed in that camp till Christmas. It was seven miles from Arlington. We had to take our own blankets. The bunks were three stories high and straw in the bottom in the bunk, no mattress. And bedbugs. I learned to count to twenty-one the first night I was there. There was a fellow laid in the bunk below me with a hammer killing bedbugs. I listened to one, two, three . . . I could count to twenty-one the next day when I woke up! Conditions were no good here then. I was getting two and a half a day. So that wasn't bad. And paid five and a half a week for board and room. The "fallers" got three and a half or four dollars a day. And the "buckers" got three dollars a day. I was, they call it "swamper." Them days there was no high leads, it was all ground logging; we had to cut and clear out, so they could get in and cut down the trees and choke the logs, so they could see where they were going with them. That was my job. I didn't go back after Christmas.*

That's really when we had a depression in Seattle; you never seen nothing like it in the other depression [the Great Depression]. I had no

*The fallers' job was to cut the trees down with minimal damage; they worked in pairs, one at each end of a falling saw. The buckers worked individually with a bucking saw (or "misery whip") to cut up the fallen trees. The swampers, as Strom describes it, cleared out the brush so these others could do their work and so the logs could be pulled out of the woods.

Ralph Strom

money. You know where Goodwill is down there on Dearborn Street? Well, it was an old abandoned warehouse. And the loggers, we had our own bedding, so we used to go and sleep there at night in that warehouse. And then walk down and keep the blanket bundle with the saloon keepers in the daytime and pick them up and go up there at night. You couldn't leave it there, they'd steal it. There was no relief them days. The Salvation Army used to give us a meal once in a while. But you had to borrow, try to get some from the other guy. I worked off and on in the woods, back and forth. I could see that I wasn't going to live that way forever.

So then I got acquainted with a German boilermaker, old country German. And this boilermaker got me into commercial boilerworks as an apprentice boilermaker. I paid six dollars a month for a hotel room. It was a small, little bitty place with just a washstand and a bed. It had a little dresser in it, too. A Japanese fixed it up for me. He was awful nice to me, that old Japanese. Otherwise I couldn't have got that low rent. I was only getting sixteen cents an hour. Ten hours a day, a dollar and sixty cents a day. That wasn't much money.

I made it fine till my clothes started to wear out. But then I told the boss—by that time I was getting along good in the boiler shop, "I haven't seen my mother for so long. I got to go home and see my mother. I'd like to get a month off." "Well," he says, "one month, that's all." So I already had a job in my pocket to work for the City of Seattle, when they were logging off the watershed up at Cedar River. I got in a month there and I made enough money to buy clothes. I went back to learn to be a boilermaker. I wanted to learn that trade in the very worst way. And then, the second time when I run out of clothes, the good Lord blessed us with one of the worst storms we ever had in Seattle, six feet of snow. And the roof started to cave in on the buildings. And me and another Swede got a contract to shovel snow and I got sixty dollars from one building and I made pretty near two hundred dollars shoveling snow in 1916.

But then the First World War broke out, and then I went to work in the shipyards. And since that time, I never had no trouble. It takes three years to learn to be a boilermaker. Well, I didn't get the whole full three years, because when the shipyards started in, they were trying heaven and earth to dig up a few experienced men for that kind of work. In 1918, I was made the riveter foreman in the Duthie shipyard.

I kind of felt at home right away, on account of being so young. Too, they were so good to me, the people everywhere. I worked hard; whenever I got something to do, I did it. And if you work hard and live right, you know, nobody abused me in any way. I was treated absolutely perfect, wherever I went. I wasn't around Swedes all the time. The kind of people that came to this country at that time, they were good people from all over the world. I had a lot of Greek friends in Seattle, and Czechoslovakians and Russians, and everything you can think of. I stayed in the shipyard till they close them down. Then I was a riveter on the telephone building on Third Avenue and a riveter on the medical building here. And then I hired out as a boilermaker for the Alaska Railroad; I went up there in 1921. I went to Anchorage first and then they transferred me up to a town called Nenana. Then when they built the bridge across the Yukon River, they moved the roundhouse that I was working in up to Fairbanks, and we all got laid off.

When I got laid off there, I started to work for miners there. And then I got the gold fever. And boy, I didn't go back to the railroad any more. I started to prospect for gold. And a bunch of fellows, we went in and took a lease on some mining ground. We didn't make any money on it. Came up with a lot of experience!

Then the U.S. Smelting and Mining and Refining Company come into Fairbanks and the manager, he said, "I hear you are an iron worker and I want you to come and work for me, because I'm going to need you pretty bad when we start building powerhouses and dredges and siphon lines. If you are a riveter and understand iron work, I give you a job." So I went to work for him in 1924. From 1924 till 1959 I worked for the same company. I didn't stay there all the time; I got vacations in the winter to come out. I was doing all right, you know. I never lost a day during the Depression.

I got married in 1922. I met my wife Edith in Seattle when I worked in the shipyards. She was born in Sweden and she was about eight years old when she came to Seattle with her mother. Her father was an alcoholic and they were divorced. That was something they didn't do in Sweden them days, is divorce. I met Edith at her mother's home. Her mother kept boarders. She had a pretty good-sized boardinghouse. I never stayed there, but I used to go up there and have a home-cooked meal once in a while.

We had it awful nice up there in Alaska. I built a house twelve by fourteen inside, a log cabin. When they seen me build that first house, they said, "When that *cheechako* [newcomer] wife of yours sees that there doghouse you're going to put her in, she go right back to Seattle. Not even a bedroom. Are you a crazy man?" Well, I had to do the best I could with what I had. "Oh, we'll have a bedroom after a while." "After a while? There won't be no after a while!" And when she seen the cabin, she said, "Oh my gosh, I always wanted a dollhouse and look at that, now I can live in one!" So we got along all right. She had her own dog and a little sled and she go wherever she wanted.

Well, then I moved into a company house. I got to be winchman, and then I got to be made dredgemaster.* I was dredgemaster for eighteen years. I had free house and light and fuel and a company pickup. So then we had nice places to live.

I had Eskimos working for me there, too. Eskimos are the finest people in the world. They're honest, reliable, and good workers, and have good characters. Their only weakness is liquor, but they don't go to extremes with that either. I had four of them that came regular every year. And I was prepared when they had to go home and hunt for seal. I let them go, but they were always welcome back next year.

I was with the company all them years and I'm getting a pension from them now, too. Pretty near forty years I worked for them, from 1924 till 1959, except for five years during the war. They shut down the dredges, because they couldn't get steel, and I worked down here at the Associated Shipyard in Seattle. I was riveting foreman, at my old trade again in the Second World War.

---

*A winchman moves heavy objects with a winch. A dredgemaster or dredgeman operates a dredge for mining metal-bearing sands from rivers and other bodies of water.

They say people go bad through bad environment. How in the name of God could anyone have had worse environment than I had when I lived in the Union Hotel? Gambling houses on Washington Street. I even got shot in the leg in a gambling house there. I used to go in and rubberneck. I didn't play myself; I had no money to play with. And a guy come in and he fired a revolver through a table and hit me in the leg here. And I didn't even know I was shot till a fellow said, "Say kid, you're bleeding, what's the matter?" I spent four days in the Seattle General Hospital. No, no, it's up to the man himself absolutely. I was with the worst—gamblers, prostitutes, everything you could think of—and no homelife. I was raised a good Christian. My mother was very religious and whatever she told me stuck in my mind. I had no use for crooked stuff. I had no use for any shady stuff.

I've been back to Sweden two times. The first time was in 1948. My mother was sick and we were moving a dredge up in Alaska and I got a letter from my brother that, golly, I don't think our mother is gonna last much longer. So by gosh I went and told the superintendent, "I'm going to Sweden and see my mother." "And moving a dredge here in the middle of the winter—no." "Yes, I say, yes. There's no 'no' about it. Your dredge moving isn't gonna stop because I go." But you see, I was dredgemaster on it and I had done the work so far. "Well," he says, "you know where everything is." "Well, it will be there when I come back. I'm going."

I only stayed twenty days. It was just to see my mother and I'm glad I did, because I would never seen her again if I hadn't gone. I told her I was coming home and she didn't believe it. The village was on two small hills and there was a meadow in between. I met a fellow on the road and I asked him, "Is that trail in the meadow open like it used to be when I was a kid?" He says, "Say, wait a minute, I know you." We had gone to school together. I had met an old lady coming up the road and it was my mother and I didn't know her and she didn't know me. "Well," he said, "there's your mother!" And I had a heck of a time to catch up with her, I was a little bit out of shape. First thing when she see me, she said, "Oh, my, but you got fat!"

Hanna Sippala

"They like Finnish girls."

*Hanna Sippala grew up along Finland's northwest coast.
She was born in 1897 and a case of "America fever" sent her
across the Atlantic in 1916. After 1919, she lived in Astoria,
Oregon, where she did housework, ran a boardinghouse, and
worked in a fish cannery. Hanna married a Finn and had one
daughter.*

When we lived Kello [Finland], we had farm and in the
wintertimes they fish by net under the ice. I was nine years
old when we moved Raahe, and then we just have a farm.
My house painted red; we had a sauna. We got eight cows and we take
milk to Raahe, summertimes twice a day and wintertimes once a day.
We have families where we take it and sell. Summertimes, we take by
bicycle. Wintertimes, we go by sled, pushing sleds, with horses, too,
sometimes.

I remember when they give Christmas present, they open the door
and throw in the presents. They don't want anybody to know who
come. You had to guess it. New Year's Eve, they melted lead and put it
in the water and what kind of things come, they figure what happens
next year.*

I go through public school, but that's all. When I get through public
school, those teachers come home and they want my folks to put me
in seminary, teachers' college. But my father said he need workers. Ja, I
have to work on the farm.

Then I want to come America. I get the America fever, they said. And

---

*The shapes of the molten lead are used to tell individuals' fortunes for the year
to come.

196

when I heard some people go to America, I said, "I want to go too." But my father and mother don't like me to go. And I said, "I lay down on the bed and you can feed me here if you don't let me go in America." And father said, "We don't want to feed grown people there. Let her go." My mother said she'd let me die before she'd let me go America!

Then they give me money; and they give enough money, if I change my mind, I can come back. First, I told them I'm happy because I want to come. But when I got over, I almost came back. But I'm so ashamed to go back, because I want to come so bad.

I stayed Kello, my brother's house, about three days. I waiting for passport to come. And then we take train to Kristiania [Oslo] in Norway. We have to pay own fare and a lot of girls don't have money to pay that fare and I pay because they give me so much money. I pay all those girls. And I never get it back, because we get to Ellis Island, they put everybody who goes in the middle land [midwest] a different way, and who stay in New York, they put a different way. I never saw them anymore; I never get those money back.

I leave the 25th of July, 1916, my home in Raahe and the 25th of August we landed in Ellis Island. They took two weeks to come in boat because war go in that time and in boat we have to come so slow between the mines. One night, they told us, don't take clothes off. And all Finn girls come to same room and we try to make it a lot of fun. When morning comes, it's all right.

I have a girlfriend in Jersey City who meet me Ellis Island. All girls have to be maid in the families; no other work there for a woman. We put [advertisement] in paper. A lot of ladies came see me same night when they get the paper. And I take the closest one; that was minister place. They like Finnish girls. They get a lot of work; they hard worker.

I get ten dollars a month first and twelve dollars next month and two dollars more every month till I get twenty dollars. My sister come here thirteen months later than I am. When my sister came, they took her. And they give me another place who can afford to pay more. I get twenty-five dollars at the other place. Clean house, do all the housework, cook, do laundry. We can't talk [English], that's why we get so little pay. They raised every time when we learn more.

Hanna Sippala

While we left Finland, my sister's boyfriend come here and he's in Astoria [Oregon]. They go together in Finland already. And he's living here and he start to want my sister to come Astoria. My sister don't want to come alone and I have to come with her. That's why we come to Astoria— 1919, November 8. We come in train and another girl came with. And they never saw us go to eat. People ask, "What you eating?" The other girl said, "No money, no food".

We stay in family two week and then we put ad in the paper. And then we go to families, maids in families. Then I get forty-five dollars a month here in Astoria. Before I married in 1921, I worked across the river on the Washington side. I get fifty dollars a month then.

When I come here at first to that family, they heard Finnish girl come to here and they come to see us. Boys come to see us. And I meet my husband there. He was Finnish. It happened he had almost same birth-place as I, Raahe. First, he work logging camp. He stayed week there and every Sunday he come home. But when my daughter born, then he quit logging camp and start longshoring because he want to stay home.

First years, we live 8th Street. Then, 1929, we rent a boarding house and two years I keep boardinghouse. Because so poor time, no other kind of work, and I took those. We get room and board there and some wages, too. We rent own house out. And they want to sell the boarding-house, and we don't want to buy it, because we afraid of poor times. We come to buy the house in Commercial Street, just one block up the hill, and we live there. Then 1939, I start to work cannery. And I work canneries twenty years, for fillet fish. Bottom fish, mostly that.

I like it, but this is so small since New York. People wonder how girls leave New York and come to Astoria because it's so small. But after, I get used to it. I find that boy. We go together two years before we married. Astoria the whole time. I like here. I got my family here.

Grethe Petersen

"We sold fresh-churned butter right out of the churn."

> *A single woman of twenty-two, Grethe Petersen met her*
> *husband at the Danish boardinghouse the same day she*
> *arrived in Seattle. After their marriage, Grethe and John*
> *owned and operated a dairy store and delicatessen for twenty*
> *years. Then they managed the Danish boardinghouse together.*
> *Both were very active in the ethnic community, including*
> *the production of Danish-language plays.*

I was born in the small town of Give in Denmark, March 8, 1900. I was baptized Elna Margrethe Jensen, but all my life I had only the name Grethe. So when I came to America and was going to get my citizen's paper, I thought I would just as well have Grethe Petersen, as people always called me. I had a sister who was working at Vejle Fjord Sanitarium and she said, "Come over here and work." That was a good job. There were about fifty girls working there. We were off in the evening; we were off on Sundays. Gee, we got good food, the best in the world! I was there for four years; but some girls had stayed there for ten, twenty years and had got to be old maids. So I thought to myself, no, I'm not going to stay here for twenty years and get to be an old maid, I'm going to get out of here. I was twenty-two years old.

I was looking for another job but didn't get it, so I went home to my mother. Then one Sunday there was something going on in Vejle and my other sister said, "Let's go to this gathering." We started visiting with a family we knew and here is that man who took me to America, Jens Lauritsen. He says to me, "Grethe, my sister is going along with me back to America, do you want to go along?" So I said, "Oh ja, that would be nice." I thought, it was just meant this way, that I wasn't going to get that job so I could go to America.

Grethe Petersen family farm, Denmark

We got on this boat, *Hellig Olaf*, Scandinavian-American Line. We sailed the 11th of August, 1922. There was a bunch of other Danish girls on the boat. We got into Hoboken [New Jersey] and Jens Lauritsen knew somebody who had a hotel and we stayed there overnight. We had one big room and we were five girls who had to sleep there. As soon as we put on the light, we saw some bugs running over the sheets. What are we going to do? There was one girl, she said, "I'm not going to take my clothes off." The rest of us, we took our clothes off. We said, "We're going to leave the light on." You know, they run away from the light. Oh, we laughed! The next morning we came down to breakfast. There was a big table and we were all sitting there. He came with two fried eggs and toast and even little fried potatoes. I had never in my life had a breakfast like that. I had never had two eggs, period. So I thought, is this America? What do you know! I couldn't get over it—two eggs!!

We came into Seattle on the 26th of August. When we came into the railroad station, some of the young fellows from the Danish Hall came down to get us.* All these young Danes that were staying in this boardinghouse were anxious to see these Danish girls, naturally. But we weren't looking our best. My hair was just like wire, from five days on the train. That night there was a party going on in the upstairs hall and we heard them singing up there, songs that we know. Jens said, "You want to go up and see it?" "Oh, no, not in the condition we are, we don't go to anything." But my husband-to-be and his friend came down to the kitchen on an errand, to look at those girls. When they saw us and saw the condition we were in, I guess black and whatever, they said to one another, going back to the party, "*Å vor Herre bevares!* Oh, good grief!" That wasn't anything for them! He told me that afterwards.

I couldn't talk the English, so I worked in this Danish boardinghouse, cleaning rooms and stuff. There was eighteen rooms rented out and there was a lot of people coming in just to eat. I saw my husband-to-be John Petersen every day; he was there for breakfast, lunch, and dinner. I got thirty-five dollars a month and my room and board. We always were invited to movies by the boarders and, of course, after the movie, we had to have coffee. And we had a little Danish society and we danced and had basket socials and necktie socials and all those things.

I was in this boardinghouse for about nine months. Everybody spoke Danish there; you have got to get out so you can learn the language. So I got a job in Laurelhurst [northeast Seattle]. There was another girl there, too, and she was a girl from Danish parents; but she spoke the English so, of course, I learned a lot from her. This was housework. I was cooking and doing all kinds of stuff. One day the lady of the house told me to "soak" something and I thought she said "cook" something. That was the only mistake I know I made, but I made that mistake.

I got married in 1924; it was just two years. My husband and this fellow [Christensen] started a dairy store. Then we moved into a new building on Market Street.† We had a churn right there in the window

---

*The Danish boardinghouse was known as Washington Hall.
†This was in Ballard, the heart of the ethnic community. The 1926 Seattle City Directory indicates 5404 22nd Avenue N.W. as the address for Christensen and Petersen dairy products, owned by Viggo Christensen and John Petersen.

and people came and got butter, milk, and all. A gallon of buttermilk for fifteen cents and a quart for five cents. We churned the butter and sold this fresh-churned butter right out of the churn. We had Kraft cheese and Banquet cheese and all kinds of Oregon cheese. They were partners, Mr. Christensen and my husband. Then they decided to part, not that there was any feud or anything like that.

Then plumber Hans Pedersen built this building over on 73rd street and we went in there. That was 1931. We stayed there until after the war. We had a good business. I started making rullepølse [cold cuts of lamb or beef] and all kinds of good things for a delicatessen. I took a trip to Denmark with my kids in 1934 and while we were there I went to Vejle. Mrs. Hansen, who I knew here, had a brother who had a business making this rullepølse and we went into his shop and he showed me how to make things. So when I came back, I started making rullepølse and leverpostej [liver pâté] and sylte [pickled pork] and all these things. Every Friday, we got a big order for the Norwegian Hall [boardinghouse]; and when the Norwegians had something going on down in Norway Hall [lodge hall], they had to have ten gallons of sour cream for rømmegrøt [sour cream porridge]. The Norwegians was good customers of ours.

I am a member of St. John's Lutheran Church and a little club we called the darning club, the Ladies Aid. We made cookies and we made dolls. We bought all the carpeting for the church, we put in a refrigerator, and the pastor got a beautiful desk; and we did that with cookies and dolls. Then when they needed money to build that church, we got into making dinners. Sometimes we made four hundred dollars on a big dinner and we thought that was good.

In Denmark we have lille julaften [little Christmas Eve, the 23rd of December]. It was tradition that we had æbleskiver [small fried cakes] and different parts of the country would have different traditions. About six years ago we started to have lille julaften at our church and I was one of the instigators, because I was just then president of the club. But it's hard to get somebody to preach in Danish. This year the minister will preach in English but the rest will be in Danish. We sing Danish hymns we have known all our lives. Then we go downstairs and have

Store owned and operated by Grethe and John Petersen, Seattle

coffee and *julekager* [Christmas cookies] and we have had a big crowd every year.

I belong to the Danish Sisterhood. I have gone through the chairs and I have been president. Also, I joined a club Harmonien [harmony], where we played Danish plays.* My husband was president of Harmony Club for twenty-some years and now I am in my fifth year being president of that club. Now we call it more of a social club, because we don't play anymore. We used to put on three plays a year. We went to San Francisco to play, to Tacoma. I played the main part, the young girl Lisbet, in *En Søndag paa Amager* for the twenty-fifth anniversary. Then when we came to the fiftieth anniversary of the club, we had this play

---

*Seattle's Harmonien was founded in 1911 and reorganized in 1921. The club presented musical and dramatic performances in the Danish language.

again and my daughter played the same part. In 1984, my granddaughter can play that same part for the seventy-fifth anniversary.[*]

Both my children speak Danish. My children went to Danish summer school at church, so they could learn Danish. They lived there; they had a big attic and they were all sleeping there. It was real nice for us, too, when we were busy. When I go to Denmark, nobody can hear that I have been gone for sixty years. I have been to Denmark eight times. The first time was in 1934. My mother was still alive and we were so glad that we made it back while she was still living in our home in Give. The second time was in 1946. My husband and I sold our business and we drove across America and took our automobile with us to Denmark. When we got there, it was right after the war and when we arrived with our big American car, people were quite surprised and impressed. Food and gasoline were both still rationed but there was a little black market going on so we got extra gasoline.

When we came back from Denmark in 1946, we were looking for a store or something to do. It happened so that there was nobody to take care of that Danish building with the boardinghouse, so they talked my husband into taking care of it. I cooked for parties and banquets and there was around twenty boarders. That was a big job, a hard job. Had to get up at five o'clock in the morning and send all those boys to work, fix up the lunch buckets and give them breakfast. I did that by myself. Since we got out of the boardinghouse, I haven't worked, just worked at home here, taking care of the house and helping my daughter with her little kids. My husband passed away the 21st of August, 1968.

I have had a wonderful life in America. In 1950, my sister Dagmar came to America. I was so busy down at the boardinghouse and help was hard to get, so my sister came over to help. And she stayed and she married that same year. She hadn't been married before; she was forty-three years old. We have been together a lot in these years. We have a sister in California and we take a trip down there every now and then. We three sisters like to get together at least once a year.

[*]The play "A Sunday in Amager," a one-act Vaudeville by Johanne Luise Heiberg (1812–1890), was the first play that Harmonien presented (November 11, 1911).

Anton Isaksen

"I have put in seventy years on boats."

*Anton Isaksen grew up fishing with his grandfather in
northern Norway, where he was born in 1903. He immigrated in 1923 and made his living as a fisherman in the
Pacific Northwest, using such varied methods as traps, dories,
and longlines. Although he spent several periods ashore in
response to family pressures, and although he had to battle
chronic seasickness, Anton found the occupation too
rewarding to abandon.*

Bøgard is in the northern part of Norway on Andøya Island,
about 180 miles north of the Polar Circle. I grew up there and I
was fourteen and a half years old when I started out fishing for
myself. Up to that time, I had been out fishing with my grandpa. He
was a real fisherman. I respect him to be the most determined fellow
for fishing.

Grandpa had his own boat. It was an open boat and that's all they
were using in the early days of my life. He looked at the weather, of
course; there you were your own weatherman. One time when the
wind came up, I was not able to row the boat against the wind and
hold it on the spot. Grandpa got disgusted with me. I was seasick by
this time. I felt like I could just lay down and die. If he threw me overboard, I wouldn't have the power to fight back. He was kind enough
to let me remain aboard the boat! And he asked me to help hoist the
sail up. It was a fairly even wind this day and the boat took off with
the wind, heading for the place to get up on shore again. And I heard
Grandpa talking to himself, "That guy, he'll never be a seaman." You
know, that was the desire of the old people, that their offsprings would
be seamen, would grow up and be somebody because they are a sea-

man. In storms, like they say, it separates the boys from the men. I, of course, had to agree with him. I just had to close my eyes because the movements of the boat bothered me. So that was my early fishing. That was anywheres from I was nine years old to about fourteen.

When I was about sixteen, I got a job on one of the big herring seiners. It was powered with steam, wonderful power, no noise from it. You could just hear a nice little sewing-machine sound from down there. The only rustle you heard was when they were shoveling coal into the boiler. I was a fisherman and we were a crew of twenty-three on this boat. I fished and put in the seasons until I was twenty years old, the day after I stepped on American soil [1923].

I wasn't going to fish here [in Washington] in the ocean. That was one reason I left the old country, because I was so seasick. My uncle had a job for me, but no, I turned it down. [Instead] we were fishing salmon in what they called traps. This was on Whidbey Island, right by Deception Pass. That was the fishing gear in those days, but it was abolished. I was with them putting in traps, and when we got them in and the season started, I was watchman on this trap. We had it real nice; we could go ashore.

When you've been a fisherman, even in the old country, you know quite a bit about different types of fishing, although this particular type of fishing I didn't know about. But I was used to hanging seines, making up seines, and this trap was another type of deal that you make up. When it was all ready, we took all this gear on scows. We took one trap at a time and we nailed these along the "capping." We called it capping, that was two by twelves put between pilings and bolted or nailed together. They would have to be real hard, because the waves of the sea were coming right in there to the beach, and backwash and everything could uproot the whole thing.

Once we had them in, then we started to watch these traps and have everything ready for the cannery tender that came out and picked up the salmon. The salmon had to go through different channels, but it finally got into what they call the "spiller." When you pulled it around, the rope was winding on the center of this wooden winch and brought the bottom of the spiller up and the salmon coming with it. Pretty soon you see hardly anything down there except foam, because the salmon was splashing around. Then you lower it from the capping, which is way up above the flood stage, and the tender come alongside, and he just put his scoop in there and raise it up and drop it into his boat and do it again. And in no time it was all empty and the cannery boat goes, and you fix up your pot again and set it for the next salmon.[*]

I got a partner, too, watching the trap, in case one fell overboard; we was always walking on top of cappings. This partner of mine came three months later, and I had fished together with him on the steamer in the old country. We knew each other, so we were happy that we could converse without any difficulty. On the salmon fishing we made eighty-five dollars a month and you got your food, bedding, and lodgings free. I paid back my ticket, three hundred dollars to my cousin.

After three months, I went to Everett completely alone and searched for a job. I started in a sawmill. I worked there only about a month. It was a hard job, terrific hard. One day there was an accident, too. That was my partner. The boss had told him to watch out for the lumber that came shooting off the rollers from the chain that goes behind you. Lumber could get caught in one end and do all sorts of damages. My partner got caught. A piece of lumber hit him in the heel; he couldn't even step on it. They took him to the hospital and I got another partner. We were unloading a truck that was wobbly with all kinds of heavy lumber on it. And we started to pull the lumber off and you just couldn't hold that load. He got caught and the load fell on both his legs and broke both legs off. So he was taken to the hospital. So I thought, "Well, next is me."

About a year and a half after I came here, I started halibut fishing. I went into fishing with my uncle that I first came to in Tacoma. He

---

[*]The salmon trap described here was a stationary trap, attached to pilings. The salmon moved through various chambers until they reached the "spiller," which could be lifted up; the live fish were then "spilled" or scooped into a tender. The Norwegians dominated the salmon trap industry; traps were outlawed on Puget Sound in 1934 and in Alaska some years later.

had built himself a schooner, *Neptune*, which was about seventy-five feet long and he carried five dories, and I was to be on one of those dories. We were two men to each dory.

For the day we might be picked up twice. You'd be put over the side once, then you set your lines. We had the gear set and it was marked with flagpoles and float, one on each end. When you were through setting it, then the mother ship picked up the empty dories and we went through the same formalities. You were two and two, and you went through your job of baiting up the gear for the next set again. In the beginning we had one hook for every nine feet. That was a lot of hooks. We could run on each dory about 3,200 hooks a day. If you got a fish on every third or fourth hook, you could have a good day. This is the way we worked. I stayed with that type of fishing for about five years.

I had a cousin as a partner, this cousin who helped me come over. He was much smaller than me, but very wiry and strong. In the dory, we had a gurdy—that's a little winch that you grind away like on a meat grinder. The one in the bow winds this in and the man in the back grabs the hook and slaps it into the fish checker. It was a competition— how fast can we beat the other guy? We got no more money, but it was in us to be competitive. It was a race and my partner and I, generally we was first aboard even if we were last over the side.

We used to go up in the Hecate Strait which is between Queen Charlotte Islands and the mainland of Canada. We used to make two-week to sixteen-day trips. Then we'd come in and sell whatever we had. Trips would vary naturally, depending on the weather and the amount of fish we were getting. I got started at the time when the great big steamers had up to twelve-fourteen dories aboard. So the grounds were pretty well fished out, for we had no conservation in those days. That year I started fishing, they put in the season; so December, January, February, we could look after our gear, work on that, and get a little time off.

Later, the dories got outlawed by federal law [1935]. No dory fishing anywheres, because there was supposed to be so many men lost. That was no problem; we became longliners. We fished from the big boat and we pulled one set at a time. There was one man at the roller and over on the power winch was a man coiling the gear and that gear had to be taken by the baiters. On the table there was cut-up bait and everything went, one thing after another, like it all was a machinery. It was no competition; you were a team. You had so much to do. Then take the gear coming in, and then dress the fish, scrape it, and clean it. You pull the viscera out, you get in there with the scraper and remove all blood, and then throw it in the checker. When you have the checker full, then a man goes down in the hole and chops up an awful lot of ice. Some of this ice needs to go into the poke or belly of this fish. You hold that belly open and you give it a swift kick with the round part of the ice scoop. You kept on doing this with the dressed fish until you had a pen full. Then you put ice around it and it would sort of freeze and stiffen. You went about doing this for every pen in the boat. If you could get on top of the hatch when it was all full and just step it down and tie it, you had a good trip.

When you came in from a trip, you had ten days to lay up on, lay in town. If you were full of energy—which I know I was in those days—there could be a job that same day. Another boat would go out and he says, "We'll be back in ten days before your boat goes out again." So here I would go out on another boat; I could do that legally. I could make more money that way. There is the main reason for staying with it, because at no time did I make that much money piling lumber in the mill or going out in the lumber camp.

In the early days of my fishing I made a promise to my wife and family, "When we have our first house paid for, I'll quit." That was a great mistake. A promise is a promise. Some people can take it lightly, but my wife didn't take it lightly. She married for to be married and have a family and she's been a real good woman. She came here [from Norway] about two and a half years after I did. She was working as a waitress in a logging camp around Tacoma. She made money, too, even paid her brother back money he had sent to her for a ticket. So, she has always been a disciplined woman and full of love for the family. We married in 1928. We had four girls. We've actually had six births in our family. We lost the first boy at birth. The second one was a twin and he lived till he was ten years old. That [son's death] was enough to make me stop fishing; I stayed home for a month and a half.

Anton and Olive Isaksen

After I got squared around, I took the boat out again shortly before Christmas. I talked to the wife from the boat and told her I was heading to a new place. It was a terrific strong tide there. I fished in the night because I would catch more of the flounders in the night than in the daytime. I was trolling and I didn't have radar and I ended up on the reef where there were all kinds of rocks. All of a sudden I'm standing right on top of a rock and we got stranded. We had no way of getting out. I had thirty tons of ice aboard for the fish, and twenty-five tons of fish aboard, plus tanks full of oil, fuel, and gear. We tried to get anchors down to hold the boat there, but with all that weight it was settling. And so it broke in the side. It just crashed like timbers out in the woods.

I called the Coast Guard. He was on the way from Ketchikan [Alaska], but he ran into a log and damaged his propeller so the next message I got was, "We're disabled and we have to be towed back to Ketchikan."

The lighthouse tender which served as Coast Guard boat too was in Petersburg and that boat came out to us. They couldn't come near us, but we had our life boats. It was dark and there were no lights aboard and the tide running about seven-eight miles an hour. The boat was gone, but we got saved by the Coast Guard. I lost no men. Thank God for that. So that was the second thing that happened to me. That was another time to stay home for a bit. I was without a boat.

Then I went into a plywood plant in Tacoma. I honestly then made up my mind that I'm not supposed to fish, maybe. I took four thousand dollars and paid for a share in that plant. I went to work there after New Year's. But then there was a friend of mine who had a boat and wanted me to take it out for him. I finally agreed. I went in the upper part of Hecate Straits outside of Prince Rupert. We fished there three days, went into the harbor there, and I was going to change over some adjustments. I stooped over and all of a sudden I couldn't straighten out. We got into Prince Rupert. I had called the ambulance to be down on the wharf to pick me up. The doctor says, "You have something to holler for, it's your appendix. We'll operate tomorrow morning." I says, "I got my wife and family in Seattle. We have had a couple of things happen, the one main thing was losing our only son." He says, "We'll see in the morning. I'll give you a shot now." I was there four or five days and he said, "You take your own chances, but I think I'll let you go down there." So I had the operation down in Ballard. That was actually the third calamity in our family. And I stayed away from fishing for about a year, I think it was.

I'm seventy-nine now [1982] and I'm still not retired. I have a thirty-foot boat laying down in the dock here. But I'm hampered like all the people that's in the salmon gill-netting here on the [Puget] Sound. We got hit hard by Judge Boldt's decision.* We have no chance to fish or to sell our boats either. I would take the boat to Alaska and fish it up

*Federal District Judge George H. Boldt issued a landmark ruling in 1974 concerning the treaty rights of Native American tribes in western Washington. In the aftermath of Boldt's ruling, fishing regulations had to be revamped to guarantee the tribes at least fifty percent of the local fish catch.

there; but I got to the point where age and my heart condition, it's all behind me.

I have put in seventy years on boats, starting when I was nine years old. I'm satisfied and very happy. I guess I've been stubborn, or should I say determined. I managed seasickness this way—I made up my mind that, well now, you've gone into this fishing, you have to make the best out of it.

Margit Johnsen

"I never did like housework."

Margit Johnsen joined her uncle in Tacoma when she was
twenty-four years old. Since she preferred cannery and outdoor
work to housework, she spent two summers up in Alaska.
Margit married a Norwegian immigrant, a fisherman, and
settled in Tacoma, where she raised a son and was active in
the Daughters of Norway.

I was born June 5, 1901, in Norway. It's a little place north of Bodø,
north of the Arctic Circle. There was farms across the fjord from
us and mountains back of the farms and the sun set on that side.
It was the most beautiful sight you ever saw! But then it could also be
storm, where you couldn't see across. It threw the water up in the air
so it was just like snow.

Fishing and farming. The farming wasn't much, because we had
about nine months of winter. Mostly was fishing; that's what we lived
on. From January to the later part of April, father was out fishing. They
stayed at the fishing ground, Lofoten, until they were through. That's
where they get big cod that are so famous and made the cod-liver oil.
We always had two or three boats. We all could fish; we had to do that
in order to eat. We salted it or dried it. You couldn't always get out and
fish it, so you had to prepare it and have it.

One thing with them over there, you never did hear them complain
about the way they lived. We had to go in the boats and get our fire-
wood, saw it up, split it, and get it in. We had to carry the water, and
we had to get all the feed for the cows for nine months of the year. The
children had to do it. We had to start in when we were six and seven
years old, so we knew what it was to work.

I was fifteen in June and we had our confirmation in June. Of course,

I was out working long before that, even. Can't say I was hired, I had to go and help out on the farms around. You got something to eat sometime. After I was confirmed, I stayed with the neighbor—he had a bigger farm—and worked until I was eighteen. I was doing everything on the farm. Then I went to the town of Bodø.

My uncle that lived here in Tacoma, my mother's brother, they came home a trip in 1920. I went and met them down on the dock in Bodø. I remember my uncle said to me, "Well, you are the only one who have nerves enough to leave home and get out on your own and start working." So, if I ever want to come to this country, to let him know and he would help me get over here.

I was doing just about everything. I worked in canneries, I laid down sardines, I worked in a store, whatever I could find. Seems to me like it was no future over there. So, in 1924, I thought, I'm going to get out of here! Then, of course, there were so many emigrants going over to this country that we had to wait a whole year, for the quota. I came here in July of 1925. I have never been sorry.

My uncle had kind of a rooming house up on 11th and J. When I'd been here about two weeks and stayed with them, I started working. I took the bus out to Sumner, or North Puyallup they called it, and worked in a cannery on the fruit, canning berries, until the season was over; it was only a couple of weeks left. Then after that I started housework. That was the only thing in those days. So I was working then for the same family for seven months, until the following May. Their name was Hansen; they were Danish. They were both born here, but Mrs. Hansen talked real good Danish, so I could understand her. They had four girls at the time; it was a great big three-story house.

I never did like housework. You got up in the morning, you made breakfast, and then you had to start in. You done the cleaning, making beds, then doing the washing. It took a whole day to do the ironing. You see, all the girls except the little one went to Annie Wright Seminary* and they had white middies and dark-blue pleated skirts. Well,

*Annie Wright School, a private girls' school located in Tacoma's North End, was founded in 1884.

those uniforms had to be starched stiff and it was my job to iron those things. The middy blouses were so stiff that you could set them on the floor. They were electric irons, but gee whillikins that was hard, too.

Then, of course, the girls came home for lunch and I fixed a little lunch for them. Then they went back to school, because it wasn't too far from where they lived. Then I cooked dinner and, of course, you cleaned that big house and everything and wash all those clothes. There was a lot of clothes to wash. I was supposed to have half of Thursday off and half of Sunday. It got to be three and four o'clock in the afternoon and everybody had gone to where they were supposed to go. And the same thing on Sundays. Before I got through with the Sunday dinner, it was about three o'clock in the afternoon and everybody had gone on picnics and things like that. There wasn't much free time, so I think that's what got me kind of soured on housework, too.

I started out at forty dollars a month, in addition to that [room and board]. Then she raised me to forty-five dollars, but then I had to take over the washing, which I done most of anyhow. I told her I might quit and go to Alaska and she didn't like that, so she said, "I'll raise you five dollars." She was mad at me when I quit.

I didn't like cooking and I didn't like housework. I like the outdoor and I like something that was altogether different. I heard of somebody that went to Alaska. They went up to those herring stations for the summer. So I thought, well, I'd like to try that. So I went to Seattle and I found the office where they hired out. I happened to run across the superintendent, who was Norwegian and from the northern part of Norway. I knew very well where he came from. So, ja, that was fine; I got hired right away.

I was working with the herring. You take the guts out of it and salt it. It is hard work and salting, it's hard on your hands. This was 1926, in southeastern Alaska. They called the herring camp Big Port Walter; it's close to Port Alexander. There was one Englishman and the rest of them was all Norwegian. The cook, he was Swedish.

When I had been there about two weeks working in the cannery area with the herring, then one of the fellows in the kitchen, he didn't like it, so he went down [to the lower forty-eight]. They were three in the kitchen; there was about seventy men to cook for. We were fourteen girls and I got picked to work in the kitchen out of the fourteen. I was tickled pink, and got good pay. Then I had monthly wages. There didn't turn out to be much herring for a long time and all the girls got sent down. I got to stay then, because I was in the kitchen. So I had the advantage of that. All I did, was took care of the dishes when they were all through and saw to it that all the vegetables were taken care of, ready to cook. Then when I come down in the fall in 1927, then I got married.* So I didn't go up anymore.

My husband, he was a friend of my uncle, so that's how I met him. His name was Enok Johnsen. He had come from Norway in 1911; he was about twelve years older than I was. He was a fisherman and a longshoreman. He used to stay at my uncle's hotel. At first when I met him, he was building a boat. And then after that, he went to Alaska up the Bering Sea in the summertime and fished, and worked longshore in the wintertime. He was gone an awful lot. My boy, when he was only about three years old, he went over to my neighbor's and he said to my neighbor, "Well, tomorrow we are going to get company." She said, "Where are you going to get company from?" "Oh," he says, "my daddy is coming home!"

I didn't work after [marriage], except once in a while I would help out a friend of mine who used to have a restaurant downtown. And then once in a while during the war I worked in the bakery down on Market Street. I just had the one boy.

I've always felt at home here. I know so many of them, they were so lonesome and so homesick. I never was because, I think, I was on my own early. I really enjoyed it after I came here. I worked hard.

*Margit spent two summers in Alaska, 1926 and 1927; in the winters, she did cannery work in Tacoma.

Ole Nissen

"We haven't got a tailor between 23rd and East Madison."

Ole Nissen was born in Ansager, Denmark, in 1887. At the
age of fourteen, he became apprenticed to a tailor; and after
arrival in the United States in 1907, he practiced his trade
in California, Vancouver, British Columbia, and Seattle.
In Seattle, Ole built and ran his own tailor shop.

In the summertime I worked with mother on the farm. In the morning, they hitched the cows all together and then I chase them across the river and up to the twenty acres we had farther up. Each one of the cows had rope on them. They were so far apart so they wouldn't run together. If there was good grass, I wouldn't have to move them very often, but if it was poor grass, then I have to move them half a circle. In between the moving of the cows, I have to look after the sheep and the young cattle. After twelve o'clock, I take them home. We had three milkings: one in the morning, one at noon, and one at night.

I was fourteen, finished with schooling, and then mother said, "I want you to learn to be a tailor." So I said, "Why should I learn to be a tailor?" "Look at your wrists," she said. "You have no farmer's wrists. You've got small wrists. You should sew, it's easy with the small bone like you have." Well, I liked the animal life, too; I got along very good with animals. Well, anyhow, mother made an agreement with the tailor in the next town for three and a half years. Then I came into a profession where I learn to make a living. I got along fine. I had no dislike for anything I had to do. That was my good part of my nature.

This was in a private home. He had a large two-story house and he had a store. Besides to learn to be a tailor, I had to run all the errands, I had to help his wife in the kitchen, I had to keep the stoves all burning and keep the fuels in. All those things I had to do besides sewing. The first year, I did only pants. The second year, I did vests. The third year, I came into coats. And the final half a year, that came into the finishing off of the garment complete. So then I had learned the whole profession, as far as the man's [tailoring was concerned]. I learned the ladies' later. I worked in the small towns around Ansager. I earned enough money so I could get over here.

My brother, he had the traveling spirit. He was in New York for five years; he learned to be a cabinetmaker. And then he came home to visit with mother and the folks. My older sister and I, we went with him back to New York. That was in 1907. My brother want to show off a little. I have to see everything there is in New York. He took us out to Coney Island. It was so crowded that you could hardly get down to the water. Everything was exciting. I had so much curiosity in my system. I saw the first colored man over the Brooklyn Bridge; my brother and I walked across. And I saw the first Indian and the first Chinaman.

My brother had one friend that he had worked together with and he [this friend] wanted him to come out and work together while they built a house in the Black Hills in Dakota. So we got on the railway. I'd never been riding on trains before. Everything was interesting.

I was just a handyman, a semi-cook. I had to help and see that they got something to eat. We stayed there July, August, September. Then we got on the work train out to Pasco [Washington]. They were building a depot and my brother being a cabinetmaker or a carpenter, that's what he was to work on. I went as a carpenter's helper. We had free trip to the place we worked and we were there for about three weeks. My brother felt sorry for me that I had to do hard work.

We got to Seattle. Naturally I was seeking a tailor field. I worked for one tailor for a little while, but the tailoring was awfully slow. So my brother, he likes to go to California and so do I. So we sailed down the coastline to San Francisco. That was 1907, the year after the big earthquake. Everything was so poor; many people were out of work and the town was all broken up.

I was out of work there for a long time. And you know, that time, just go and buy a glass of beer, what they call the schooners, at noon.

You got the schooners for five cents and then they serve lunch at noon. There were crackers and sandwiches and there were enough anyhow, so you scouted around and found out where you got the most food.

I found some work in one tailor shop, but that was only about a week and a half. I decided it was so hard to seek free lunch, that I was going to get into some place where they had food to eat. So I called into cafés. And here I come into a café close to the ferry building, number fifteen Market Street at that time, they called it Alameda Café. The man that owned that, he was Danish, too. "Well," he said, "young man, you hang around. If I should need to hire a new man, I will get your address and then I can let you know." Then a short time after that a man came in from the café and he told me, "You can get a job down there at Market Street if you want to start tonight at six o'clock. The man that had the job he quit. He won too much money on the horse races." So I said, "I have no clothes." "Well," he said, "there's always some of the men leave their clothes and you can wear that for tonight. And you can see if you can find clothes for tomorrow." So that worked out pretty good.

I waited on table. He took me around and showed me everything. They had a table for four and table for six and so on. And he told me what was the manner the waiter has to have: "You have to be easygoing and be friendly to everybody you see. Seat them friendly. When you bring any of your food, you set it down nice and softly just like you would be at home, don't throw it down. And show that you're interested in they are taken well care of. If you do that, they'll come back again. And that's how we expand." I got twelve dollars a week. Well, we had our own [room], my brother and I, in a Gentlemen [boarding-house] in San Francisco that they put up just for the hard times. They had twenty rooms, we only had one toilet.

But then I saw an ad in the paper that they wanted a coatmaker down in Selma, near Fresno. And so I wrote to them. I had more luck than a little bit. He happened to be Danish, too, and he said I could come right away to be a coatmaker. So I went over and told my boss that I was quitting. "Oh," he says, "You quitting? What's the matter with you?" I told him I was a tailor by trade. "Well," he said. "You're a café man now." I said, "I have seven years in tailoring. What do you think? I have a chance to get a job as a coatmaker." "Well," he says, "That's up to you, of course. You come back when you get hungry."

I was down in Selma for one year. I worked piecework. I got nine dollars for making a coat. We used to say two coats and a quarter would be a week's wages. A tailor in Eureka came down to visit. Selma, or Fresno, is very hot place and he said to me, "Young fellow, you better come work for me and get out of this heat in the summer." And so I quit and went up and worked for him in Eureka. I was there one year, coatmaker. I had lots of novel experiences while I was in both places.

Mother wrote that she'd like somebody to come home after her, and so we pooled our money and sent my brother. They came over to Vancouver, Canada. So my sister and I packed our goods and up we went to Vancouver, 1910. We rented a house and there we lived all together for four years.

Vancouver was a very good tailor town. Up there I had the best kind of a job in tailoring you can get. T. C. Morgan, he had two shops. He had one shop down on the lower floor of the building and then upstairs he had the ladies' shop. That's where I got my ladies' training and that was my big success. I was a proficient ladies' tailor. The ladies' cutter, he quit and started in business by himself. He had trained me and he want me with him. I know just exactly how he wants things done. So I went with him and worked for him for a couple years. Then I decided I wanted to go back to the States.

I like Seattle. It had a friendly influence on me the first time I was here. So I went to the American consul and I said I'd like to go back. I hadn't taken my first [citizenship] paper, but anyhow, I had already been here and it was for mother's sake that we went into Canada. He said, "Bring your folks down to the office, and we'll see what we can do." I brought the folks down and then he said, "Which one has the most money?" I happened to have the most money, because I'd been working on prosperous conditions and had lots of overtime. "Well now, you'll be in charge of your mother." That was 1914.

We had a big six-room house on Lake Washington Boulevard [in Seattle]. And the neighbor came in, a tall man, six-foot seven, and he

Ole Nissen in front of his tailor shop, Seattle, 1928

looked at me and he said—I was just a peewee—"Well, little fellow," he said, "what do you do?" "Oh," I said, "I'm a tailor." He says, "You're a tailor? For heaven's sake. We haven't got a tailor between 23rd and East Madison. We need a tailor. You can start the shop right here." He had it all figured out how I could do it. I said, "You don't know what kind of tailor I am." "I will know it," he said. "I'll bring you my coat over and you put in a lining. If you put in a lining right, why then I'll boast for you." So I got free advertising. So I opened up the shop there. The first suit I made, twenty-nine dollars; he was a Swedish fellow. After that, thirty-five dollars was the cheapest one I made.

I belong to the [Danish] Brotherhood and they used to play card the last Wednesday of the month. I played whist with a vice-president of the Washington Mutual Bank; he was Danish, too. They all know I was a tailor, so he asked me if I would make his wife a blue serge suit. I said,

"I'd be glad to." So I made her a blue serge. The bankers, they meet every month and they take their wives with them. And the men, they meet together, and they talk money and business. And the women, they huddle together and talk clothes and children. So this way I had four bankers' wives I made clothes for. And they introduce me to the senators', governors', and mayors' wives. I got all the top through that vice president of Washington Mutual.

I did all my ladies' work. But with the men's work, I cut it, arranged for the fitting, fit it down, then I sent it out to coatmakers, vestmakers, and pantsmakers. At any time I had more than I could do myself.

I bought a piece of property on 28th and East Madison with one house standing in the front of it. The lot runs from street to street. I went to a contractor. We decided to raise up the house and move it to face the back and then put up two stores in front. I was just going to put one, but he says, "Why don't you put up two? You can have income from renting that out, enough to pay for all expenses you have on this." So I did that. I rented out to a barber shop and a beauty parlor. I had a nice store. It was up-to-date and modern. I had my name in front. Nineteen twenty-five was when the building was completed; I was there from 1925 till 1967.

I went down to the office where we had to put in Social Security when I was in business. I said, "I'm eighty years old now, and I'm thinking about [retiring]." He told me, "If you're eighty years old, it's about time you retire."

Jenny Pedersen

"Everybody's gonna eat and
everybody's gonna wear clothes."

*Jenny Pedersen was trained as a dressmaker in Denmark
and she put out a "Sewing done here" sign when she and
her husband moved to Seattle. The Pedersens had two children
and the family relocated to a farm east of Seattle so that they
could produce much of their own food. Jenny grew up in an
urban environment and was a somewhat reluctant emigrant.*

I was born in Esbjerg, Denmark, on October 5, 1899. It's on the west
side of Jylland [Jutland] by the North Sea. Esbjerg is a big fishing
town and ships come in from all over to load and unload. My
mother started a delicatessen shop and my father started a fish market.
He went to the harbor every day and get the fresh fish and took home
in a wheelbarrow; that became a pretty big business. He would clean
it, sell it, and weight it. Some of these young women that come in to
buy fish, they would say, "Is that fresh, that fish?" "Well, lady, can't you
see it's jumping off the scale?" he'd say.

We young kids would help in the delicatessen shop when we come
from school. Mother had head cheese and pigs' feet and she made
meatloaf and she made *frikadeller*, meatballs. I had to grind the meat for
meatballs and she would say, "Now Jenny, you fooled me today; it has
to go through the meat grinder *three* times before I will use it. So you
do that or otherwise I'll have to get somebody else to do it." And she
would make a big batch of fishballs and fishcakes and fishpudding. She
was very good with fish. We learned to cook, us kids, even the boys.

When I got out of school when I was fourteen, I started to learn
to sew. There was a big complex; they had lots of girls that came, we
were about ten there, to learn to sew. I stayed there about half a year. I
got sick and my mother took me to the doctor and he said, "That girl

Jenny Pedersen, eight years old

should be out in the fresh air more than she is." I stayed home a half a year running errands and that got me out in the air, on the bicycle. Well, after that time, I guess I looked pretty good, so I got that job in the factory.

By the time I was sixteen, I started to go out and sew to people. Since my father delivered fish, he got to talk to everybody and they would talk to him. And they would say, well, they needed a dressmaker. So my father would say, "Well, I have a girl that's a dressmaker." So I had to go and see them. Over there they have a dressmaker come into their home and I would get a job for a week, or maybe two. Most people had their clothes made. I had several jobs where the daughter got married and I stayed there and made her trousseau.

Later on my folks decided I ought to learn designing. So I went to Copenhagen for half a year to learn to cut out patterns and try it on the person. See, we didn't have patterns we could buy. We had to measure the person and then just cut a big square. And then out of that you cut the neck, the sleeve, and they had a pleat here and one here. You learn to cut the sleeves out and the skirt and everything, just by putting it down with a pencil. Then, of course, we have to try it on. We usually had first paper and then we had some of the very thin material and then tried it on a person. Out of that foundation, you can make hundreds of designs.

One day in 1921 my husband-to-be came to visit us in the store. He had greetings from my sister over on Bainbridge Island [Washington] and he had a shirt for my father and ribbons for the girls. He came again and again. And one day I came out from the family I'd been sewing with and he was standing out there waiting for me. I kind of liked him. Krist was dressed a little different; he had on American-style clothes. He wasn't the same type as we met at home. Well, it developed into a love affair. One thing led to another and he bought me an engagement ring. We were married on Pentecost day, June 4, 1922.

Then we moved to the town where he lived. That was on the east coast. His uncle had put him up in business, so he had a store where he sold woodenware, shovels, and axes and all these things. In the meantime, he'd been talking about this here United States—it's such a wonderful place and you have to lay on your back to see these sky-scrapers! I said, "I don't want to go there; don't talk about it. I have two sisters that went over there and we hardly ever hear from them." You'd get a letter that looked like they'd been crying their heads off, because you could see how the writing had been running.

Our son in the meantime was born at home. We had a boy, Niels. Kind of a depression had started in there; the business wasn't so good. We went to look for tickets and they could only get some to Canada, they said. So we started selling furniture and all the things we had gotten for wedding presents. My mother was so mad.

We came to Halifax on March 16, 1925. And then we went to Winnipeg and we put an ad in the paper. There was a farmer, Johnson, he answered that. He had 165 acres of wheat, so he wanted a farmer from Denmark. They were laying for those European guys, because they were hardworking people. When we come outside of Winnipeg a few miles, I said to Krist, "My goodness, looks like that's awfully far away from town." I was a town girl; I was scared to get too far away from town.

After several miles we were there at a little farm. The next morning, well, I had to get up five o'clock and start in working—feed the chickens which he did, too, but he said he'd rather I'd do it because he thought that was a woman's work. And I got into making butter. They had a big, round keg, very old-fashioned and I almost blowed the house up one time with that. There was a cork and you were supposed to take the air out of it every ten minutes or so; well, I forgot it one time and the milk started running out of the barrel on the side.

And I had to make bread; I had never made bread before. I said to Krist, "Read the recipe there, what it says. I'm not that dumb I can't understand that." What I got was a yeast cake, the Red Star yeast, just like a rock. Then Krist talked to the man, "My wife don't seem to understand that kind of yeast. Are you sure that's all right?" "Yes, but we have an Indian woman that live a couple of miles. I'll go get her and she can maybe show her how." Well, if she had showed me how, but she told me how and I didn't know Indian language. They were talking Indian to me and they were talking English to me and I was talking Danish. And I tell you, we were in a mess there! But finally I got something out of it. The first loaf, well, I was ashamed to show it to anybody, because I threw it in the river and it sank right to the bottom. I had to learn lots of things.

We decided that we'd better go out west to Vancouver. I still remember Hastings Street to this day, because I bawled my head off. I stood there with a suitcase in one hand and Niels in the other hand, and I prayed to the Lord to give me a home somewhere. When we stood there, Krist put an ad in the newspaper. And the next morning there was a call [from a man], he had a hundred cows. Of course, we packed

Jenny and Krist Pedersen and sons

up and went out on that farm. Krist started milking the next day. Somehow we got along. They had a big garden. We were supposed to get our milk, all our vegetables, and then forty dollars a month. I didn't have to work there. So I stayed in and took care of things, but no sewing machine.

We tried to get to the United States all along. So finally, I think it was about a year and a half or so, we heard from the consulate. And then we packed our things and off we went. We took the train and came to Seattle. So we met all our family. That was getting into '29.

We moved to Ballard.* My husband went to the waterfront; they put him on right away longshoring. I was getting better with my English and I got acquainted with the four girls [where they rented an apartment]. They belonged to the Lutheran Church and right away they took me out to the Ladies [Aid]. They found out I could sew, well, then I had lots of work right there. I put a sign in the window, "Sewing done here," and I had a lot of people come. Then I found out I was going to have another baby; they are six years apart.

Nineteen forty, that's when we had moved out to the farm. Krist was on a five-month strike. We talked about it. I said, "We have to do something. Couldn't we get out a little further and have a garden?" We bought the cow as soon as we could, and, of course, the cow had a calf. Before we knew it, we were in the farming business. A few years later, we bought a lot of turkey chicks and raised those and sold them. What we couldn't sell, we cooked and invited all the neighbors around and our own family to have a picnic. Then, of course, we raised many things in the garden.

I did more sewing out here. I made good money on my sewing, but then still, it wasn't enough for what we needed to pay out for things. My husband said, "We'll be home in ten years. We'll make so much money over there. The streets are paved with gold in the United States and blah, blah, blah." Well, I didn't find no gold on the streets of Seattle. I knew beforehand I have to work for it. That was just his talk.

I got in the canning business. We planted a few peach trees and we had prune [plum] trees. I didn't know what to do with all them prunes. Fed them to the cow and the chickens and the turkeys and told people to come and pick them and they never did. So I tried to find out what we could do with the fruit we had; we had so much we couldn't use it ourselves. So someone said, "Call up the school. They want plums." The war [World War II] had come on and the mothers all work and they had to feed the kids. That's when hot lunches start in school. So then, they asked if I would pick them and take them up there. Well, I didn't drive and my husband worked all day. So I got a neighbor who

*Area of Seattle with a heavy population of Scandinavians.

was home. When we come up there, the manager of the kitchen said, "Well, I wish you would come and help us can them." I thought, well, it isn't enough I pick them and take them up there; I have to come and can them!

So before I knew it, I was in the cannery down in Kirkland* and we were canning and I was down there the rest of the summer. Besides my own canning at home, I was down there canning. The big sacks of celery and onions and everything came from somewhere, I don't know where, but they needed someone to help can. That was free; we got nothing. Well, that was all right. I was out for learning. I never mind that.

My mother always said, "You can never learn enough. You get too old to learn, then you are getting old." Then she said another thing, too, I always remember, "You learn to sew and you learn to cook because wherever you go in the world, they're gonna eat. Everybody's gonna eat and everybody's gonna wear clothes." That always stuck with me.

---

*Community to the east of Seattle, previously quite rural, now part of the metropolitan area. The Pedersens' farm was located close by.

Part Four / **New Lives: Family**

T
he vast majority of the immigrants married other Scandinavians, typically someone who spoke the same language. An
analysis of the marital patterns of seventy-two women interviewed for the oral history project who were single at the time of
immigration revealed that almost ninety percent of them married en-
dogamously, that is, within the Scandinavian ethnic group. Five of
these marriages were between different Nordic nationalities and seven
joined the first-generation immigrants with members of the second-
or third-generation; but the obvious tendency was for a Norwegian
immigrant to marry a fellow Norwegian immigrant, and so on. Even
the mixing that took place within the Scandinavian community was
linguistically compatible, as when Swede-Finn Anna Johnson married
the son of Swedish immigrants.[1]

Women were in scarce supply, especially in the rural areas of the
Pacific Northwest. No wonder, then, that the Scandinavian bachelors
were eager to make their acquaintance. When Hanna Sippala arrived in
Astoria, Oregon, the women newcomers were greeted by a reception
committee: "Boys come to see us. And I meet my husband there. He
was Finnish. It happened he had almost the same birthplace as I." A
similar story is told by Grethe Petersen about the Seattle Danes.

According to the 1910 census, Swedish and Norwegian males in
Washington state outnumbered their female counterparts by a ratio
of 187.9/100 and 177.7/100. Even though the percentage of women
in the local Scandinavian population increased steadily between 1900
and 1940, females remained in the minority. Demographic data from
Seattle illustrate the trend. In 1900, women made up less than thirty
percent of Seattle's Danish population; by 1940, this had risen to nearly
thirty-eight percent. Similar patterns can be ascertained for the other

Scandinavian nationalities in the city. In the United States as a whole, Scandinavian immigrant men outnumbered the women; however, the discrepancy was greatest in the western states. This helps explain why some men pursued long-distance courtships or had an eye out for likely mates on a return trip to Scandinavia, where the sex ratio was more favorable. Jenny Pedersen found herself attracted to a visiting Danish American who cut a rather exotic figure—"he had on American-style clothes." Gertie Hjortedal's husband undertook a fervent transatlantic correspondence and later traveled from eastern Washington to Chicago to propose. Anne Hansen encouraged her sister to emigrate and marry her bachelor brother-in-law—"Hans wanted to know if I had a sister, because he wanted to marry."

The women immigrants married at about the same point in life as they would have in the homeland. During this period, women in Sweden, Norway, and Denmark were, on average, twenty-six years of age when they married; these women immigrants were, on average, just under twenty-five. But courtship practices changed in the urban environment of the Pacific Northwest. The definition of a suitable mate was no longer intertwined with familial expectations of property ownership and social standing. The single wage earners attended social events together and made individual decisions about whom to marry. While hardly reluctant brides, the Scandinavian women had little economic incentive to marry, since they were, for the most part, earning good wages and supplied with comfortable accommodations.

Weddings in the old country were elaborate and involved large numbers of family and neighbors. Ina Silverberg and Else Goodwin (Part One) mention festivities lasting over three days. The immigrants replaced this stylized ritual with a simple ceremony, often in a parsonage parlor rather than a church, and quietly began their lives together. Sometimes friends staged a party or modest meal to celebrate the occasion.

As immigrant workers, the Scandinavian women exhibited both economic independence and a sturdy self-reliance. Therefore, they brought to the domestic sphere expectations about playing an active role. In town, there was no strict formula concerning paid employ-

Christine Emerson (second from left) and siblings (see p. 249)

ment after marriage. Some couples even arranged complementary work schedules so they could share child care. In instances where the husband fished or otherwise worked away from home, virtually sole responsibility for the household and child rearing rested with the wife. On rural homesteads, they faced daunting challenges like primitive housing, limited medical care, and isolation, as they worked to raise animals and gardens where sagebrush or virgin forests had stood not long before. The rural women delivered their babies at home, assisted by supportive neighbors. A trained nurse like Gertie Hjortedal could render valuable service to her neighbors, treating them herself when possible, "and I never charge them a penny."

Strict child-rearing practices and expectations of family loyalty carried over into the new environment. Christine Emerson says of her father, "We had to kind of toe the line. But we learned; he taught us.

And he wanted things done just right." For Christine Emerson and Hans Fredrickson, obeying parental authority meant sacrificing their own ambitions. When her mother died on their eastern Washington farm, Christine had to abandon plans for a high school education, since "it was up to me to take care of the rest of them." She speaks honestly about the pain and disappointment this caused her, though the reward was watching her siblings succeed. Olaf Sivertson had planned to return to Norway for teachers' college, but changed those plans when family members followed him to America—"then it was natural that this would be my permanent home."

The immigrant families placed special emphasis on the achievements of the younger generation. Nurturing the children's success meant that first-generation parents stressed education, encouraged entry into white-collar professions, and in some measure at least, passed on the Christian tradition from their own upbringing. Interestingly, both Anne Hansen and Gertie Hjortedal compare themselves with an unhappy sister who never felt at home in America. Satisfaction, they conclude, derives from cultivating rewarding associations with family and friends and from defining happiness in terms of domestic realities. As Anne states, "When I see my kids and they have good homes, I can say, if I didn't have anything else, I have lived to see my kids didn't have to struggle like I did."

NOTES

1. For further details on marriage and courtship, see my article "'I met him at Normanna Hall': Ethnic Cohesion and Marital Patterns among Scandinavian Immigrant Women," in *Norwegian-American Studies*, 32 (1989), 71–92, and its sources. See also Lovoll, *A Century of Urban Life: The Norwegians in Chicago before 1930* (Northfield, Minnesota, 1988).

Anne Hansen

"The women had their babies at home."

*Anne Hansen and her husband, Holger, homesteaded in
central Washington. Anne traveled with Holger to the United
States in 1908. She reared three children and saw the farm
through many improvements. The family spoke Danish in the
home, but they were not part of a Scandinavian settlement
and Anne never returned to visit the homeland.*

In Denmark my name was Schmidt, which is a German name. My
folks lived near Germany and I think they used a German name
because they could get along better. I was born in 1888, at Aastrup
near Holsted in Jylland.

We were a big family of twelve kids, six girls and six boys. My father
was a *gårdmand* [farmer]. It was a big farm, but it was raw land. There was
lyng [heather] and it wasn't improved yet. I could do anything on a farm.
I could even beat a man at hoeing weeds. There were so many of us, we
could hardly live on the place. I hired out. Sometimes I was paid by the
month and sometimes by the year. We harvested wheat and rye with a
scythe and tied the bundles. If we farmed in this country like we did
over there, we'd never make a living.

My mother had cancer. She was sick for three years and I was allowed
to stay out of school to take care of her. She suffered awfully. I wasn't fifteen years old yet when she died. The worst thing of my life was when
my mother died.

I came over here when I was twenty. The man who became my husband came home from this country and I like to go over here. He took
me over. He was from the community where I was working. My husband's name was Holger Hansen, he was four years older than me. I
must have been eighteen when we met.

Anne Hansen, 1983

Holger settled in Stratford, Washington; that's where our homestead is. He had sisters and brothers over here, several of them. His brother Hans was here in central Washington, he raised wild horses. My sister Mette came over here after I was here. Hans wanted to know if I had a sister, because he wanted to marry. They were married in Wilson Creek.

I learned English by listening to others. I could have learned to talk perfectly if I had had a chance, but I didn't. I was living out there on the homestead by myself. My husband had to go out working to make a living. We didn't make a living on the farm, because we didn't have the machinery. Holger farmed and worked in the harvest fields. In the wintertime, he used to trap coyotes and get bounty and sell the hides. My husband was a hardworking man.

The place where we homesteaded had been homesteaded before and they had given it up to the government. So we bought what was there. There was a little barn on the place. Our first house was ten by eighteen. It was a two-room house; that was the whole house. We lived in the little house at least eighteen years. I should have died long before that. I don't see how we ever did it.

We were allowed 160 acres and then we were allowed to take additional. We had a little place where we raised dry land potatoes and they were wonderful potatoes. Onions and berries and things like that in the garden. I had the best kind of garden soil; we fertilized with barnyard stuff. Otherwise it was a wheat farm. We raised wheat.

We only went to town when we had to. We had to walk, we had no transportation. After we got established so that we had our own horses, we would raise potatoes in this low land and we'd haul them to town in the fall. And then we'd buy supply like flour and sugar, a hundred pounds of sugar at a time.

All it was was sagebrush country. Sagebrush everywhere. That was the only thing we had to burn to keep warm and to cook with, the sagebrush. We'd go out in the fall and cut the brush and haul it home and stack it up in a big heap outside the house and that lasted all winter. It was dirty, but it made a heat.

We didn't have water and we didn't get it. That was our drawback; there wasn't any water. We got water from the neighbors. When I had my first baby, I carried my baby in one arm and a bucket of water in the other arm. And the woman told me, "Don't waste the water!" They didn't have too much; it was just a shallow open well. Then my husband, when he was home on Sundays, he got some barrels and hauled it in barrels, for washing.

We packed water for a long time and then we had somebody drill a well, and we didn't get enough. We finally had to buy a drilling machine to drill a well. Then we had to hire a man to run it and that's

Anne Hansen

237

when we had water. Now of course it's not like a homestead used to be. You should have seen it then and seen it now. One of my grandkids has a solar-system house.

I knew my neighbors out there better than I know my neighbors now across the street. Back there I knew them for miles. I had good neighbors. I used to bake rye bread and you should have tasted my Danish pastry. My husband just loved the dark bread. My old neighbors remember the food I used to make. I still like good food, I miss having it now.

I guess I was a tough old egg. The climate didn't bother me. We had good health. We didn't have to have doctors, even when the babies were born. I had two boys and a girl. I still have my boys, but my girl died from cancer in her early thirties. That was hard, but if it's God's will, you have to take it.

Our neighbor Ellen was having a baby and her husband asked if I could come and stay with her while he got the doctor. "Well, sure," I said, "I can stay with Ellen." We had the doctor at their home and he tried to take that baby with the forceps. I was never so scared when one of my own children was born. I thought she was going to die and I didn't think the baby would live. It was a young doctor and he said, "I have to get help. I'll have to go to Ephrata and find the doctor. Can you wrap her up and go with her in the car?" I said, "Sure I can." So we started out for Ephrata. It was in the spring, it was muddy and water puddles all the way. And we gone a ways and she said, "The baby is coming." I said, "O.K., if the baby comes, I know what to do." So I cut the cord with his pocket knife and I tore a strip off of my white underskirt.

You would think that the baby would have died from roughness like that. We were between her home and my home, and I didn't have much of a home, and so I said, "Ellen, do you want to go home or do you want to come to my house?" She said, "I want to go home." So I went with them out there and we got cleaned up and went to bed. Then in the morning it was getting daylight, here comes the doctor we were supposed to find in Ephrata. He comes to see if he [the first doctor] had hurt the baby by taking it with the forceps. But he hadn't. The baby is still living.

Most, but not all, of the women had their babies at home. When I had my own baby, the last one, I didn't have a doctor. I was all alone. My husband was out working and I had two boys—one was about eight years old, the other seven or so. We had cows. The boys would go out on their own with the cows and when they were to come home, I'd hang up something white, like a tablecloth, so they could see to come home with the cows. Well, I finally hung up the flag. The first time, my oldest boy said, "There's the flag. We're supposed to go home, but the sun is up too high, it's too early to take the cows home." So they waited a while and then it come up again. Then he said to Charlie, "It must be that we have to come home."

So they started home with the cows. The baby hadn't come. The water had broke, but I was walking in and out, on needles and pins. Then when they got the cows in the corral, I knew they couldn't close the gate, so I said to Charlie, "You stay by the gate so the cows can't come out," and I said to Hank, "You get your bike and get dad and tell him that mother is sick." I had to use my mind to know what to do. When my husband come home, he could hear the baby cry.

My oldest boy is Henry and he lives in Ephrata. He is an auto mechanic and electrician and handyman. The youngest one, Charlie, runs the farm. He raises cattle and sweet corn and everything. I remember when Charlie was a kid and we used to milk cows, he said, "Pop, why don't we let the calves do the milking? They like it, we don't." So we decided to raise beef cattle.

We spoke Danish at home. My daughter Linda could talk Danish and even read the letters that we got. But I don't hear from Denmark any more. Linda got a bang out of talking Danish to me when there were people around. The boys can understand it, but they don't talk it. They feel foolish.

I never went back to Denmark. When I would have like to have gone—when I was younger—I couldn't afford it. My sister Mette was just crazy to go back, but they couldn't afford it either. She never liked it here, like I did. I made myself like it. I could go out and make friends. I couldn't make money, but I could make friends. My sister would have given her eye teeth if she could have gone back to Denmark. We talked Danish most of the time.

I'm not ashamed to be Danish, but if they tell me I'm not American, that hurts my feelings, because I am a true American. My husband was a citizen, so I became a citizen by marrying him.

We didn't have any wedding. This is my wedding ring and I didn't get that when we were married. His folks thought I should have a ring and we didn't have money and we were going out here homesteading and start life all over. So we figured better than buying a ring, buying something we had to have. But they wanted me to have a ring—they wanted me to have one of theirs to wear for my wedding. He says, "No, if you want a ring, I'll get you a ring, but you can't have somebody else's." So we just skipped it. When we had our golden wedding anniversary, I got it.

We was always progressive. We always went ahead, regardless of how poor we was. We never went in debt unless it was absolutely necessary. And that's what I consider our luck. Nowadays they buy things on time and they never pay for them. That wasn't the way we did it. It was paid for on time; we were honest people. When I see my kids and they have good homes, I can say, if I didn't have anything else, I have lived to see my kids didn't have to struggle like I did. That poor old homestead out there, now Charlie has over two hundred new calves.

We stayed on the homestead until we were worn out. We never lived any other place. I couldn't stay out there alone, otherwise I'd still be out there and raise the garden. I compare my homesteading to climbing a big mountain, starting on the steep side. It was really steep, but we got to the top!

Olaf Sivertson

*"I started out just like the pioneers did
in the wild timbers."*

*After Olaf Sivertson had settled in Tacoma in 1902, he was
joined by the majority of his family from Norway. In 1910,
he began clearing land at Mountain View, east of Tacoma.
With his wife and seven children, Olaf contributed to the
development of the Mountain View church and community
and transformed the forest into a modern farm. Olaf Sivertson
was an ardent amateur historian and prepared histories of his
church, family, and local community.*

I was born December 15, 1884, at the place called Raftsund [Norway].
My home place was just about in the middle of the sound, where
it was the narrowest and where the tide ran really swift. We were
five children; there were three boys and two girls. I was next to the
youngest.

I finished grade school. And when I was fifteen, then I went to
Lofoten* to fish codfish. The boat looked like one of the old Viking
ships only shortened a great deal. It was an open boat and during the
wintertime it was often stormy and cold. It was always my intention
to become a teacher, so the fishing, that was to save up a little bit of
money for my education. After I came home from fishing in the spring
of 1902, I sent in my application to Tromsø to the college and got the
reply that I was accepted and was to report the first part of June.

In the meantime, there was a family and a couple of single men getting ready to leave for America, and one of the men was a cousin of
mine. He started to talk me into keeping him company to America. One

*Rich fishing banks off the Lofoten Islands in northern Norway.

reason they would like to have me along was because I could help them with the language. My father had a book of instructions in English, a hundred lessons in English, and he gave that book to me to have something to study while I was away fishing. In any case, I began to think it would be nice to take a trip to America. I could stay for five years and still I was young enough to go to school and become a teacher as I had intended. We left the 22nd of May, 1902. I was only seventeen and a half years old, but I was a grown man.

A neighbor from my home community had left for Tacoma a couple of years earlier. Of course, this neighbor that was leaving, he had been writing forth and back to this neighbor that lived in Tacoma. So Tacoma was definitely the destination. These people I went with, they had heard about the nice climate out here and how it looked like Norway and the fishery on the West Coast.

We took the immigrant train across Canada and landed in Tacoma in the evening. We were eight altogether, six adults and two little children. That was the group and we stayed together. We hired a cab and went up the hill to 25th and L Street where this neighbor of ours had a small three-room home. We came there in the evening and we bedded down on the living room floor. That took up almost all of the living room floor! The next morning we went out looking for a house to rent. We found a house and rented it and the eight of us stayed together.

After we was established in our new rented home, then we went out and looked over the town. This family we came to, they were very helpful—took us around and got us to meet friends of theirs. At that time, it really was a Norwegian colony up on the hill, around K Street and from 11th Street to 23rd, and we were right in the middle of it. There was grocery stores owned by Norwegians, a butcher shop, and things like that.

I got work at a sawmill. I was living down closer to where I was working, but every Sunday I would be up there with the rest of them [Norwegian friends on the hill]. I tried to save money. Five cents for the breakfast and ten cents for the lunch. In the evening, I would generally go to a Japanese restaurant where you could get a pretty good hot meal for ten cents. If you wanted to go to a little fancier restaurant, you paid fifteen cents. But I was going to save money for my education, so I cut corners wherever I could.

One of the only luxuries that I allowed myself—I was a great reader. There was a Scandinavian bookstore down on Pacific Avenue, really there were two Swedes that owned it. I would go down there and browse. And they had these Norwegian papers coming out, the *Skan-dinaven* and *Decorah Posten* and *Tacoma Tidende* and they had Norwegian books, paperbacks. They were twenty-five cents apiece. Generally every Saturday night I would go there and buy a Norwegian book. That was just about the only luxury I allowed myself.*

At the time, there was very little paper money. We were paid in gold and silver. One of the first things after I got my first paycheck was to buy a money belt. You would put your gold coins in the money belt and you wore it all the time next to your skin. That was my bank. During the summer and winter, these gold coins multiplied in my money belt.

There was a man running one of the planing machines—an American, Clinton Flowers, and he had a fine wife and two little girls. We talked about our personal affairs. He had built a little house and a chicken house up on McKinley Hill. But then he had to borrow money, and he paid three percent a month [interest]. Well, that was thirty-six percent a year. We come to dicker about a deal: I would let him have money to pay off that debt and I could come to live with them and that way, I would eat up the money that he borrowed from me. The result was that I stayed with that family for a year.

So I got into a very fine American family. One benefit was that they were speaking only English. I was lucky that I got away from the accent that so often hangs with the Norwegian immigrant that mostly associates with his own countrymen.

Mr. Flowers quit his job [at the sawmill] and started to work at the planing mill up on Center Street. And he got me a job at the mill up there as a tallyman and lumber grader. I had a pencil and a sheet of paper on a board and I just took tally of the lumber. So I didn't do

*Olaf Sivertson donated his library to the Scandinavian Immigrant Experience Collection at Pacific Lutheran University.

any hard work. That was one of the benefits of being connected with Mr. Flowers; he was a smart man.

Sometime later that year, during 1903, I got a letter from my sister in Norway that they were going to rent out the farm and then they were coming to Tacoma. That was my sister Inga and brother-in-law Ole and they had one little girl. They thought I was doing well in Tacoma, so they was going to join me here.

With the help of Flowers, I bought two lots and decided to build a house. That was on J Street, close to Center Street. So by the time they were ready to come here in April of 1904, I had a house ready for them. Not only did they come, but my mother and youngest sister came, too. My father was going to sell the farm, so he stayed behind, but then he took sick and died shortly after. Well, there I had my mother and sister, too, so I had to build a cabin for them. In the meantime I had built a little cabin for myself so I was living there, too. The whole family was together on Center and J.

So that changed my plans. I was going to go back to Norway and become a schoolteacher. Well, that was out the window. I was the anchorman; I was here first and I was pretty well established. And after I built the house, why then I was a property owner and a taxpayer. I had the biggest part of the family here and then it was natural that this would be my permanent home.

My mother was a practical nurse and midwife. She made a living for herself; as a matter of fact, she was quite the financier. She saved money. She was very independent. My sister started to work as a housemaid. She supported herself. I didn't have any financial responsibility for them.

When it was established that I wasn't going back to Norway, then I applied immediately for my first citizenship paper, the declaration of intention as they call it. Five years later when I came up to take the examination for my second paper to become a citizen, then it was discovered that I wasn't twenty-one when I took out my first paper. I had to be of legal age. Then I had to take a new first paper and wait to get my second paper.

In December of 1906, Helga Johnson and I were married. In the spring of 1907, I bought lots up in the west end, up on Grant Avenue and 23rd, and built a five-room house up there. And in 1907, my brother Magnus came. He and I formed a contracting firm and started to take cement contracts—sidewalks, foundations, basements, and things like that. We were contracting with cement work until 1917.

For some time, I had in mind that I would like to raise my family out in the country, where the air was clean and where there was lots of room. In 1910, I bought a piece of land about ten miles east of Tacoma on the Edgewood hill north of Puyallup and Sumner, at a place that was called Mountain View. I built a small house and moved my family out here, a boy of two and a girl only a month old. From then on this was my permanent home and I rented out the house in Tacoma.

The name Mountain View hadn't been heard of before 1908. Then they started a mutual telephone company and they needed a name. Well, they thought Sunrise would be a nice name. Then at a meeting, one was sitting there looking to the east and said, "Why not call it Mountain View? There's such a nice view of the mountain [Mount Rainier]." The name appealed to them and it became the Mountain View Telephone Company. Then the community took the name; it became the Mountain View community. Then the congregation changed the name from Puyallup Lutheran Church to Mountain View Lutheran Church. And it's been Mountain View ever since.

The land was covered with virgin timber just about like it was down in the valley when the first pioneers came in 1850. My brother-in-law and I pitched a tent and started to fall timber, saw it up into four-foot lengths, and split it into cord wood. My brother-in-law had a seven-foot crosscut saw that we used to fall the trees. The trees were mostly from three to six feet in diameter. There was one granddaddy tree that was almost eight feet across; that was the biggest on the place. After the cord wood was cleared out of the woods, I started to clear land.

It took a long time. You did pretty well if you cleared an acre of land each year. I could clear land only when I didn't work somewhere else, because I had to work out in order to make a living for my family and to pay the expenses for improvements.* First I built a two-room house. That was sufficient for me and my wife and my two little children at the time. But as the family grew, I built an addition to the house, so eventually it was a six-room house.

It was an enjoyable life out here. The family was busy; there was no idleness. Our land was just a mile north of the Mountain View church and the Norwegian settlement at Mountain View. We became a part of that settlement. They were all fine neighbors. Really it was like a big family out here.

The church was something the immigrants brought with them from the old country. There the church was a state church and everybody belonged, so it was part of the Norwegian culture. Mountain View [Lutheran] Church was a small church, eighteen by thirty [feet], at the time. It was the center of all community activities. In the fall of 1910, they organized a young people's society that met in the church. It was the social nub. As a matter of fact, the members of the young people's society, some were over fifty! We would come together twice a month and have a little program and refreshments. We organized a choir that would sing at church services, which to begin with took place once a month. We started the Sunday School in 1910. And it was all Norwegian. In 1918, we started the first English Sunday School class. Then there was one class in English and the rest were Norwegian. Well finally, in 1922, all the classes were English.

I seemed to be useful in the community. It seems like I was picked to do many different things and to serve in many different offices. It wasn't anything exactly I was looking for, but I was willing to help in any way that I possibly could. I was secretary for the church from 1912 to 1955 and Sunday School superintendent for forty-two years. I was school director for nine years. I was in the berry association, water company, and the telephone company. Name it and I was in it!

In 1922, I was appointed road foreman for the district by the county commissioner. I had been in cement work and street work and was

---

*Olaf took seasonal jobs in Alaska for several years, worked in the sawmill, and also tried his hand at berry farming.

familiar with road work. Then in 1928, I was appointed supervisor for all the roadwork in the district. In the meantime, I tore down the old barn and built a new one and I tore down the old chicken houses and started to build new and modern chicken houses. I continued to build from 1926 till the time I quit the county [1932].

Then I had chicken houses and a flock of chickens, about twenty-five hundred. I kept on to 1956. I was seventy-two years old then and I figured I had worked long enough. So I sold out the cows and the chickens, everything on the place, and retired.

We had seven children. Two of them were born in Tacoma; the rest were born right here. We spoke Norwegian at home for some time, but eventually, when the children grew up, we turned mostly to English. My oldest boy couldn't speak English when he started to school; but then after he learned to speak English at school, the next one started to school and they started to speak English among themselves. All the children had some kind of a profession. Two of them became teachers and graduated from Pacific Lutheran College. Magda, she also graduated, but she took a business course. Olive was a registered nurse.

This has been my home since 1910. I still take care of my lawn and try to keep the place neat and clean, take care of my house, do my own housekeeping. I do this by myself. My wife took sick around 1960 and never got well again. I've been happy here since, by myself.

I'm satisfied with the move I did. I've had a very interesting life and a full life. And I've had a happy family. I have no doubt that being a schoolteacher in Norway is just a shade above the average, so then that would have been all right. But I've been very satisfied here. I've been busy, probably sometimes too busy. I've been too busy to even seriously think about a trip to Norway. My brother Sigurd and his family, we corresponded regularly; the contact was very good between us. He died in the early '50s. Then, of course, his children kept up the contact.

Mountain View is a beautiful community, a good community, and a community that is unique. It used to be a very close-knit community and I would say it still is. The church started out with six Norwegian families and a minister. It has grown during the years. We are now over twelve hundred members in the congregation. I think the church is the reason for this community to be what it is—a good, peaceful community. Our Sunday School has helped to bring up good Christian people. And that reflects on the community as a whole.

When a person get old, then he looks back and remembers. I often think back. That is probably why I am so interested in early history. It brings back the time when the whole country around here was wild timberland. And then follow the first immigrants that came out here, the first homesteader down in the Puyallup Valley. I feel I'm part of it, because I started out just like the pioneers did in the wild timbers, and cleared a little spot, put down a cabin, and kept on clearing and developing, and helped to make a community. Yes, I'm part of the land, part of the history, and I feel very close to the development of this part of the country.

Christine Emerson

"Dad needed someone to stay home."

*Lacrosse, Washington, was the new home for the Slind family
from Selbu, Norway. Daughter Christine attended school
through the eighth grade, and then had to forgo high school
because she was needed at home. When she was twenty,
Christine married Joe Emerson. They had four children.*

There was eight of us altogether, six children. We all came to this
country in 1922. I was eight, my oldest brother was twelve, and
the youngest was three years old. Mother died in 1930, so then
it was up to me to take care of the rest of them. So I practically raised
another family before I got married.

I was born in Selbu, Norway, February 21, 1914. My parents, Ole
Slind and Ingeborg Klegset, were both born in Selbu. They were dairy
farmers and my dad worked in the timber. He was gone in the wintertime quite a bit. They had less than a dozen cows which they milked
and sold their cream and butter. It was pretty hard, eight of us on a
small place. Dad knew something about this country. He had been to
Minnesota 1904 till 1908, and he thought it would be easier to make
a living for all of us. We were all excited, naturally. Getting ready, we
probably weren't much help, but we were excited about it. We got new
clothes, new dresses, which we paraded around in. Before we left, it
was the Seventeenth of May celebration [Norwegian constitution day],
and we got to wear our new dresses. I can remember how all the kids
were saying, "Look at them. They're going to go to America!"

Someone had told my folks that just the oldest and youngest had to
be vaccinated before we could get on the boat. Well, we got ready and
came to get on the boat and here four of us weren't vaccinated. So they
had a special taxi come and get us, take us to the doctor, and we were

On Slind farm, Lacrosse, Washington

all vaccinated. The boat waited for us. Of course, the vaccination didn't set so good with us; I remember I was quite sick. One day, my sister and I decided we were going to tour the boat by ourselves. And we were having a good time until one of the sailors spotted us and told us we had no business down in there. He frightened us pretty bad—they were going to throw us overboard, if they caught us down there! So we didn't venture out by ourselves very much anymore.

While we lived in Norway, we didn't see apples or oranges much to speak of. On the boat they would put an apple by our plate noon or night. That was special. And there was one man that didn't eat apple, so he'd give it to my sister and I, and we would take turns. When we got off the boat in New York, a man came around and handed us a banana. It was quite expensive and dad said, no, he wasn't going to buy a banana. The man took them all back. Well, that didn't make any difference to us, because we didn't know what a banana was, if it was something to eat or what.

We came to Lacrosse, Washington, to my mother's uncle. It was June, hot and dry. And talk about dust! We'd never seen such dirt. We were living with this couple until September, then dad rented a place of our own. They were hard times, no money. It seemed like each year got better. Where we came was a Norwegian settlement. We had a lot of relatives around Lacrosse. If we had stayed with my uncle, we would have gone to a school where they knew Norwegian and English. But our place, we went to a school where there were no Norwegians, there were mostly Germans. It was a good thing, or we probably would not have learned it as fast. We seemed to get rid of our brogue. I can't re-member anyone making fun of us. I mentioned it to someone [of our former schoolmates] now, that they never made fun of us. They said, "You think we dared make fun of you? If our folks would have found that out, we would have got it." They all understood.

Dad took out citizenship papers. In those days, when the father took it, the rest of the family became citizens. He was really up on his gov-ernment. And it helped us, too, because we'd drill him on it. We'd learn it as he was learning it.

I'm pretty sure my mother was lonely. She was just forty-one years old. She was ill that summer and had surgery, and she only lived about a week. I had just finished eighth grade and I was planning to go to high school. But dad needed someone to stay home. It was hard. It was hard on everybody and it was very hard on me, because I had thought I would go on to school. The others did so. My sister became a nurse, my brother a doctor. I think about that now, if there was something else a person could do besides housework. Of course, my children try to tell me that was a profession too. Just the same, you get the urge, you wish there was something else you could have done.

It was a lot of work. We were up early and late. We had hired people and there was a lot of cooking to do. I cooked three big meals a day. I did the bread baking. Washing and ironing wasn't convenient like it is now. I had a washing machine that had a motor that you had to stomp on to get started. Sometimes you would, and sometimes you wouldn't. We did a lot of canning in the summertime. The children were all home. They went to high school and then went on to college. You did things for them while they were in college like you did when they were at home, their laundry and things.

After mother died, it was just a lot of work. You didn't feel like a young girl. You had more things in common with the older people. I always said that if something happened to me, I didn't want my husband to have my daughters stay home and take care of things. I don't believe it's fair. But times were different in those days. Dad helped as much as he could. He was a strict father. We had to kind of toe the line. But we learned; he taught us. And he wanted things done just right.

I was almost twenty-one when I got married. Joe Emerson. He was in that same community. His folks were from Norway. He went to the same church we did and then he worked for my dad some. I had just a home wedding, not a big wedding. Joe and I were in Lewiston, Idaho, for a few days. And then we came back and stayed at dad's and helped him some more till we moved to Moscow, Idaho, on the farm. Dad was capable of cooking and taking care of the place. I was there in harvest after we were married; my sister was there some of the time, too. Between the two of us, we did it. And then it wasn't too long until dad got married. He remarried the year after I was married.

We lived in Moscow for about three years and then we moved to Dayton, Washington. We rented a place. We lived there till 1970. Spent most of our years there. I had two girls in Moscow, and the boys were born in Dayton. Inez is the oldest one and she's a media technician at Pasco Community College. And then Camille, she works at Pacific Lutheran University. Vern is on the farm; he's renting the farm we were on. And then my youngest son, Lewis J., is in Spokane; he's with the school system up there.

We belonged to the Selbu Lutheran Church in Lacrosse. We lived in Dayton, but we went to the Selbu church. It was about thirty miles, but

Joe Emerson and baby

we just felt like that was our home church, so we kept going there. That was the pattern and you did it. We had to get the youngsters there for confirmation. It's just like now, you have obligations, and you do them.

Dad saw that the future over here was better. And it was. It has been good to us. I did something that was necessary. It's all been well paid for. My brothers and sister, they've all amounted to something.

Hans Fredrickson

"You're gonna go to school if I can help it."

Hans Fredrickson, born 1909, was raised on a farm in
Småland, Sweden. He settled in Washington in 1929 and
held many short-term jobs during and after the Depression.
He married a woman of Swedish descent in 1934; they had
four children, all of whom attended college. Hans kept close
ties with his nine siblings, both those who stayed in Sweden
and those who came to Tacoma.

ig family, six boys and four girls; there are five of us here [U.S.]
and five over there [Sweden] yet. Besides, two girls died in
whooping cough. The later years when mother was in the rest
home, the nurses asked her how many kids she'd had. And she said
she'd had six and a half dozen. The nurses thought, "No, she's all mixed
up." But after they got to thinking, she had six and one half dozen—
that makes twelve. Ja, she was pretty bright.

Dad was up north building railroads when he was young, before he
was married. But after that, he took the farm and stayed all the time.
The farm wasn't big, but there was work for all of us even so. We had
five times as much woods as we had cultivated land and that was the
backbone of it really, selling timber. Dad was a tough one—you had to
work. We were broken in, all of us the same way.

When the kids were coming on smaller, I had to take care of the little
ones. I liked kids; I still do. I helped my mother in the house if she
wasn't feeling well, so I learned cooking at quite a young age. When I
got a little older, my dad said, "You can have *et öre* [a penny] to milk a
cow, if you learn to milk them." And my God, that was big money for
us; we weren't used to no money. We were plugging away and milking
all we could, and pretty soon he said, "Well, now you know how to

Hans Fredrickson and family in Sweden

milk, you don't have to get any paid anymore." And that was the order of the day after that. Morning and night, holidays and Sundays, you had to be there and milk, no matter what. We grew lots of potatoes. In the fall, my dad said, "Stay home from school and pick potatoes." I would much rather go to school, but I had to take orders from my dad. If I didn't do what he said, boy, that would have been the end of it. It was kind of a rough life, but now, looking back on it, I appreciate it. I'm happier with [being] raised that way instead of just running around with your own will.

I had six years of school. I was quick in the head for anything arithmetic—it was amazing. The last year we got a new teacher. Boy, he was a dandy. He had me in after school to instruct me, especially in arithmetic. He said, "Hans, you are not gonna quit school and just go work with your arms and your back. That don't bring you anything. You

Hans Fredrickson and traveling companions

should go to school." Well, we didn't have the money. My dad didn't have too much to spare, you understand, with ten kids to feed. I regret that I couldn't have gone to school. My God, I would have loved it.

Here now, we got four kids. And I told them, "Boy, you're gonna go to school if I can help it." And they are all bright. They all went to university. Matter of fact, one is a doctor in nuclear physics.

When you are young, you want to get out and see the world and I was tired of all the Sundays and holidays milking the cows. I was the oldest one left and I had to do all of it. My oldest brother was in Chicago and the one next to me was in Tacoma. My sister was here in Tacoma. And my uncle was here, too, and cousins which I had never seen.

I came over to Chicago in 1928. Right quick, I got a job where my brother was working, concrete work. In August of 1929, the depression started to move in there; we could see it. So we were thinking that we had a brother and sister [in Tacoma] and uncle and cousins we'd never seen. We heard it was nice, warm winters, so we decided to get away from that cold in Chicago. When that wind came off Lake Michigan, it was just like daggers through your head. You could hardly stand it!

We had an old '24 Buick, touring. We drove out to Tacoma and came to the place the uncle lived, down on South 19th and M. I went to the door and knocked and his wife came out and said, "Oh, my God, is it Hans?" She knew me because I looked so much like my brother Sven that was boarding with them. I was so surprised when she said "Hans"; she'd never seen me, I'd never seen her.

I met my wife Elsie up at the Swedish Order of the Valhalla; they had dances there every Saturday night and I liked to dance. I didn't have much to eat, but she would invite me to dinners, especially on Sundays, and that filled me up—held me over to the next Sunday. Her parents were from Sweden. We had a wedding at her house in Puyallup, December 29, 1934. That must have been about three years [after we met]. She was after me; she wanted to get married before we were twenty-five. Well, I wanted to get married, too. There were maybe a dozen people for the wedding, some neighbors there and my sister and my brother.

We rented a big, new beautiful apartment. Thirty dollars a month for the rent. Right then, I wasn't working. We'd come in from [lumber] camp and there was no work. I was the cook, dishwasher, and bed-maker. She was working. She was a stenographer. Well, I worked some after that, out in South Prairie, and the guys I worked for asked me how much I paid for rent. "Are you crazy? Thirty dollars a month for rent!" They never heard of a thing like that. Anyway, we stayed there one month; that was our honeymoon. Then we moved to an apartment in J Street. Four rooms—front room, kitchen, and two bedrooms, for fifteen dollars. So that was quite a difference.

I got it in my head to take a trip to Sweden. She was working, too, so we saved up and went to Sweden in 1936. Wonderful! We were there all summer. Dad and mother were both in good health. That was the reason I wanted to go there. That was a beautiful summer; we liked it.

I built houses in my spare time. I was a crazy working fool! We bought this place, there was just a little house. Then I added on, first the kitchen, then the back bedroom, then the upstairs. Then I dug out the basement all by hand; it was mostly hardpan. At night I'd come home, I'd get in there with a pick and pick. It was just [like] concrete most of it, it was so hard. But I dug it all out by hand, wheeled it out by hand.

I almost went nuts because we didn't have any kids. I love kids. Nineteen forty-two, before we had any children. Four kids and they're all nice. They're all wonderful. The oldest is an engineer at Boeing. He's married and has two boys. The second one, he is not married. He is a doctor in nuclear physics at the University of Washington. The third one is a librarian in California. She's a beauty; she's not married either. And the younger guy, you know what he took up? Anthropology. As a subject, it's useless. He had long hair, whiskers all over. His mother was so disgusted. Everytime he came home, she asked him, "When are you going to cut the hair and the whiskers?" Then later on, he got married and he was a changed man after that. He bought a five-acre place and they have two rentals. Now they have a baby, the cutest little boy. He's a chunky, heavy guy—happy! Oh, I love him. I babysit with him.

We used to go to the Lutheran Church over by Wright Park. That's where all the kids went to Sunday School. After that, I haven't gone to church, maybe to julotta—an early service on Christmas morning—the same as we used to in Sweden. We are here Christmas Eve every year, all the kids. Just like home, big meal in the evening and then presents. We have the Christmas tree in the corner like we used to at home. Now it's getting outrageous, so full of packages and presents so you won't believe it.

My brother, the next older brother to me, plays accordian. He used to play when he was smaller. I started much later, took lessons from my cousin. We played lot of dances and parties, sometimes just the two of us, sometimes a piano player with us, some[times] a whole orchestra. All the kids play piano. The oldest boy, he's really good. They all took lessons on the accordian after they broke in on the piano.

We chipped in and had my mother come over here after my dad died, to take her off the grief. We wanted her to fly over. No, sir, she wouldn't think of flying. She took the boat. Then my oldest sister here and her husband went to New York and met her because she couldn't speak a word of English, of course. Later on, Boeing was showing a new plane and I had her along. When she saw that plane, she said, oh boy, next time she was going to fly!

Nineteen thirty-six was the first time we were back in Sweden. I've been there four times. My brother had the [family] farm when we were home last. Now he has it rented out. I have three sisters and two brothers, they live within an area of seven miles. Then I got lots of cousins.

Nineteen fifty-nine, I bought a Volvo in Göteborg and then drove home right across Sweden; we were there with all the four kids. They knew we were coming and there was a big reunion. Nineteen seventy-four, did the same thing. One brother came and met us in Göteborg in his car. We were both driving. He was poking around, and so I said, "What's the matter? Aren't you going to drive so we can get home?" No, he said, because the brother on the farm didn't want us to get there until seven o'clock so he would be through with milking the cows.

Of course, then there was a big reunion. We had a big supper and he served drinks, brännvin. And then he asked me, "How do you tycke om Sverige?" How do you like Sweden? I said, "It's pretty nice, but it's långt mellan suparna." That means, it's far between the drinks. Boy, he jumped up and brought more to drink. I'll never forget that; that was comical!

Anna Johnson

"There is nobody that can take a mother's place."

*Anna was born in Finland in 1899. She lost both parents
and emigrated at the age of thirteen to live with an uncle in
Minnesota. In 1920, she moved to Everett, Washington, where
she married Frank Johnson. Anna and Frank had three children;
their work schedules were arranged so the children were not left
without parental care. The Johnsons relocated to Tacoma in 1945.*

We had a three-bedroom house in Esse, Finland, close to Jakobstad. It was very pleasant. My mother was a very religious person. She done lots of singing and we all had to learn how to sing. She also taught Sunday School in the house. In Finland, in wintertime, you could not travel very far because it was too cold, and so it was better for children to come to the house and have Sunday School there. In Finland, you had to have more than one job in order to make your living. Father was a tailor by trade, but he also was the school superintendent and teacher in school. He played the organ and was a deacon in the church. After dad died, mother done practical nursing to make a living.

We were five children. I am the only one left from the family. My sister Marie died in 1973. The others died when they were children. My mother drowned when I was nine years and nine months old. She was going to buy some yeast from a bakery across the river and it had snowed during the night. Somebody had chopped a hole in the ice— when they were rinsing their clothes, they would chop a hole and rinse the clothes in the river—evidently she stepped into that and couldn't get out. All we could see was the marks of her fingers around the hole, that she tried to get out and couldn't. I was taken over to my uncle's place to live.

My uncle's son had a new-born baby and I had to look over that. So very little schooling I got. We all learned how to read and write, learned our catechism by heart, some of the Bible history. [But] mostly you learned how to work and that was it. Then my father's cousin came in 1913 from America, and she asked me if I wanted to come to America and I said, "Anything, just to get away from here." I didn't even know how far it was or anything. My uncle Emil in Bemidji, Minnesota, paid my way and it was ninety-two dollars on the boat.

So I went to America. I left my sister behind. I was thirteen; she was sixteen, going on seventeen. In Finland, it would have been very hard for me, because if you work for a farmer, lots of them expected the ladies to do the plowing, the harvesting, and everything. I don't think I would have been living if I had to live in Finland. I wouldn't have had so good opportunity as I had here.

We passed so many beautiful places and then to come to this little house in Bemidji! They were renting a house at that time and just living in, I think it was, four rooms. We had beds even in the living room and I was not used to that. Later on, we moved to uncle's house that he had been having remodeled, but that was not very large either. It was two-story, but he rented the upstairs. He was a millwright, and in 1913 all the men made in the sawmill was $1.75 a day. So it was not very much to feed a family and, of course, I was additional burden. My uncle and aunt had five children at that time and my auntie was not very well and that's why I helped to take care of the children and to do the washing and so on. In those days, you didn't see a washing machine, you had to scrub the clothes on a board. The same with the living condition, it was just plain food.

I was with my uncle off and on till 1915; then I went to work for a lady that was running a boardinghouse. I was waiting on the table and washing the dishes and help with the cooking and peeling the potatoes and so on. And, of course, we had to clean the rooms for the boarders and change the beds and everything. I think it was $2.50 a week, but then some weeks I didn't get anything. Some weeks she would maybe sew me a dress, which I needed, so she took that out of the wages. Then when the war broke out, why she quit with the boardinghouse because food got so high. So then I went to work in a restaurant in Bemidji and I was there until 1920.

God had plans for me. I went to Canada to visit Aunt Hanna, that is what I called her, that brought me to this country, and I stayed there for not quite a month. And then I took the train and come to Everett [Washington]. It was God's plan. After I got to Everett, I stayed with my father's cousin, Selma Johnson.

I got married. My husband Frank Johnson had been into the service in World War I. Then he come to Seattle and hired out on a boat to go fishing to Alaska. I know him before—just slightly acquainted, that's all; he sang in a church choir in Bemidji, Minnesota. He had his good suit stored over to Selma Johnson's place and he come over there to get his suit. He was of Swedish parents. It must have been about a year and a half, maybe not that long [before they married]. We just went to Pastor Peterson and got married in the parsonage. We had our witnesses and that was it. We didn't have a honeymoon.

He was working in the sawmill; he didn't follow his fishing trade after that. I worked some after I got married. The Depression came in 1929 and lots of the mills went down, so I worked in a restaurant. I always did restaurant work. As long as you are good and honest and keep your nose to the grindstone, why you are O.K. We got a union in, so we had $3.00 or $3.30 a day. I think it was good with Cooks and Waitresses Union, because you get to talk to each other and make friends.

And when Frank got a job, the children were in school, and so I kept on working. My work was sometimes from five o'clock in the afternoon and then sometimes it was from ten until five. So I was always home when the children were home. I didn't want to go and leave my children, because the mother will never know what the child is doing while she is going to work. A child around twelve, thirteen years old needs to have a home life; it's not good for them not to have the parents around home. There is nobody that can take a mother's place.

We have three children. The oldest one, he was in the Second World War, his name is Rudy Johnson. He's pastor of Our Savior's Lutheran Church, Seaside, Oregon; they have four children. Clifford Johnson, he's a graduate of Pacific Lutheran University. He took up accounting and he's an accountant for a firm in Portland, Oregon. He has three children. Then Roger, he bought our share at Puget Sound Plywood and he's working over there. He has three children.

I am called either one—Finnish or Swedish; it doesn't make any difference. Swedish is the language I speak. My children didn't learn the Swedish language. I tried to teach them the Swedish and my husband kind of make fun of it, because it was not so modern then for a person to teach the Swedish to children. Now it's more modern that they learn more than one language.

The Finnish were the only country that paid their debt to America and I think that I can look up to Finland and be proud of it.* I have contact still. I hear from my brother-in-law; I have cousins living over there and lots of friends. My husband and me went back to Finland first time in 1954. The second time was 1967, then again in 1969, and then 1975.

You don't see the hard times in Finland now like the first time I went over there. Then I did not want to stay with my sister more than maybe two weeks, because it was hard to buy things. I went to the grocery store and I wanted to get some meat for Sunday; the lady she says, "How much do you want?" I says, "I take the whole piece." She says, "No, you can't have the whole piece; there are other people that have to eat, too." It was just like a small pot roast and I had to just take what she figured she would sell me. Now they have the meat.

*After the Second World War, Finland had to pay massive reparations to the Soviet Union. The obligation was met through great sacrifice and determination and with the short-term aid of loans from Sweden and the United States.

Gertie Hjortedal

*"I saw the little, beautiful girl
and I was happy and satisfied."*

Gertie Hjortedal was a trained nurse of thirty-one when she
came to America to visit her sisters. She married a Norwegian
who was employed by the railroad. Gertie and Osten lived
in rural eastern Washington for several years. After their
daughter and son were born, the family moved into Spokane;
there Gertie held various nursing jobs until she retired at the
age of seventy.

I was born at Storebø, Huftarøy, Norway, September 24, 1894. My
parents had a farm. They had a lot of land that wasn't developed,
timberland, and we had up to ten milking cow. We had forty-five
sheep, three pigs, forty or fifty chicken. We girls was the one that had
to take care of it, because daddy was busy down in his shop. He was a
boat builder and so was my grandfather.

Daddy want so bad a boy and the boy never came. He didn't like us
girls. We were eleven girls and I'm the ninth. He was so mad because
he didn't get a boy. Like we could help it. Ignorant, that's all. We heard
it daily; he should have a boy. When we were big enough to do any
work, we wasn't spared. It was hard to work out on the farm and we
didn't have the latest equipment like we have now. No, we have to cart
the water home. Washing clothes, we have to walk, carry water home,
warm it, and wash the clothes. We have to carry water to the cow, to
the pig, chicken. My mother made and sell quite a bit of butter. And
we made some cheese.

Every Sunday I remember my daddy was reading in Johann Arndt and it must be a mile long. Long, long sermons.* The kids was out play-ing and we couldn't go because we had to wait till he was finished with reading that Johann Arndt. And when he say amen, out we go and play like the rest of the kids.

I was fifteen years old and I asked my daddy if I could get enough money to take the business college, and he turned me down because I happened to be a girl. If I had been a boy, I could have got anything I wanted. But my mother give me money and I went to Bergen. I got a house job and I worked for six month before I could get enough money to go to business college and pay the tuition. When I went to college, I work till about four p.m.; and from four to eight p.m., I went to the college. And when I come home, there was a big, big shelf of dirty dishes for me to wash and I washed those dishes and I wasn't through with my work before it was ten or eleven o'clock at night. And I was so tired that I didn't have time to study much. I took business college in a half year and I'm sorry to say I didn't get good mark. I made it, but that was all.

I work in several grocery store. I work in Bergen. I work in Odda. I went in the nurses' training in 1921. And I finish my nurses' training in '24 with good marks. I had no trouble to study. I love it. I took the courses at Ullevål hospital in Oslo. They was very particular who they took in, but they took me in. We had to work twelve hours a day. I liked to help people, so that was my idea—to be God's little messenger girl. And I was. Many time I took care of the patient, they told me, "God must have sent you," and I say, "I know He did."

When I was just finished, I could get the night supervisor job in Oslo, Rikshospitalet. That was a very good honor, but I turn it down because there was night duty and I accept a job in Haugesund [west coast of Norway] and I didn't know we have the night duty there. I had been there a month—back to night duty and I hate that. So one day I had

*A German pastor and the author of numerous religious books, Johann Arndt lived from 1555 to 1621. His theology was influenced by medieval mysticism and he in turn influenced the Pietistic movement.

night duty and here come in a fellow from America. He was a friend of my sister's husband. I had already asked for my passport and I told him, "I'm coming to America." And after he find that out, he just write and write every week and I don't know how often.

Four of them [sisters] left and went to America. Oh, they were bragging, it was so wonderful over America. Daddy paid money for them to go, but he didn't pay for me because I wouldn't accept no money. I was too proud to take money when I was turned down so badly [for school tuition]. I made my own way. I was thirty-one years old. I had enough money to come home, when I had seen my people, but this fellow I met in Haugesund, he come clear to Chicago and asked if I would marry him and I say yes.

So he went back to his job and I was working in Cook County Hospital for two years. And there we get married in Chicago in a big church and we had a wedding dinner in a mission home right across from the church. We had many guests and we get lots of beautiful sterling.

So we went from Chicago. And when we went by Spokane, I say to my husband, "In this city I want to live and want to die, right here." But we went clear out to little godforsaken country they call Marlin. There was a new house—four room, no running water, no electricity. And I got so discouraged, I think I cry the whole day. And I sent application to Deaconess Hospital in Spokane, if they could make use of a registered nurse. They said, "Not right now, but maybe later." Then I get pregnant and then I was stuck.

One day, we went visiting somebody and they had a chicken with eight little baby chicks. So I say to my husband, "I like to buy that." And I got so attached to that little baby chicks, they come and eat out of my hands. And the baby chicks grew; I didn't lose a single one of them. One day, I was going into the chicken coop and feed my chicken, there was a great big rattlesnake. It stood with its head, it was just going to grab one of my chicken and I close the door and went and get a big stick. I open the door and I hammer and hammer on that head till it fell off. And my husband came home and I say, "I have killed a snake." He says, "No, you wouldn't have nerve." "Come and see," I say. So he come and see. And you know the chicken ate the meat of that snake and he had nine rattle!

I went to Glasgow, Montana, two weeks before I expect the baby. That was pretty risky, but I did. Two weeks later on, a beautiful little baby was born and she was baptized in Glasgow, Montana. My sister was a nurse and I expect her to take care of me and she sure did. I have a doctor that came and he was going to give me some medicine. And I say, "Forget it! My mother had eleven and I can stand one." I didn't took no medicine. I saw the little, beautiful girl and I was happy and satisfied. After two weeks I went home to Marlin. And we was there till Gladys was a year and three months.

Then we went to Edwall. My husband made sixty-five dollars a month. On that sixty-five dollars, we give to God's kingdom—that's the first time we started to tithe—and the six-fifty was awful hard for us to give to God's kingdom, but we did; we trust God will take care of us. We had money enough to buy a cow. We bought some chicken and with the big garden, you'd be surprised how much we had. And lots of hobo come around and ask for something to eat. I always give them something. And I give a tract in each packet I give.

One day a hobo come round and he say, he was hungry. And I say to my husband, in Norwegian, "Poor fellow, *han ser så elendig ut; vi må be ham inn* [he looks so miserable, we have to invite him in]. And he understand Norwegian and before we had said one word to him, he came in and say, "*Takk, takk, mange takk*" [many thanks]. I got so surprised and I gave him a big chunk of headcheese, two bottles of milk, and a loaf of bread and butter. He clean it up all. He was hollow inside. And he thank us so long he see us. I never forget that. And one day daddy [her husband] was working someplace, and they come twenty-seven hobo and I have just made, I don't know how many loaf of bread, quite a few, and I was scared, too, I had those little kids. And I gave the last bread I had. So next day I made some more.

Every neighbor round there come to me [for nursing] and I never charge them a penny. I remember one woman, she had got the insect way in her ear and it was singing and I put a drop of alcohol, killed the insect, and took it out. I never saw her since but she thanked me for it. There was lots of people come round and I help them. If it was something bad—one had infection in the side and he want me to fix it—I say, "No, that's out of my line. You go into the hospital." So I know what I could do and what I couldn't.

We was there for two years. Then our little son was born. And daddy was going over to call the doctor to come and help me. He come back and say, "I just can't wake up that man." We didn't have telephone, and I say, "For God sake go and get the neighbor woman." When the neighbor woman came, the baby was there. [Our] little girl, she was twenty-three months old and she say, "Mama, see baby." Then the neighbor come; she was just shaking like that. And I say, "You take it easy and do exactly what I tell you. Everything will go fine." And I told her to hold the baby on his leg and give him a spanking, so you could see the life. She did and he holler. "That's fine," I say, "You clean him up and when he is clean, you come and take care of me." That was one o'clock at night. About three o'clock I was cleaned up, the baby was in his crib, and the woman was laying right beside me, and everything went just perfect.

Spokane looked so very much like Bergen. We have been here fifty years.[*] And here I will live and here I will die. So this is my home.

Our son Erling was seven years old when the neighbor boy put a stone in a snowball and hit his eardrum. At that time I had a nursing home; I had about eight patient in a large, beautiful place, and we had a doctor and the doctor say he's getting better. And I say, "Doctor, you is a liar." I took his temperature; he had 103 and he say, "Momma, I can't stand it, I have such a pain." The doctor say, "If you not satisfied, why don't you call a specialist?" I did, and he told me, in one more hour, you wouldn't have no boy. So I got somebody to took care of the patients and I went to Deaconess Hospital and he was operated on and I thought I was brave enough to stay in when the operation was on and I fainted. They had to carry me out. Everything turn out O.K. I give up

[*]Gertie Hjortedal was interviewed at the Riverview Terrace retirement home in Spokane in 1984.

my patients, sell the house, and took care of my son. He is still alive, thank God. It was a whole year before it healed up. He is the Director of Finance for Spokane Falls Community College in Spokane.

Gladys lives in Denver, Colorado. She went to St. Olaf College; she was a registered nurse. Then she got acquainted with this Hans Jansen and after a couple years, he come over here and they got married in Our Savior Lutheran Church. He is a lawyer. He was born in Minnesota and he can talk Norwegian.

I was private duty nurse for seventeen years. I took care of one Mr. Myklebust and I guess he thought I was O.K. and he asked me, "Would you be interested to be a head nurse when Riverview Terrace [retirement home] will be ready to be occupied?" I say, "I am getting pretty old now so I don't know if I should or not." And he said, "Please put your application in." So I did, I was accepted and I work here till I was seventy. Then my husband say, "That's enough. You are not going to work anymore," because he had to take me to work and back; I couldn't drive.

I find out since I was married to an American citizen, I did not need to take my own citizen papers. But I did. I went to school three months and I learned a lot. The judge told me, "You have such a terrible name, you have to at least change the first name. Change it from Gjertine to Gertie." So after I got my citizen paper, my name is Gertie Hjortedal. Everybody say, Gjertine is so much nicer name.

My sister Anna that was a nurse in Glasgow, Montana, she say, "I'm so sorry I came to America." She was head nurse in Trondheim in a hospital there, and the sisters that were just a few years older than she had talked her into coming to America. She told me, "I have never felt home in America." She had no children. I got children and she didn't. I think that was the difference. I wouldn't have felt at home either, if I hadn't had children. I have two lovely children. They love us dear and we love them.

Part Five / **New Lives: Tradition**

Although they were sometimes reluctant to pass the language and traditional family names on to their children, the immigrants did acknowledge and uphold the Scandinavian heritage in a variety of ways. In the home, they prepared special foods and celebrated holidays in traditional fashion. In public, they socialized and nurtured aspects of the cultural history like music and folk arts. They united to found clubs and churches, to erect buildings, and to mark important events; in so doing, they fostered impressive ethnic communities.

Many of the Scandinavian organizations that flourished in the Pacific Northwest, indeed throughout the United States, were geared toward a specific segment of the ethnic population. The temperance cause engaged some immigrant energies; both women like Marie Berglund and men like Julius Tollefson appreciated the alcohol-free atmosphere and civic engagement of the Norwegian Good Templars. There were singing and dramatic societies, some of them gender-specific, others like the Danish performing society Harmonien in Seattle open to both men and women. Among the Norwegian immigrants in particular, groups formed to perpetuate ties to a specific rural valley or district in the homeland, the *bydgelag*. Most important among the secular organizations were the broadly-based lodges—the Swedish Order of Vasa, the Finnish Brotherhood, and their counterparts. In the days before federal legislation mandated financial safety nets for workers (Social Security, Workman's Compensation), these lodges acted as mutual aid societies, making sickness and funeral payments available as key membership benefits. In addition, they sponsored an active calendar of social events and involved many people in the life of the organization, as the interview with Signe Steel suggests. The scope of these national organizations was impressive. At its peak in 1930, the Vasa Order had over 72,000 members spread across 438 local lodges.[1]

The oral testimony reveals that fellowship with other Scandinavians provided a welcome antidote to the initial loneliness and awkwardness of immigrant life. Most couples met either through friends and relatives or through the churches or one of the secular Scandinavian organizations and so, as discussed above, a pattern of endogamous marriage prevailed. Interestingly, the women who emigrated as children were less likely than those who emigrated as adults to marry within the ethnic group. While ready exceptions are available, the generalization appears to hold that the younger the emigrant, the weaker the ethnic tie.

The early church congregations maintained a strong ethnic identity. Choirs, ladies' aids, young people's societies, and lending libraries were typical features of well-established congregations. Although Lutheranism held a favored position within the immigrant population, the lively theological debates within the various Lutheran synods and the attraction of other denominations like the Baptists and the Methodists made for a complex religious picture. The more pious saw the church as the organizing principle for all social and charitable activity, and certainly the institutions that grew out of a church affiliation, among them Pacific Lutheran University (founded 1890), constitute a significant legacy of Scandinavian-American values and energies. Yet it must be pointed out that the Pacific Northwest was, and remains, a less churched region than the Midwest. For various reasons, including occupational and settlement patterns, fewer Scandinavians joined a Lutheran church out west.[2]

The Scandinavian-language press played an important role in maintaining links with Scandinavia and stimulating ties with other Scandinavians in North America. Reading reports and advice in the ethnic press also helped the immigrants grow accustomed to American ways of life. The competition for readers was fierce among the various foreign-language publications and, over time, with the American newspapers. An indication of the precarious nature of the ethnic press in America is provided by the statistic, quoted by Sture Lindmark,

Emmy Berg with folk dance group, formed in Seattle, 1918 (see p. 180)

that 3,444 foreign-language newspapers were started between 1884 and 1920 and that 3,186 folded during the same forty-year period. Most Scandinavian-American publications appeared weekly and were targeted to a local audience; for example, only a dozen of the estimated 1,500 Swedish-American publications could be called national in scope.[3] Scandinavians in the Pacific Northwest subscribed to such well-known newspapers as the Swedish-language *Svenska-Amerikanaren* (Chicago), Norwegian-language *Decorah Posten* (Decorah, Iowa), and Danish-language *Den Danske Pioneer* (Omaha, Nebraska); in addition, they benefited from several newspapers published in Tacoma and Seattle.

Arnfinn Bruflot, who edited *Western Viking* in the 1930s, argues in his interview that the Scandinavian-language press no longer has a useful role to play. Only a handful of newspapers remain, among them *Western Viking*, and the once flourishing book-publishing industry has long since disappeared. With his Norwegian-language poetry and prose, Bruflot continues the tradition of literature written by immigrants about the immigrant experience, albeit he has chosen to publish his work in Norway for the Norwegian reading public, since the Scandinavian languages have virtually disappeared from use in present-day Scandinavian-American communities.

At the Magnusson home in Ballard, Iceland's linguistic and literary traditions were preserved for many years in the form of a community library. Jon's mother lived with Gudrun and Jon and "there was Icelandic spoken a lot in our home." In later years, the children lost the ability to speak Icelandic, although "they understand quite a bit." Frederik Madsen enjoyed singing in his native Danish, and Hilma Salvon was encouraged to use Finnish in church and at home. In contrast, Astrid Lovestrand (Part Two) was reluctant to give her children Swedish names, fearing that they would be laughed at. For the same reason, she also promised her husband that she would not teach the children to speak Swedish.

In daily life, but especially at holidays, the immigrants cultivated Nordic traditions. Food customs, and to a lesser extent handicrafts, were important aspects of the domestic heritage. Gudrun Magnusson shares information about typical Icelandic dishes, and Hilma Salvon emphasizes the importance of rye bread as a Finnish staple. If at no other time, traditional Scandinavian foods were a mandatory feature of the Christmas celebration in Scandinavian-American homes.

It should be remembered that, as white northern Europeans, these first-generation Scandinavians blended rather easily into the mainstream of American culture, even as they nurtured strong ethnic ties. A dilution of linguistic and cultural identity occurred, starting with the second generation. An upsurge of Scandinavian ethnic enthusiasm during the 1970s, shared with other ethnic groups, underscored the need to transmit to the younger generations the legacies of Scandinavian and Scandinavian-American culture.

In defining their ethnic identity, the oral history narrators suggest specific values and characteristics that make them proud to claim a connection with the Scandinavian countries. Frederik Madsen speaks warmly about the influence of the Danish folk high schools, for example. For him, the folk high school songs and other cultural activities provide a means of reflecting on the meaning of life and of establishing one's priorities. The values so transmitted stress responsibility to the commonweal and this, Madsen believes, translates into good citizenship. Further, he contrasts the Danish farmers' commitment to agricultural cooperatives with the self-centered approach of American farmers. Other individuals emphasize the work ethic, honesty, Christian charity, and self-reliance as typical Scandinavian traits. Ethnic pride, not chauvinism, is the point. As Signe Steel puts it, "I admire all cultures, not just Swedish." Nor need ethnic pride dilute loyalty to the adopted homeland. Like Frederik Madsen, many would claim that the cultivation of one's Scandinavian roots makes one "a better American."

The immigrants' twin loyalties—to their upbringing and to their new country—are captured in these lines from Arnfinn Bruflot's poem: "They came to America in order to be one nation. And they took with them the hymn book, the Bible, and the [home] valley." Or, as he phrases it when speaking directly about his own life: "This new country has given me a lot. I might have had some small influence on making this a better country, too." Reflecting on her new life in the new land, Elsie Odmark gives voice to the familiar divided heart: "I don't suppose I would want to be anything but a Swede. But I also very much love America."

NOTES

1. The Vasa Order is discussed in some detail by Sture Lindmark, *Swedish America, 1914–1932* (Uppsala, Sweden, 1971), 304–312.

2. Lovoll in *The Promise of America* (Minneapolis, 1984), 163, notes that in 1906 only fifteen percent of all Norwegians in Washington were members of a Lutheran congregation.

3. Lindmark, *Swedish America*, 221–223.

Jon and Gudrun Magnusson

"*We had the Iceland library in our home.*

Jon Magnusson brought his mother along when he emigrated
from Iceland in 1913. After three years in Canada, they relocated to Seattle, where Jon earned his living as a carpenter.
He married the daughter of Icelandic immigrants to Canada,
Gudrun Lindal, in 1921. Jon and Gudrun played a leading
role in local ethnic organizations and at home maintained the
Icelandic language and food customs. The first-person voice
here is that of Gudrun. She supplied details that Jon himself
could not remember at the age of ninety-six, when this interview took place.

When Jon first came to America, he was eight months old
[1887]. He came with his parents. His father died after a
night in New York, sunstroke. His mother was shipped back
to Iceland as an undesirable emigrant, [because of] the very young children. She worked for farmers and was allowed to keep Jon with her.
So he did all kinds of chores for his keep, too. But then, when Jon was
sixteen, he moved to Reykjavik to learn the carpenter trade. And his
mother joined him there and kept house for him.

Jon came to Winnipeg, Canada, in 1913 with his mother. He was
twenty-six years old. In Winnipeg, he rented a couple of rooms with
my auntie. I was a boarder there; I was just in Winnipeg for three
months for vacation, because I was teaching school out in Saskatchewan. We got acquainted because we were in the same house, but we
didn't go out together at all. But we were impressed with each other's
characters; we could see what we were like, our lifestyles. But then
I went back to teach in Saskatchewan and Jon kept on working and
staying with my auntie. He knew all about my people in Winnipeg.

Jon and Gudrun Magnusson

Then Jon left Winnipeg and came to Seattle in 1916. He brought his mother and they settled in Ballard. In 1920, my sister Kristin, who was already in Seattle, was very sick and they called me. So I got a substitute teacher and came out and never even thought about Jon being here. But the next morning he came to see me. That was the beginning of our acquaintance.

I stayed two weeks to take care of Kristin, until she was well enough. Jon took me to see the city, but nothing developed there except hospitality. But then, after I came back to Canada, he wrote me a serious letter, wanted to start a correspondence, a serious correspondence. So we corresponded for a whole year. And that was the courtship.

We were married in Winnipeg and all my relatives were there. We were married at my brother's place, a large house. We took the train that night to Vancouver, B.C., where we stopped for four days for our honeymoon. Then we came to Ballard to his little home and his mother. We lived in Ballard for the rest of our sixty years. His mother passed on in 1939. She was with us for eighteen years.

I was born in 1891 and my parents had been in Canada for four years then. They came from Hunavatnssysla in Merkeferd; that was in west Iceland. They came to Winnipeg first. One son was born there, so that was the fifth child. Then they moved to the country in Saskatchewan and I was born there in 1891. Altogether in our family there was twelve children. My father was very ambitious to get along. He was impatient with the hardships of pioneer farming; he wanted education and was interested in world affairs.

We all learned to read Icelandic and write. And of course, when I married him—such an Icelander—and his mother could never talk English, so while she lived, there was Icelandic spoken a lot in our home. We have three children. The older two, that was while grandma was still living, they learned Icelandic real well. But then when they went to school and had English-speaking friends, they quit talking Icelandic. They don't talk any now, but they understand quite a bit.

We had the Iceland library in our home for thirty-eight years—two hundred volumes, most all of the books were Icelandic. The club was called Icelandic Literary Society, Vestri. It was founded in 1900 and in 1965 it disbanded; we could not keep the books any longer. We sold our house and had built a smaller one. We had no room any longer and nobody offered to take it over. But the books were not thrown away; they were given to the University of Washington library and also the main [city] library, and then lots of people bought them. So, many of these books are still in the community. But now the situation is such that our descendants, our children and our children's children, don't read Icelandic well enough. And the new ones that come from Iceland are not many enough to keep a library. They have so much other things to read; they can read some Icelandic, but they want to read English literature, too.

There was all kind of Icelandic activity. They formed a kind of Icelandic congregation; they bought a church right in Ballard. Both of us were very active in all that activity with the Icelanders and the social life [with the] Norwegians and the rest of the Scandinavians.

We make skyr. It's served as a pudding and it's made from buttermilk. That's warmed and then strained and strained until it's the consistency that we want for pudding. Little bit of cream and little bit of sugar, and then you serve it in a little bowl with cream and sugar as the party wants. That's very popular. Of course, we're fond of fish, and that's cooked any way that the Americans do. They mostly boil it. And then the hard fish. That wasn't really considered as food, but a delicacy. Hard fish is cod, dried cod, dried so you have to beat it to be able to chew it. It has a strong taste. And hangikjöt, that's smoked mutton. They smoke the leg and the ribs and the neck; in fact, any of it is smoked. You serve it cold and slice it and it's very tasty.

The brown bread is a special bread. Whole wheat or partly, whatever you want, but there has to be brown wheat in it. And molasses; that's what makes it taste. You can steam it and that tastes very good or you can bake it. I used to make them both, lots of brown bread. Pönnukökur is another delicacy. They make real thin pancakes and you roll them with sugar. Sugar is all we ever put in, but some of the Icelanders put jelly, too, or jam and berries. We had to make them thin. I have a special skillet for that.

Vinarterta, of course, was the chief coffeecake. That was sort of a cookie dough and it was baked in cake tins so it came out as layers. Then you put it with prune jam. You cooked the prunes real well, then stoned them and then put whatever flavor you wanted—lemon was one essential—and you boiled it again until it was thick. Then you see, the cakes, whether they are square or round, they're placed one on top of the other and the jam put in between. This is left to soften; it's hard to cut at first. But if you've kept it for a day or so, it cuts up better. We'd have at least five layers, [often] seven or eight. It looks nice. We cut it in layers and serve, with whipped cream is our favorite. The girls now don't do as much baking. They're keeping the recipes in case they do.

I'd like to tell you something about the Christmas in the early immigrant days in Saskatchewan, Canada. Christmas was very wonderful to us children when we were on the farm; there were so many of us. When I was a little girl, my oldest brother started in November to make the candles. We had to use tallow for wax, because we couldn't get any wax in the grocery stores. They made the wax candle holder by breaking off the neck of a large whiskey bottle. They used that for the candle holders and the tallow was hardened and then we could have our own candle. Every child got a candle and we could walk around with them. And I always remember the thrill, the wonderful thrill, that I felt when I was walking around with a candle that was all my own.

Six o'clock Christmas Eve, everybody had to quit working. Christmas has come. We didn't eat till about eight o'clock, but we always had something special—smoked mutton, the thin pancakes, brown bread, vinarterta. We were allowed to stay up till twelve o'clock, or as long as we could stay awake. We enjoyed what we got. One time, I got a little doll with a china head that was fastened on the body. Christmas Day was just another good day. The real Christmas was Christmas Eve.

Julius Tollefson

"It was just like getting a letter from home."

Born in 1890, Julius Tollefson grew up near Rognan, Norway,
just north of the Arctic Circle. He apprenticed himself to a
blacksmith and in 1907 traveled to America on a ticket supplied by his brother. While Julius worked in the lumber mills
of Tacoma, he developed lively connections with the local
ethnic community. He made seven return visits to Norway.

I always felt attached to Tacoma, because I got acquainted with so
many Norwegians here. I arrived the 19th of May, 1907. I was on
the train and I was thinking about getting here for the Seventeenth
of May [Norwegian Constitution Day] and I didn't make it.

There was nobody to meet me and I was at the hotel for two days.
I walked through town and I walked J Street all the way through till I
got to 17th and J, and I saw a church there that looked almost exactly
like the church we had in Norway. All right, so I was curious to see
what it was. And I walked across the street and here is a sign, all in
Norwegian: *Vår Frelsers Evangeliske Lutherske Kirke*; it means, Our Savior's
Evangelical Lutheran Church. So Sunday, I went to church there. That
was my favorite church. I've served in all capacity in that church and
our children was baptized and confirmed there. The church was built
in 1903 and it was there till somewheres in the 1960s.

It's quite a history with the first organization here in Tacoma. In 1889,
a Norwegian missionary got a young people's club organized [as] an
athletic club and that was the first functioning of the Norwegian young
people, you may say. And he started a Ladies Aid society and a singing
society. In 1893, we had the Cleveland depression, President Cleveland's depression. Then this athletic club changed their name to the
Norwegian Commercial Club, to give an impression on the city coun-

cil and the county, for job purposes. Every nation were trying to get a job through the county or the city because industry was shut down, there was no other jobs, and so the Norwegians weren't going to let the Germans and the Swedes and the other nationalities get ahead of them. The Norwegians were dependable and good workers. They went on under that name until 1898 and then they changed the name to the Ancient Order of Vikings.

The Sons of Norway was organized here in Tacoma, 1904. And then the Norwegian Good Templars were organized about 1906. In 1908, I joined the Good Templars. The Good Templars were working against the liquor, because we had a saloon nearly on every corner downtown at that time and they had the red-light district down on A Street, between 15th and 13th. Then the Sons of Norway got quite active and a fellow from Bodø that was typesetter got me to join the Sons of Norway in 1909. Then I belonged to the two groups.

All right. Then they started Nordlandslaget here in March, 1912, and I was with the founders of that organization. We were about twelve, I think, to begin with. Nordlandslaget was to carry on the tradition that we grew up under in Nordland [northern Norway]. Norway is quite a long country; it's far between the south and north and we had certain memories that we really loved from our childhood. We had with us the history of our forefathers and we felt that northern Norway had been neglected.*

I dropped the Good Templars, since I had the Nordlandslaget and the Sons of Norway. One thing I don't think should exist in our organizations—the Sons of Norway are the only organization that have come to a tendency of using liquor at their socials, and that's something I have never approved of. In fact, it was part of the downfall of the Ancient Order of Vikings; they ended in 1955. I'm still a member of Sons of Norway. I'm the longest continuous member in the whole United States.

---

*This association of immigrants with ties to a particular geographical area in Norway was typical for the movement known as the bygdelag. See the major study by Lovoll, A Folk Epic: The Bydgelag in America (Boston, 1975).

We met at the Fraternity Hall on Tacoma Avenue. We were down at the Swiss Hall, or over at the Danish Hall. We were sort of chased round, because we had no solid place. In 1912, we started to discuss the question of building a center for all our Norwegian activities here in Tacoma. Without having a meeting center for Norwegian organizations, we'd eventually disintegrate. In 1914, we got to the point where we decided to sell stock in the building and have a regular Board of Trustees. We got permission from the state to sell stock, ten dollars a share. We did buy four lots on 15th and K Street for a building site. We had bazaars and other activities to raise money. In 1922, we had sold twenty-five thousand dollars worth of stock and started to build Normanna Hall.

All right, it was quite a financial set-up. We almost had the roof on the building and we were out of money. We were building it with the labor of the organization instead of letting it on a contract, because one of the fellows says, "If a contractor can built it for twenty-five thousand dollars, we can, too." It didn't happen, because there was much delay and it's more costly to build in the winter. All right, we had to borrow three thousand dollars to finish it up so we could move in. Here we had a mortgage on our hand and we had financial troubles. We finally decided it was a poor way of financing it, by socials. So we issued five-dollar bonds, instead of stocks, and we raised enough money to pay off our mortgage. Then we were on our own.

It was just the members in the various organizations financing the hall. There were two Good Templar lodges, the Ancient Order of Vikings, the Sons of Norway, and the Daughters of Norway. They were represented through a directors' corporation. In 1927, I was elected on the board.

We had our regular meetings, one meeting a week for each organization, so it kept the hall quite occupied. Then we had the socials and bazaars. The Seventeenth of May we had speakers and we had a program; we had decorations and refreshments. We had as many as fifteen hundred people in that hall and charged them an admission. I wouldn't say that it was entirely the organization that was interesting all the people—it was from a social standpoint. Various socials drew the people together and they'd join from time to time. They'd meet people from their own communities from Norway. It's important because, you take for instance me now, I was here and someone would come from the place where I came from and they knew the families and they knew the situation from year to year. It was just like getting a letter from home.

It was very little English to begin with. But during World War I, it was a cycle of patriotism for United States and the various ethnic groups felt that they didn't want to be set aside. They want to be with the patriotic atmosphere of the country, so they gradually [switched to English]. When I have been in Norway, they have been so surprised how well I have kept up my Norwegian language. Of course, I've taken a pride in it. I use it whenever it's possible.

The greatest solidarity that the Norwegians have ever shown was the Seventeenth of May, 1914. That was the centennial of the signing of the Norwegian Constitution. They claim there was ten thousand Norwegians here in Tacoma at that time. We gathered on 11th and A Street at the Tacoma Hotel and we marched all the way up to Wright Park. We had flags, decorations, and colors of all kinds. All these people walked up to Wright Park. Fawcett was the mayor and he was to congratulate us on the day, and I'll never forget the first thing he said as he got up there on that platform: "You know, I've met a lot of Norwegians in this town; there's some good ones and some bad ones." That was the beginning of his speech. Well, true as it was, usually a public speaker wouldn't start out that way!

I've been active. Except for Nordlandslaget, I've never held any office, except as a trustee. I'd be a good deal out of town and I'd just as soon serve on the committees. I wouldn't be tied down. I could speak more from the floor than I could from the chair! I served fifteen years on the Board of Trustees at Normanna Hall and I know all their functionings and the corporation. It was originally incorporated for fifty years and the fifty years was over and we had an amendment made to the corporation papers to extend indefinitely.

The question that has come up is that we don't have any young people coming in. Our average age in Nordlandslaget is getting to be above the sixties. So you can see what we are up against. At the present time the Sons of Norway is working for scholarships a good deal, and Nordlandslaget is, too. We formed the Leif Erikson Committee principally for scholarship. They do want to keep up the Norwegian culture and art and so on.

We immigrants came here and started from nothing. We were considered illiterate because we didn't know the language. We were dumbbells, just starting with the rough work. All right. Our children, it reflected upon them, this immigration tradition and they never took up the Norwegian culture and the Norwegian language, because they were heritage of the "dumb" immigrants. Now the third generation, they are waking up to the fact that they got a heritage that's unique. The history of the past generations is very interesting and worthwhile. I'm glad to be part of it.

Signe Steel

"Everybody were your friends."

Signe Steel nurtured a lively connection with the Swedish community in Seattle, even though she was only four when she arrived in America in 1906. Her husband Jack was also a Swedish immigrant. After their marriage in 1923, Signe stayed at home and cared for two younger brothers who lived with them. Later, she took employment in an upholstery shop, cutting and sewing.

I was only four when I came to this country. Dad had been foreman in this sawmill and he was laid off. His sister and family lived here on Fir Island near Mt. Vernon [Washington], so they borrowed some money and came to America too. We arrived in 1906. My uncle met us in Mt. Vernon. They were farmers and he was wearing overalls. Mother felt insulted. She had never seen anything like that meeting a train! We laughed about it later.

Dad got a job at the Cedarhome mill. They bought five acres in Cedarhome and we had cows and chickens and pigs. We all started in the first grade when we were seven years old. There was no problem whatever going to school. Mother read all the time, even the American papers. Then she also took the Swedish papers, one from Minneapolis and one from Chicago. When I was in the first grade, as soon as I had learned our alphabet there, I kept reading the Swedish paper and picking up the words. I can read and write Swedish as easy as I do English.

Mother developed a goiter and died in 1917. Dad had died four years before; he was killed in a horse runaway. I was a month less than fifteen when mother died, so from then on, I was mother and father. Two brothers and one sister younger than me—Elsa, then Fred, and Harry, the baby, was five years old. So I was in the barn milking cows and I

Signe Steel (upper right) and siblings

sewed and baked; no running water and no electric lights. When I got married in 1923, the two boys came to live with us. I loved them as my own, my mother's children.

Christmas time, mother always had my cousins from Arlington. And when there was a single young man [who] had no family, my dad and my uncle would bring him home for holidays to our place. Sometimes, if they were too many, they would go sleep in the barn. We always had the branches of fir out by our porch, because that's a Swedish custom. Of course we always baked Swedish coffee bread with cardamom and all the cookies. We had to have all that at Christmas. They stayed overnight. Morning, they all would walk over to the church for *julotta* [Swedish Christmas worship]. I'm the only one stayed home and saw about breakfast. Christmas Day then, we all were invited over to my auntie.

I left Cedarhome in 1920. That made me eighteen. My cousin here in town [Seattle] was doing housework. Fifty dollars a month was good pay. So I talked it over with my uncle and my sister and they thought it was O.K. Every month I sent home twenty-five to thirty dollars, so that was a good thing. Of course, I had to wear a black dress and a white apron. I had to eat in the kitchen and they sounded the buzzer when I was coming in to serve. But I had no problem at all; they were my friends. I thought I had it so easy, because I had running water and electric light and bathroom.

When I came to town, I got busy with everything. I joined the Order of Vasa, Klippan, soon as I came, because I had friends [there].* I became active immediately. The week after I joined, I was chaplain and on the coffee committee. Of course they were all young people I thoroughly enjoyed. You knew everybody and everybody were your friends. We had plays and dances and all kinds of things that we were doing. I was captain of the drill team and I was recording secretary. I was on committees constantly. That was the main organization here then. They were organized to retain the Swedish culture and sick benefit. I've belonged there now for sixty-two years. Now young people aren't willing to join to partake in committee work and all that. There are just a few people that go to the meetings.

I met my husband Jack Steel through other friends, because he was not active in Vasa. He was nineteen when he came to this country, so he grew up in Sweden, learned his trade there. I guess he was interested, so he joined the Klippan, Order of Vasa. Later, he joined the Harmony Singing society, too; we had a singing society that had pro-

---

*Each lodge had its own special name, in this case *Klippan*, which means "the rock." The Order of Vasa was founded in 1897 on the east coast and developed into a national organization for Swedish Americans. The Seattle lodge was formed in 1912.

Signe and John Steel

grams and dances every Sunday. Many of the same people I knew from Vasa belonged there.

We were married on February 10, 1923. A friend of mine wanted to give me a big wedding at Order of Vasa. But I said no, I didn't want that. They would all feel they had to come with gifts and everything. So we just went to Reverend Friborg's house, he was at the Swedish Baptist Church.* But they had a big shower for us first and a great big party for us afterwards at this summer home.

*Pastor Emil Friborg served the Central Baptist Church.

Everyone knew Reverend Friborg, because he was active in the culture society and they often had him speak at Klippan and things like that. The Swedish Foundation was organized by Reverend Friborg. Years ago, there was the Swedish Sanitarium in Denver and all Swedish organizations and churches would contribute to it. Then, when t.b. was almost eradicated, they sold the building and sent a fund to each city that had been helping, to set up a foundation. We are only about twenty-five people that belong. They invest the money and the interest that's earned, donate every penny to charity. We meet only once a year. We allow ourselves a dinner and then we make our report of how we spent the money.

I got on the Welfare Committee eight-nine years ago. We are given one thousand dollars a year to work with and we give direct to the people that are hard up. Before, when I was driving my car, I would drive over to their home and see them. But now I have them meet me at the store, so I can get food and shoes [for them]. And it's like I always say in my report, I have respected every one that I have met. There's always illness or something that has caused the problem. For the foundation, I keep every single receipt and thank-you note and hand that over then when we have our meeting.

Once a month, I went to the nursing home. I would make some coffee bread and a cookie and I would get a program. Many of those in the nursing homes are on welfare. When I found out they need clothes, I get clothes for them. My friends know about it, so they give me good, clean clothes. And then if there are things I can't use there [nursing home], I take it to the Clothes Closet, where they give families in need.

I worked up on Broadway in an upholstery shop and there was a Swedish man rented a room from the boss. He was a wino. But I could tell that he comes from a fine home, because even if he's drunk, he's such a gentleman. Well, he had a stroke, so I told the boss, someone should notify his people in Sweden. If you can find an address, I can write to them in Swedish. So I wrote to his brother then and kept them posted. I kept visiting him for three years in a nursing home and looking after him till he died. He wanted to go home so bad, and they wanted him to come home so he could be in a nursing home near them. I talk to the Swedish consul to see if we couldn't get him going. And there was a trip arranged; one was gonna look after him, because he'd be in a wheelchair. But he had another stroke and died.

They [this man's relatives] kept telling me that they wanted me to look them up, if I ever came to Sweden. Well, 1971, I got cheap fare through the Swedish Club and I did notify them. They couldn't do enough. We had planned to stay overnight; we couldn't get away for five days. They were such lovely people; we became very good friends.

I feel everyone should retain their own culture. I admire all cultures, not just Swedish. I don't believe the one is better than another. I think there is good and bad in everybody. I know some Swedish I don't care for a bit and others that I think are just wonderful. And the same thing with every nationality. Wonderful Oriental people and wonderful Black people, beside all the others. We're all here in this country, so we all actually come from somewhere. All should be treated as equals; I believe in that. And then, it's a joy to learn things from each other.

Frederik Madsen

"Because I am a Dane and have gone to folk schools,
I think I am a better American."

Frederik Madsen spent the first eight years of his life in the
United States. He returned in 1922, at the age of seventeen.
As a young man, he worked on the family farm in upstate
New York, where they attempted to establish a dairy co-
operative. In the 1930s, he took up gold mining in Nevada.
Later, he moved his family to Washington and began a heavy
equipment business. He was greatly influenced by the Danish
folk high school movement.

I was born in 1904 in Brainerd, Minnesota. My father was kind of modern. He had his own dairy and he was the first one in Brainerd to use bottles for milk. Otherwise, they used to come around with milking cans and dip it out into your container. I don't know the year my father came to America, but I think it was something like 1890. He met my mother in Canada. My mother came over as a young girl, just about fourteen years old, because it was hard times in Denmark and there was a relation in Canada that would take her, so there would be one less mouth to feed.

In 1912, my father sold his dairy business. I guess he had made enough money. His intention was to go to Denmark and buy a little farm and spend the rest of his life in Denmark. My youngest brother was born earlier the year we went to Denmark. We were six children, two girls and four boys. Father bought a little farm north of Vejle. This was good ground; it was farm country and beautiful country. The land used to be part of an estate and it was a fellow that had been in America that had built the buildings. We had a big woods close by.

When I started talking, my parents taught me Danish to start with. But when I went to school, they had us start talking English. We spoke

English [at home] in order for us to get used to it. By the time I went to Denmark I had forgotten Danish—couldn't speak Danish or read or anything. But right close, there was a little private school where the teacher could speak English. So father made arrangements so we could go to school there for the first three months and then we transferred to the regular school.

My mother never did like it in Denmark; she yearned to get back to America. My father and mother finally decided that they were gonna get back to America. But they didn't know how times were. So my father and I, we went over first in 1922, because we could both get jobs. I was confirmed then and I had worked for farmers two winters.

I feel very fortunate that I got to work for people that had been on Danish folk schools. The Danish folk school is a school that mostly farm youths could go to. There is no grades, no degrees at all; you don't graduate from anything. It's a school for life, a school that you learn to live. Now, the people I worked for, a custom they learned in the schools was to sing. We sang a song every morning before breakfast. And in the evening we also sang. Then after the singing, the man we worked for, the owner, would read out loud from some of the choice books in Danish.*

It was a good life; I could see that it was a good life. And I wanted to stay in Denmark so I could go to a folk school, because I wanted to be like them. But I couldn't do that. My father wouldn't let me stay over there, because if I stayed half year longer, I would have to register for the draft. And he didn't want me to do that, because we were American citizens. We were born in the United States.

My father and I came over on the Scandinavian-American line in

---

*Known as folkehøjskoler, the folk high schools are a legacy from N. F. S. Grundtvig, a nineteenth-century Danish poet and clergyman who advocated adult education as a way of promoting citizen democracy. The first folk high school was established in 1844. Serving principally rural populations, these residential schools offer short courses and are geared, as Madsen notes, toward learning for "life," rather than learning a vocation. Such schools have been established in the other Scandinavian countries and, as described below, Danish immigrants also brought the concept with them to North America.

1922. My uncle met us in Chicago. I got a job right away because there was a Scandinavian-American employment agency and people knew that the Danes were good workers, so Danes never had any trouble getting jobs. I could speak enough English to get along, but I had forgotten an awful lot. I bought an American book, *The Call of the Wild* by Jack London, and I read that and that's all it took.

It [America] was altogether different and I longed for Denmark to start with. But people seemed so interested in what I could tell about Europe, so that kind of made up for it. I got along real good. I know I was a good worker.

My father worked a year at a dairy and then sent for my mother and the rest of the kids. Mother had a sister whose husband had bought a farm in New York; and they talked my father into coming there, because there were quite a few Danes that were getting together and it was a good place. They bought a farm there and it was a good life. I wanted to be with my parents and the rest of the kids, so I went to New York. I got a job at the creamery and I worked for the highway department.

In Denmark, there was much smaller farms, but every bit of soil was utilized; it was all intensely farmed. In America, things tend to be much bigger all the way around, and farming was not so much of a science as it is in Denmark. One of the cradles of farm cooperatives was in Denmark; they bloomed in Denmark. In a cooperative, people join together and control the means of production and the means of selling. It doesn't have to go through a lot of middlemen. A cooperative creamery, the farmers own that creamery. Other companies, they just pay so much for your milk and they don't care whether you make it or not. But the cooperative does; the cooperative is part of life. Farmers in Denmark, nearly all of them were members of the cooperatives.*

In upstate New York, in Delaware county, we tried a dairy cooperative. It was dairy farm country. There were three creameries—a cooperative creamery and two other creameries, and the tactics of the

---

*The Cooperative Movement took hold in Denmark in the 1880s, especially but not exclusively among the dairy farmers. By 1913 the country had almost 1,200 cooperative dairies.

big creameries were to pay a little bit more to the farmer for his milk and get them away from the coop. After the coop had to give up because too many farmers left, then they lowered the price of the milk. The members of the cooperative tried to keep it together and keep people from falling for the few cents more they got for their milk; but, of course, American farmers, they are not very good cooperators. If someone offers then ten cents more a can of milk, why they'll take it!

Then I heard about the Danish folk schools over here, the Danish-American folk schools. So my brother and I and another Danish boy from that area, we spent a winter in Nebraska at that folk school.[*] That was a wonderful experience. Before I went, I was awfully bashful and I was scared of girls. I got over that completely there. It was a Danish community and all the people living around there invited us out. They had folk dancing and gym. We did a lot of singing. Everybody lived right on the school and there was both Danish and American lectures. It brought me up on my education, my American reading and speaking. They were all pretty much young unmarried people. School just lasted three months.

The next winter I wanted to go to the folk school in Minnesota. My father said he wanted all four boys to go. So us four boys from New York state went to Tyler, Minnesota. After this folk school in Minnesota, three of us went to California. We had heard so much about California; it was something we wanted to try. That was during the Depression and work was scarce. We went to a Danish town in California by the name of Solvang. There was a Danish folk school in that town and that was the core of the town; a Danish church, too. I figure that's the best years of my life, being a young fellow in that town, because we had so much folk dancing and had so much fun.[†]

I met my wife there. That's close to Santa Barbara and a lot of farm girls from the Midwest came to Santa Barbara and worked as maids and

---

[*]The folk high school in Nysted, Nebraska, was founded in 1887 and functioned until 1936. Coeducational courses were offered starting in 1911.

[†]Danebod was the name of the folk high school near Tyler, Minnesota. It opened in 1888 and in 1923 forty students were enrolled. The Solvang school, Atterdag College, was also attended by Laura Foss (see Part Two).

cooks. They would come up to Solvang for the monthly young people's society meeting. There was always something good at the meeting like lectures. After the meeting, we had the folk dancing. My brother and I and another guy played for the folk dancing. I played accordion, my brother played violin, and the other fellow played piano. I just bought an accordion and learned it by myself. Once in a while, us young fellows from Solvang were invited down to Santa Barbara, because the girls got together and put on something.

I was interested in machinery and I got a job on highway construction and I got to run a bulldozer! The job ended. There was a Danish couple that used to live in Nevada; his brother was going to start gold mining and he needed some help. This couple talked me into going along up to Nevada. I got started mining. He sold that ground to me, so I had my own gold mine in Nevada, up in the sticks, seventeen miles from town, no water. I bought myself a small bulldozer and had a scraper behind it. I made real good on cleaning bedrock, much better than if I had worked for wages. I went to Solvang during the winters. This was in 1934, '35, '36, '37.

In 1938, Esther and I went to Viborg, South Dakota, to get married. It was a Danish town. Nearly everybody in Viborg were Danish. All the friends of the family were invited to the wedding and my parents came from New York too. We went on a honeymoon, drove down to New York, around through the southern states, and back up to Nevada. When we got up to Nevada, I had ordered a bed from Sears Roebuck, but it hadn't come yet. I had a tent and a cot I had been sleeping on, but we didn't have any bed. So we piled up a whole bunch of sagebrush and made a mattress of sagebrush, and there we slept for two or three nights.

She was pretty brave to go up, because we didn't have a house to live in and we had to haul all the water. We lived in the tent that summer, slept outside. It was just wonderful sleeping outside up in Nevada, because the air is dry and nights are beautiful. You are up so high; you can see twice as many stars as you can at sea level.

In 1972, we were back in Denmark. That was fifty years after I came over. That was a wonderful trip. We were in Denmark three, four weeks and every day was a banquet. You can't go to Denmark without gaining weight; it's just impossible. They sure know how to put on a festivity. Every place we went, they would have a big dinner in their homes and have friends and other relatives along too. We went to a wedding and I got up to make a little speech in Danish. But I spoke dialect. And they had not heard that dialect for many years!

The Danish people are a happy people.* It's a small country, but I think they are much more mature in what the world should be like. It all goes back to what the Danes learned in the folk schools. The folk schools have changed the outlook of the Danes, even though it's a small proportion of the Danes that attended a folk school.

There has been four Danish-American Folk Schools; I have attended three.† There are no more. In Tyler, Minnesota, they don't have folk school anymore, but they have the building and they have doings there. Every fall, they have a Danish folk meeting there that is pretty much like a week at a folk school—singing and listen to lectures and folk dancing and learn to live the good life. We learn to realize what is worthwhile in life and what isn't, to make life rich. It's only for four days and it's a long ways to go for that, but I wouldn't miss it for anything. It's really important to me because I'm together with people that think pretty much as I do. They're all people of Danish descent. Once in a while, there is somebody that has married a Dane that's gotten so Danish they come. We don't speak it so much, but some of the lectures are in Danish. Most of the singing is in Danish.

The singing part of my Danish heritage means an awful lot to me. We have a book, songbook for the Danish folk in America. It has transla-

---

*In everyday speech, "happy Danes" is the expression used about the segment of the population that has been influenced, directly or indirectly, by the Grundtvigian movement within the church and the folk high schools, in contrast to the pious "Church Danes."

†In fact, there were five folk high schools in the United States and one in Canada. See Enok Mortensen, *Schools for Life: A Danish-American Experiment in Adult Education* (Solvang, California, 1977).

tions from Danish. A favorite song is #290, one of Grundtvig's songs. It's basically on playing an active life in this world. You sing about every part of life in this songbook; that's real important to me.*

To be aware is also important to me. I have learned to be aware of the whole world, not just to be selfish about the country we happen to belong to, but also to see that there is things wrong in the world that should be righted, and work in a small way towards that. I have been active lately in the peace initiatives, for a nuclear freeze. I attend all the groups that work for peace. If I was a good speaker, I would do a lot more.

I have been active in a church. I have usually been on the church council. I think being active in church work comes partly from being a participant in the folk school, because the folk schools were part of the religion, too; they were church connected. Also, it [folk school] made me interested in the community that I lived in. We were some of the forerunners in getting a community club started. I also served as water commissioner for many years, and fire commissioner, too.

I have had a real satisfactory life. I am happy that I have been able to contribute a little bit to the world and have a good insight in what needs to be done. Because I am a Dane and have gone to folk schools, I think I am a better American.

*The hymn referred to here begins: "Et jaevnt og muntert virksomt Liv paa Jord . . ."

Hilma Salvon

"All my life, I've been eating rye bread."

Hilma Salvon was born in Finland in 1895. She emigrated
with her family in 1906 and settled in Astoria, Oregon.
Confirmed in Finnish and married to a Finn, Hilma retained
her language and food customs. The Salvons enjoyed a very
positive return visit to Finland.

We never had a farm; we never had a cow. We didn't even
own our home ever, because my father, he did logging.
It was a combination Swedish and Finnish logging outfit;
father had charge of the working crew. They were logging way up in
Lapland. The logs were floated along Ounasjoki, past Rovaniemi, and
then to Kemijoki. It's a big river, Kemijoki, and they would float it to
Kemi, where the Swedish took their share of the logs and the Finns
took their share. Father was foreman ten years for this outfit.

Rovaniemi is the last city when you go to the Arctic Circle. The family
stayed in a little village ten kilometers from Rovaniemi. We rented a cot-
tage there, mother and us children. It was made of logs. It was painted
red and it was trimmed in white. It was a very nice and cozy house.

Finland was under Russian rule then.* Russia demanded soldiers
from Finland and they were protesting against it, the whole Finland.
They were going around with these lists, everybody to sign. There was
a general strike. Everything was in confusion and everything was standing still. Father and many Finns, if they could, just flew to America. He
wrote to his cousin here in Astoria that he'd like to come to America

*The 1890s saw the beginning of a particularly strident era in the relationship be-
tween Finland and its neighbor to the east, as the tsar's policy of Russification was
implemented.

and he sent a ticket. And when somebody sends a ticket from America
—well, you go. My father came in 1905. We were left in Finland, because mother was expecting. Then that baby was born in January and
then we left in 1906. There was four of us [children]: Matt and me and
Kate and then the nine-month boy, Tanna.

There were many boardinghouses in Astoria because many single
men came here. Father was eating in a boardinghouse and he had a
room with this family near the boardinghouse. That part of Astoria is
Finnish town, Uniontown.* We stayed this short time with this family
and then we rented a house next to it. It had two bedrooms, a living
room, a dining room, and a kitchen—five rooms. I went to school right
away. A neighbor there had five girls. The oldest girl, she is yet living,
said she would take me to school because I didn't know how to speak
English. We've been friends for seventy-five years.

Evangelical Church was right near the house we rented. I went to
summer school there. It was in Finnish, the ministers were Finnish,
and mother thought it was good that I wouldn't forget Finn. I went
to that and so did my husband. We were both confirmed from this
church. The first ministers had to come from Finland. But then, when
years went on, Suomi College in Michigan started to train ministers.†
They are not training them anyplace anymore. The last Finnish ministers and the Finnish immigration people, that old generation, passed
on, and the young generation, they have intermarried with different
religions, different churches, and different nationalities, and there was
no patronage. The language is going, too. It's many years ago that the
last Finnish minister was here. The same thing happened in Swedish
church. The attendance was low, so they consolidated. Peace Lutheran
is a consolidation of the remnants of Swedes and Finns.‡

---

*Uniontown on the west end of town was named for the Union Cannery, an early
Finnish business. It was home to Astoria's Finnish community and housed all the
necessary business and cultural institutions.
†Suomi College, a Lutheran college founded in 1896, is located in Hancock, Michi-
gan, in an area of heavy Finnish settlement.
‡The Finnish Evangelical Lutheran Church, founded in 1883 and part of the Suomi

There was all kinds of Finnish newspapers published at that time. I used to read those Finnish newspapers and my folks used to read Finnish books. And if it was kind of easy to read, well, I used to read Finnish books [too]. There was many Finnish people in Astoria. Some of the business places required that you speak Finnish, because there was so many of the old generation that couldn't speak English.*

My husband Jalver came from Finland. He came before I did, 1902. I didn't meet him in school. When I got through the eighth grade, I got a job at a department store; it had just about everything in it. He and the lady that raised him lived nearby and he came to shop there and I got to know him. And I used to eat my lunch at the Finnish boardinghouse and he was eating there, too, sometimes. We were married 1917. We stayed here ever since.

We visited Finland and we stayed four months, from May until September. We studied Finland, my husband and I. We traveled all over and we learned many things. We didn't stay too much with relatives—the summer is short and they are so busy; we stayed in travelers' inns. We were treated very well and it was very interesting. We found out about the social security, about the medicare system, about their farming, about their school system. And it seems that there are valuable things that might work here too. The lunches are free in Finland for all school children, furnished by the government. In the summertime the school children are taken to camps for vacations and like that. We learned so much about Finland. Believe me or not, Finland's flag was put out in five places for us!

I am proud of my Finnish heritage because I like Finland's culture and the Finnish population. There is no illiteracy; they all know how to read. The Finnish people living in a poor country like that, they are

---

Synod with direct links to the Lutheran church in Finland, later changed its name and affiliated with the Lutheran Church in America. In 1974, it merged with another congregation to form Peace Evangelical Lutheran Church.

*Astoria boasted the largest Finnish community west of the Mississippi. The 1905 census showed a foreign-born Finnish population of 2,000 out of a total population of 11,000.

very resourceful people. When we visited there, whatever they do, they do it so well and everything is so clean and orderly.

I like Finnish cooking. All my life, I've been eating rye bread. I have never eaten white bread. We liked the rye bread, the way it was made in Finland, and mother used to make it here. Then us girls used to make it. But now I don't have to bake it. This Finnish baker that came from Finland, he taught the baker here in Astoria to make real solid rye; I get it from him. And now the health stores are starting to make the sour rye. And it's just like the sour rye mother made.

Arnfinn Bruflot

"I have my language from Norway, and my tradition."

Arnfinn Bruflot has published poems and a novel about the
immigrant experience. He was born in western Norway in
1904 and arrived in Tacoma, Washington, in 1928. During
the 1930s, he worked for a local Norwegian-language newspaper. Otherwise, he earned his living as a laborer in the
lumber industry and a painting contractor. In 1948, he
married a second-generation Norwegian woman and they
had one son. Arnfinn's literary endeavors blossomed during
retirement.

It was only the oldest that could have the farm. Because I was the
youngest, I had to figure out something else. After the First World
War was very good times. So everybody thought, well, get yourself an education and then you've got it made. But it didn't turn out
that way. By the middle '20s there already had gotten to be a surplus
of teachers and almost any occupation you could think of. I had borrowed a lot of money [for education] and I had to do something to pay
back the bank. So the only way I could take care of my responsibility
and meet my obligations, why I had to emigrate.

I graduated in 1927. The next year I emigrated. There were lots of
people from my home community right here in Tacoma. I thought
Tacoma was very nice, and very different from what it is now. You had a
good feeling when you went out and talked to people, went to lodges,
Normanna Hall. If you were [out] late at the meeting up at the Sons of
Norway, you were safe. You could go out any time, day or night, and
people were very friendly and very helpful. They talk to you any place
you meet them. I mixed with everybody, all kinds of people—different
nationalities, the Americans, so to speak. It was marvelous.

Bruflot family farm in Norway

The *Western Viking* was printed right here in Tacoma, up on K Street. The Norwegian newspapers had hard times because the immigrants got Americanized and some of them started to keep American papers. A fellow by the name of Hans Lavik bought the *Western Viking*. Lavik was quite a man here in Tacoma. He was a promoter, in the right sense of the word; he was a very good advertiser and he was a go-getter. But he couldn't write. So Lavik called on me, if I wouldn't help him. He knew that I had some education and he wanted to give me the job there.*

I was writing the editorials and I was doing some artwork. I was

*The Norwegian-language newspaper *Western Viking* was founded in 1890 in Tacoma. Arnfinn Bruflot was recruited to serve as editor in 1937. After many years of publication in Tacoma, it was bought out by its Seattle rival, *Washington Posten*. In 1959, the name *Western Viking* was restored; the weekly newspaper continues to be published in Seattle, now with articles in both English and Norwegian.

Part Five / NEW LIVES: TRADITION

supervising the articles and seeing to it that it was done well. The articles were about community things, about people here and there. But we were shorthanded and didn't have a good printer, and some of the good work got spoiled by misprints. That couldn't be helped.

You could say I was a left-winger at that time. I had liberal views and I was more for common ordinary people. I wasn't too much for the money class. So I wrote the editorials in that way. They were really getting some people mad. One time Axel Oxholm, he was a big shot here in town, called me down to [his] office and he was really pounding the table! I was saying the good neighbor collections didn't get out to where the money belonged; they were spending too much money on organization [administration]. Well, Oxholm was the head guy for that; he was just irate.[*]

Then Lavik sold the newspaper to a paper in Seattle called *Washington Posten*; the two were competitors. I could have been a correspondent later on, but I told them I wasn't interested. The Norwegian newspapers always have had a rough time here in the United States, except probably *Decorah Posten* in Decorah, Iowa. In 1920, in fact, *Decorah Posten* was the largest Norwegian newspaper in either Norway or America.[†] But the subscription fell off. All these papers have merged. It is definitely a losing cause, because the people from the old country are dying off. Let's face it.

When the immigrants came to the United States, they had to learn English on their own. They had their own language, but the children was learning English. That's what made it one country. That's the unifying force in any country—one language. Keep up your ethnic culture, yes, but not the language. The ethnic interest, that's beautiful, that's fine. You always feel proud of your old country. But let's face it, the new generation are not going to have the same enthusiasm as the old

[*]Axel Oxholm was a Norwegian immigrant who, according to Bruflot, developed a successful career with the Weyerhaeuser Company. Arnfinn Bruflot wrote a poem about Oxholm for the 1975 collection *Dei kom til Amerika*.
[†]Founded in 1874, *Decorah Posten* merged with *Western Viking* in 1973. In the 1920s its subscription list peaked at 45,000. See Lovoll, "*Decorah-Posten*: The Story of an Immigrant Newspaper," in *Norwegian-American Studies*, 27 (1977).

people had, you can't expect that; and I don't even know if that would be good. My idea is that with all the forces and all the different things we have, a multiracial nation, the more we can unify the country, the better. And the best way you can unify is through the language.

Writing's been a hobby all my life. Let's say a person has a dream. You are thinking about something you dream and so when you have spare time, why then you take pencil and paper and start writing. [At home in Norway] I was writing some poems. I remember one that got splashed all over the first page in the local paper there and, of course, that made me very happy. So I tried to write in some national news-papers and I got a few of them in. I suspect I probably would have been a writer, tried to make my living of it, if I had been back in Norway. But serious writing didn't take place until I retired here in Tacoma.*

Junibåten, boat in June or boat of June, was published first, in 1969, and Det Storkna Havet was published the year after that, in 1970. "Det Storkna Havet," the dried-up ocean—that is symbolic. That's about our society and the various forces at work, quite a little bit about pollu-tion. Prœriekveld, evening on the prairie, was published in 1973. And Dei kom til Amerika [They came to America] in 1975; that's centered on the immigrant theme.

The novel Inn i Amerika [Into America] was published in 1980. It's about immigrant life in the city of Tacoma, and also out in the woods. It's life in the Northwest as I saw it at that time, the late 1920s and the Depression. Some of the reviewers back home [in Norway] have sur-mised that it is an autobiography. Well, it isn't. Every author will take something out of themselves in their writing, but in the main it isn't my experience. It's an observation of a lot of people.

Modern writing has to include social questions. We have to be con-scious of the way the world is going and write about things that are good and constructive. Of course, we have the racial things and poverty. These things are difficult to include in poetry. But it can be done. You

*Arnfinn Bruflot has published several collections of poetry and one novel. Since this interview, a fifth poetry collection has appeared—På andre sida av havet [on the other side of the ocean], 1986.

Arnfinn Bruflot as a student in Norway

have to put it into a form or style that is original and effective. You have to use images a lot; that is, to my notion, the best way of writing.

Norway is a country with two official languages. According to Norwegian law, they are of equal standing. I can write either one of them, bokmål or nynorsk.* I wrote bokmål when I was editor up at the *Western Viking*, because the paper was all bokmål. Maybe there is an advantage to

---

*Norwegian appears in two official written forms: bokmål means "book language" and nynorsk "new Norwegian." In school, Norwegian children are required to learn both versions.

bokmål in writing prose; *nynorsk* is a new language and not yet formed into a very pliable tool. But in poetry, *nynorsk* certainly has the advantage, because it's more beautiful and more expressive. And it's not a worn-out language, so you can be more original. That's the reason that in later times, when I wrote poetry, I wrote in *nynorsk*.

I spoke a dialect which would be closer to *nynorsk* than *bokmål*. It's this way. You have to be yourself if you are going to have roots. Roots have gotten very popular the last few years. And if you are going to think about your ancestors and where you came from, naturally you would favor the language you were brought up in, which in my case would be *nynorsk*.

I must have rewritten them [the books] quite a few times. I live in a different country, so it's much more difficult. I got criticism, but there was always encouragement to keep on. Finally, Det Norske Samlaget published it [first poetry collection].* Very good [reviews], as good as you can expect, or even better than I can expect. That gives me a good feeling. It's unique. Actually, the last one that did it successfully was Ole Rölvaag when he wrote *I de dage*. He wrote in Norwegian and Aschehoug publishing house in Oslo published it in 1924. It was translated into *Giants in the Earth* [1927] and that became a best seller.†

There is no way I could publish in this country and make any money. The Norwegian language is failing all over here. I am doing some writing in English now. Getting something published nowadays is a difficult thing. I should work harder at it. I try to do a couple of hours every day. I belong to the Tacoma Writers' Club; they have fiction classes and poetry classes. I used to go quite a little bit.

I have my language from Norway, and my tradition, and some good things working for me. It has been very important in my life and a good influence. I certainly have no regrets. This new country has given me

---

*Det Norske Samlaget in Oslo has published all of his books. They are the leading publishing house for works in the *nynorsk* language.
†Ole Edvart Rölvaag (1876–1931) is the best known Norwegian immigrant writer. *Giants in the Earth*, as Bruflot notes, was first published in Norway and later translated into English. More typical for immigrant authors was publication with a Scandinavian-American press.

a lot. I might have had some small influence on making this a better country, too.

"Bygdefolket" [The people from the valleys]*

They came from all over Norway but mainly from the valleys. The city could be expanded at home, but the valleys were expanded in the settlements in America.

America was not a welfare state for immigrants; whoever was able to cope, made it. You had to tackle the world with only two empty hands.

The people from the valleys came to America and they took up the struggle for a living. The people from the valleys were blessed, [in] that they were hardy and had enough stubbornness to make it.

The people from the valleys had dreams and they were dreaming when it looked the darkest. They [saw] new settlements and small towns and generations [who] were going to have it better than themselves.

The people from the valleys came to America and they were planted into new earth. They entered a society that almost took the breath away. The new country pressed them to their utmost power. They were either going to live, or they were going to die.

They came to America; they were poor, but they were willing to work. They came to America in order to be one nation. And they took with them the hymn book, the Bible, and the valley.

*From *Dei kom til Amerika*, 1975. This is Bruflot's spontaneous oral translation of the Norwegian text.

Birthplaces

I

ICELAND

*Born in the U.S.

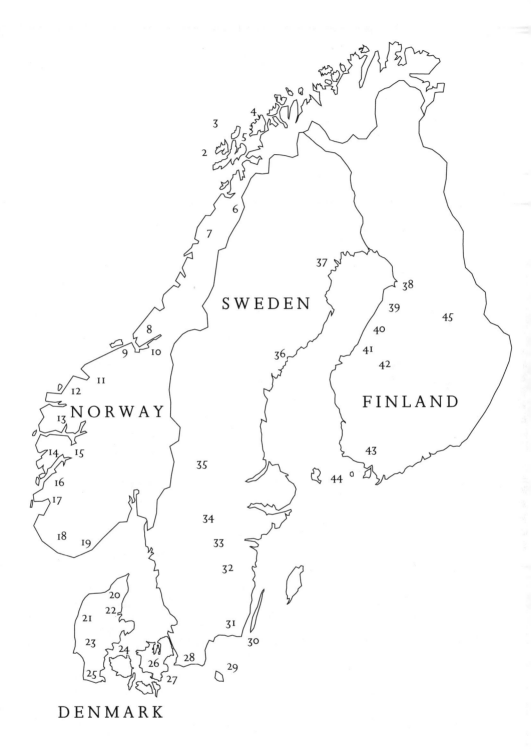

SWEDEN

NORWAY

FINLAND

DENMARK

3

4

2

5

6

7

37

38

39

45

8

40

9   10

36   41

42

11

12

NORWAY

13

FINLAND

14   15

35

16

17

43

34   44

18   19

33

32

20

22

21

31

23

30

24

28

26

29

25   27

DENMARK

Appendix

''NEW LAND–NEW LIVES:

SCANDINAVIAN EXPERIENCES IN THE

NORTHWEST''

An oral history project of Pacific Lutheran University

INTERVIEW QUESTIONNAIRE

This tape will become part of the Scandinavian Immigrant Experience
Collection at Pacific Lutheran University. The date today is _____.
The interview is taking place in/at _____ and is being conducted by
_____.

I. Personal Background:	What is your full name, please?
	When and where were you born?
	What were your parents' names? Tell me about them— occupations, characteristics, etc.
	How many children in your family? Names of brothers & sisters.
	Do you remember your grandparents? Tell me about them.
	Do you know the background of your family name(s)? Original or changed?
	Please describe your childhood home?
	How did you celebrate Christmas and other special days? What foods were traditional in your family? Have any of the recipes been handed down?
	What Scandinavian customs and folk beliefs do you recall from your childhood?
II. Emigration:	When did you come to the U.S.? With whom? Was family separated?
	Why did you come?
	Did you know anyone in the U.S. before you came over?
	How did you feel on the day you left?
	What kinds of things did you bring with you?
	What do you remember of the trip over? Conditions, length, cost, etc.
	Tell me about the day you arrived—port of entry, problems, first place you stayed, feelings.
	How did you get across the country?

III. Settling In: Did you have difficulties because you didn't know the
language?
Was there any prejudice against you?
Did you go to school in the U.S.?
What seemed most difficult/most exciting about America?
How long before you felt at home?
Did you have any contact with minority groups?
Are you an American citizen? When/how?
If married, how did you meet spouse?
What was your wedding like?

IV. Family: Tell me about spouse; children; grandchildren (limit if necessary):
names, dates, occupations, education, outstanding
accomplishments.
What aspects of family life do you remember best? Values,
responsibilities, activities.
How did you contribute to the family income?

V. Occupation: How difficult was it to find work?
Did you try your hand at a variety of jobs?
What were the working conditions like—workday/-week,
pay, benefits?
Did you work among Scandinavians?
Describe some typical activities/days. What major changes
have you witnessed over the years?

VI. Church and   Have you been active in a church? In what ways?
Community   Scandinavian congregation? When was English used?
Life: Are you involved with Scandinavian organizations?
Describe typical activities.
What other kinds of groups or organizations have you joined?

VII. Heritage: Have you revisited country of birth? What was that like?
What contact, if any, do you still have with people there?
How would you describe the (Finns, Swedes, etc.)?
What has it meant to you to be (Swedish, Norwegian, etc.)?
Does your family have reunions? What are they like?
Any special objects that represent family history and
heritage—photos, keepsakes, albums, etc.?

In what ways do you still use native *language*?
    Passed on to children?
Can you share a prayer, song, or saying in your language?
Is there anything else that you would like to share?

Thank you very much.
This concludes our interview with _____.

Selected Bibliography

Scandinavian-American History

Blegen, Theodore C. *Norwegian Migration to America: The American Transition.* Northfield, Minnesota: Norwegian-American Historical Association, 1940.

Gulliksen, Øyvind T., Ingeborg R. Kongslien, and Dina Tolfsby, eds. *Essays on Norwegian-American Literature and History. Volume II.* Oslo: NAHA-Norway, 1990.

Hasselmo, Nils, ed. *Perspectives on Swedish Immigration.* Chicago: The Swedish Pioneer Historical Society, 1978.

Haugen, Einar. *The Norwegian Language in America: A Study in Bilingual Behavior.* Bloomington: Indiana University Press, 1969.

Hoglund, A. William. *Finnish Immigrants in America, 1880–1920.* Madison: University of Wisconsin Press, 1960.

Hvidt, Kristian. *Flight to America: The Social Background of 300,000 Danish Emigrants.* New York: Academic Press, 1975.

Jalkanen, Ralph J., ed. *The Finns in North America: A Social Symposium.* Hancock, Michigan: Michigan State University Press for Suomi College, 1969.

Janson, Florence Edith. *The Background of Swedish Immigration, 1840–1930.* Chicago: University of Chicago Press, 1931; reprinted New York: Arno Press, 1970.

Lindmark, Sture. "End of the Great Migration: Decline, Restriction, and Press Reaction 1929–1932." *Swedish Pioneer Historical Quarterly,* 20:1 (1969).

——— . *Swedish America, 1914–1932.* Uppsala, Sweden: Läromedelsförlagen, 1971.

Lovoll, Odd S. *A Century of Urban Life: The Norwegians in Chicago before 1930.* Northfield, Minnesota: Norwegian-American Historical Association, 1988.

——— . *A Folk Epic: The Bygdelag in America.* Boston: Twayne Publishers for the Norwegian-American Historical Association, 1975.

——— . *The Promise of America: A History of the Norwegian-American People.* Minneapolis: University of Minnesota Press, 1984.

Marzolf, Marion Tuttle. *The Danish-Language Press in America.* New York: Arno Press, 1979.

Mortensen, Enok. *Schools for Life: A Danish-American Experiment in Adult Education.* Solvang, California: Danish-American Heritage Society, 1977.

Nelson, Helge. *The Swedes and the Swedish Settlements in North America.* Lund, Sweden: Gleerup, 1943; reprinted New York: Arno Press, 1979.

Nielsen, George R. *The Danish Americans*. Boston: Twayne, 1981.

Norman, Hans and Harald Runblom. *Transatlantic Connections: Nordic Migration to the New World after 1800*. Oslo: Norwegian University Press [1988].

Ohland, Ann-Sofie. "Utvandring och självständighet: Några synpunkter på den kvinnlige emigrationen från Sverige." *Historisk tidskrift*, 1983:2.

Ostergren, Robert C. *A Community Transplanted: The Trans-Atlantic Experience of a Swedish Immigrant Settlement in the Upper Middle West*. Madison: University of Wisconsin Press, 1988.

Qualey, Carlton C. *Norwegian Settlement in the United States*. Northfield, Minnesota: Norwegian-American Historical Association, 1938.

Rasmussen, Janet E. " 'I was scared to death when I came to Chicago': White Slavery and the Woman Immigrant." *Fin(s) de siecle in Scandinavian Perspective*, ed. Faith Ingwersen and Mary Kay Norseng. Festskrift in honor of Harald S. Naess. Columbia, South Carolina: Camden House, 1993.

————. " 'We were brought up to work': Familial Values and Scandinavian Immigrant Women." *Selecta*, 7 (1986).

Ross, Carl and K. Marianne Wargelin Brown, eds. *Women Who Dared: The History of Finnish American Women*. St. Paul, Minnesota: Immigration History Research Center, 1986.

Runblom, Harald and Hans Norman, eds. *From Sweden to America: A History of the Migration*. Minneapolis: University of Minnesota Press, 1976.

Semmingsen, Ingrid. *Norway to America: A History of the Migration*. Trans. Einar Haugen. Minneapolis: University of Minnesota Press, 1978.

Scandinavians in the Pacific Northwest

Arestad, Sverre. "Bibliography on the Scandinavians of the Pacific Coast." *Pacific Northwest Quarterly*, 36 (1945).

————. "Norwegians in the Pacific Coast Fisheries." *Norwegian-American Studies*, 30 (1985).

Bergman, Hans. *History of the Scandinavians in Tacoma and Pierce County*. Tacoma, Washington: Hans Bergman, 1926.

Bjork, Kenneth O. *West of the Great Divide: Norwegian Migration to the Pacific Coast, 1847–1893*. Northfield, Minnesota: Norwegian-American Historical Association, 1958.

Dahlie, Jorgen. *A Social History of Scandinavian Immigration, Washington State, 1895–1910*. New York: Arno Press, 1980.

Forslund, Stephen J. *The Swedes in Tacoma and the Puget Sound Country, 1852–1976*. Ed. Doris Gundstrom King. Tacoma, Washington: privately printed, 1976.

Hegstad, Patsy Adams. "Citizenship, Voting and Immigrants: A Comparative Study of the Naturalization Propensity and Voter Registration of Nordics in Seattle and Ballard, Washington, 1892–1900." Ph.D. dissertation, University of Washington, 1982. See also her article, "Scandinavian Settlement in Seattle, 'Queen City of the Puget Sound.'" *Norwegian-American Studies*, 30 (1985).

Hummasti, Paul George. *Finnish Radicals in Astoria, Oregon, 1904–1940: A Study in Immigrant Socialism.* New York: Arno, 1979.

Johnson, Walter, ed. Special Number "Swedes in Washington State." *The Swedish-American Historical Quarterly*, 34:4 (1983).

Kvelstad, Rangvald. "The Pioneers of Dog Fish Bay." *Norwegian-American Studies*, 30 (1985).

Lovoll, Odd S. "*Washington Posten*: A Window on a Norwegian-American Urban Community." *Norwegian-American Studies*, 31 (1986).

MacHaffie, Ingeborg Nielsen. *Danish in Portland: Past and Present.* Tigard, Oregon: Skribent Press, 1982.

Pottsmith, Marie Holst. "Pioneering Years in Hamlet, Oregon: A Finnish Community." *Oregon Historical Quarterly*, 61 (1960).

Rasmussen, Janet E. "'I met him at Normanna Hall': Ethnic Cohesion and Marital Patterns Among Scandinavian Immigrant Women." *Norwegian-American Studies*, 32 (1989).

———. "Women and Domestic Service: An Oral History Report from the Pacific Northwest." *Norse Heritage 1989 Yearbook.* Stavanger, Norway: The Norwegian Emigration Center, 1989.

Sehmsdorf, Henning K. "Assimilation, Adaptation, Survivals: Norwegian-American Traditions in the Pacific Northwest." *Northwest Folklore*, 7:1 (1988).

Slind, Marvin G. "Norse to the Palouse: The Selbu Community." *Bunchgrass Historian*, 10:4 (1982).

Slind, Marvin G. and Fred C. Bohm. *Norse to the Palouse: Sagas of the Selbu Norwegians.* Pullman, Washington: Norlys Press, 1990.

Stine, Thomas O. *Scandinavians on the Pacific.* 1900; reprinted San Francisco: R & E Research Associates, 1968.

Tingelstad, Gertrude. *Scandinavians in the Silverton Country: Their Arrival and Early Settlement.* Corvallis, Oregon: Tingelstad, 1978.

Veirs, Kristina, ed. *Nordic Heritage Northwest.* Seattle: The Writing Works, 1982.

First-Person Immigrant Accounts

Arestad, Sverre. "What Was Snus Hill?" *Makers of an American Immigrant Legacy: Essays in Honor of Kenneth O. Bjork*, ed. Odd S. Lovoll. Northfield, Minnesota: Norwegian-American Historical Association, 1980.

Barton, H. Arnold, ed. *Letters from the Promised Land: Swedes in America, 1840–1914.* Minneapolis: University of Minnesota Press, 1975.

Birkeland, Torger. *Echoes of Puget Sound: Fifty Years of Logging and Steamboating.* Caldwell, Idaho: Caxton Printers, 1960.

Blegen, Theodore C., ed. *Land of Their Choice: The Immigrants Write Home.* Minneapolis: University of Minnesota Press, 1955.

Eide, Harald. *The Alaska Adventures of a Norwegian Cheechako: A Greenhorn with a Gold Pan.* Anchorage: Alaska Northwest, 1975.

[Erickson, Beda.] "Beda Erickson's Journey to Chicago, 1902." ed. and trans. Walter Johnson and Ruth Ingeborg Johnson. *Swedish Pioneer Historical Quarterly,* 32:1 (1981).

Fries, U[lrich] E[nglehart] and Emil B. Fries. *From Copenhagen to Okanagon: The Autobiography of a Pioneer.* Caldwell, Idaho: Caxton Printers, 1949.

Hale, Frederick, ed. *Danes in North America.* Seattle: University of Washington Press, 1984.

Hought, Anna Guttormsen, with Florence Ekstrand. *Anna.* Seattle: Welcome Press, 1986.

Iverson, O. B. "From the Prairie to Puget Sound," ed. Sverre Arestad. *Norwegian-American Studies and Records,* 16 (1950).

Knaplund, Paul. *Moorings Old and New: Entries in an Immigrant's Log.* Madison: State Historical Society of Wisconsin, 1963.

Lind, Jens. "Memories and Autobiography of Jens Lind." *The Bridge,* 13:1 (1990).

Morrison, Joan and Charlotte Fox Zabusky. *American Mosaic: The Immigrant Experience in the Words of Those Who Lived It.* New York: E. P. Dutton, 1980.

Storseth, John. "Pioneering on the Pacific Coast," with a foreword by Einar Haugen. *Norwegian-American Studies and Records,* 13 (1943).

Wilson, Elmer. "A Swede's First Logging Camp," trans. Henry Axel Person. *The Swedish-American Historical Quarterly,* 34:4 (1983).

Zempel, Solveig, ed. and trans. *In Their Own Words: Letters from Norwegian Immigrants.* Minneapolis: University of Minnesota Press, 1991.

On Immigration and Ethnicity

Archdeacon, Thomas J. *Becoming American: An Ethnic History.* New York: Free Press, 1983.

Bodnar, John. *The Transplanted: A History of Immigrants in Urban America.* Bloomington: Indiana University Press, 1985.

Neidle, Cecyle S. *America's Immigrant Women.* Boston: Twayne, 1975.

Seller, Maxine. *To Seek America: A History of Ethnic Life in the United States.* [Englewood, New Jersey]: Jerome S. Ozer, Publisher, 1977.

Taylor, Philip. *The Distant Magnet: European Emigration to the U.S.A.* New York: Harper & Row, 1971.

Thernstrom, Stephan, ed. *Harvard Encyclopedia of American Ethnic Groups.* Cambridge, Massachusetts: Harvard University Press, 1980.

On Oral History

Baum, Willa K. *Oral History for the Local Historical Society.* 2nd edition. [Nashville:] American Association for State and Local History, 1971.

———. *Transcribing and Editing Oral History.* Nashville: American Association for State and Local history, 1977.

Bennett, James. "Human Values in Oral History." *Oral History Review,* 11 (1983).

Okihiro, Gary Y. "Oral History and the Writing of Ethnic History: A Reconnaissance into Method and Theory." *Oral History Review,* 9 (1981).

Plummer, Ken. *Documents of Life: An Introduction to the Problems and Literature of a Humanistic Method.* London: George Allen & Unwin, 1983.

Starr, Louis M. "Oral History." *Encyclopedia of Library and Information Services.* Volume 20. New York: Marcel Dekker, 1977.

Sundberg, Edvard F. and Gerda. "Ribbons of Memories: An American-Scandinavian Oral History Project." *Swedish-American Historical Quarterly,* 33:3 (1982).

Thompson, Paul. *The Voice of the Past: Oral History.* Oxford: Oxford University Press, 1978.

Background Works Consulted

Andenæs, Johs., O. Riste, and M. Skodvin. *Norway and the Second World War.* Oslo: Tanum, 1966.

Browning, Robert J. *Fisheries of the North Pacific.* Anchorage: Alaska Northwest, 1974.

Carlson, Gordon. *Seventy-Five Years History Columbia Baptist Conference.* Seattle: Columbia Baptist Conference, 1964.

Cipolla, Carlo M., ed. *The Fontana Economic History of Europe.* Volume 4. *The Emergence of the Industrial Societies, Part Two.* London: Collins, 1973.

Denmark: An Official Handbook. Copenhagen: Royal Danish Ministry of Foreign Affairs, 1970.

Derry, T. K. *A History of Modern Norway 1814–1972.* London: Oxford University Press, 1973.

———. *A History of Scandinavia.* Minneapolis: University of Minnesota Press, 1979.

Fullerton, Brian and Alan F. Williams. *Scandinavia: An Introductory Geography.* New York: Praeger, 1972.

Hambro, C. J. *Amerikaferd.* Oslo: Tanum, 1935.

Haugen, Einar. *Ole Edvart Rölvaag.* Boston: Twayne, 1983.

Henrikson, Alf. *Nordens historie: Et illustrert overblikk.* Oslo: Den norske Bokklubben, 1987.

Historisk statistik för Sverige. I. Befolkning. Stockholm: Statistiska Centralbyrån, 1955.

Hovde, B. J. *The Scandinavian Countries, 1720–1865.* 2 volumes. Boston: Chapman & Grimes, 1943.

Katzman, David M. *Seven Days a Week: Women and Domestic Service in Industrializing America.* 1978; reprinted Urbana: University of Illinois Press, 1981.

Lantz, Monica. *Emigrantvisor.* Stockholm: LTs förlag, 1981.

Moum, Sidsel Vogt. *Kvinnfolkarbeid: Kvinners kår og status i Norge 1875–1910.* Oslo: Universitetsforlaget, 1981.

Mykland, Knut, ed. *Norges historie.* Volume 15. *Historisk atlas,* by Rolf M. Hagen, et al. Oslo: Cappelen, 1980.

Nicandri, David L. "Washington's Ethnic Workingmen in 1900: A Comparative View." Paper delivered at Pacific Northwest History Conference, Portland, Oregon, April 7, 1979.

Puget Sound Plywood: A Cooperative Association 1941–74. Tacoma, Washington: Board of Directors Puget Sound Plywood, 1974.

Schmid, Calvin F. *Social Trends in Seattle.* Seattle: University of Washington Press, 1944.

Scott, Franklin D. *Scandinavia.* Cambridge, Massachusetts: Harvard University Press, 1975.

Van Syckle, Edwin. *They tried to cut it all.* Seattle: Pacific Search Press, 1980.

Wuorinen, John H. *A History of Finland.* New York; Columbia University Press for the American-Scandinavian Foundation, 1965.